T0121163

STUCK IN
THE MIDDLE
WITH YOU

▼

FEATURING CONVERSATIONS WITH
RICHARD RUSSO, TREY ELLIS, AUGUSTEN
BURROUGHS, EDWARD ALBEE, TIMOTHY
KREIDER, ANN BEATTIE, SUSAN MINOT,
AND OTHER PARENTS AND FORMER
CHILDREN

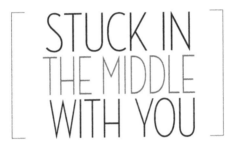

# STUCK IN THE MIDDLE WITH YOU

## A Memoir of Parenting in Three Genders

# JENNIFER FINNEY BOYLAN

WITH AN AFTERWORD BY ANNA QUINDLEN

B\D\W\Y
Broadway Books / New York

Jennifer Finney Boylan is available for select readings and lectures. To inquire about a possible appearance, please contact the Random House Speakers Bureau at rhspeakers@randomhouse.com.

Published in the United States by Broadway Books, an imprint of the
Crown Publishing Group, a division of Random House LLC,
a Penguin Random House Company, New York.
www.crownpublishing.com

BROADWAY BOOKS and its logo, B \ D \ W \ Y,
are trademarks of Random House LLC.

Originally published in hardcover in slightly different form in the United States by
Crown Publishers, an imprint of the Crown Publishing Group, a division of Random
House LLC, New York, in 2013.

Library of Congress Cataloging-in-Publication Data
Boylan, Jennifer Finney, 1958–
Stuck in the middle with you : a memoir of parenting in three genders /
by Jennifer Finney Boylan; and featuring conversations with Richard Russo, Trey Ellis,
Augusten Burroughs, Edward Albee, Timothy Kreider, Ann Beattie, Susan Minot &
other parents and former children; with an afterword by Anna Quindlen.
1. Boylan, Jennifer Finney, 1958—Family.   2. Novelists, American—20th century—
Biography.   3. English teachers—United States—Biography.   4. Male-to-female
transsexuals—Family relationships—United States.   5. Parents—United States—
Interviews.   6. Children—United States—Interviews.   7. Gender identity—
United States. 8. Families—United States.   I. Title.
PS3552.O914Z478 20013
818'.5403—dc23            2012025579

ISBN 978-0-7679-2177-0
eBook ISBN 978-0-307-95284-4

*Book design by Lauren Dong*
*Cover design by Anna Kochman*
*Author photograph: Jim Bowdoin*
*Frontispiece photograph: © Heather Perry*
*Photograph, page viii: Courtesy of the author*

First Paperback Edition

147468846

FOR DEIRDRE

[ BRIGHT STAR ]

*AND*

ZACH AND SEAN

[ SONS FOR THE HOUSE OF FRANKENSTEIN ]

*The Boylans in Maine, summer 2012.*

# CONTENTS

## CAVEAT EMPTOR

IT IS NOW customary for literary memoirs to begin with a little note in which the author analyzes the egregiousness of her various fabrications. While I hope my sins are venial, a full disclaimer for this book, along with a realm of other entertaining material, may be found at www .jenniferboylan.net. There's a contact tab there as well, for readers who want to write.

In my earlier nonfiction I have used pseudonyms for everyone I know, with the exception of public figures. As I set about writing this book, I asked my boys how they would feel about my telling the story of our family. My son Zach turned to me and said, "Look, that's fine. But this time, can you make me one promise? *Use our real names for a change.*"

This wish, among so many others, has been granted.

—*JFB*

All women become like their mothers.
That is their tragedy.
No man does. That's his.

—OSCAR WILDE

# 1 [ DADDY ]

▼

"I DON'T THINK SO," SAID MY FATHER.

"HE'S NOT MUCH."

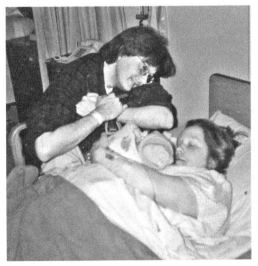

*James and Deirdre Boylan, with newborn Zach.*
*February 11, 1994.*

# RED CARD

She sat alone in the stands as the duel unfolded. Like me, she had no visible husband. I had a lump in my breast. She seemed sad. Our sons had swords.

I slid next to her on the bleacher, put my purse on the floor. Then a group of dads two rows ahead of us leapt to their feet, yelling. A boy was on the ground. His adversary stood above him, foil extended.

"Red card!" shouted one of the dads. "Red-card him, ref!"

The trainer from my sons' school, Kents Hill, stepped toward the ring to protest. But a penalty was not called.

"Are you blind, ref?" shouted one of the dads. He was really upset. I'd never seen a dad all red in the face at a fencing match before.

"They don't understand," said the woman to my right. She was a tiny thing, like a budgie. In her hands she held a copy of *Cooking Light* magazine. "He was flèching him."

"Fleshing?" I said. A lot of the minutiae of fencing was beyond me. Offhand this sounded like the word you'd use if you accidentally encouraged someone to wind up naked.

"Flèche," she said. "That's Ethan's secret weapon."

The dads in front of us were still hollering and booing. The boy who'd been upended was back on his feet, and now I recognized him. This was a young man we'll call Chandler, the smallest boy on the Kents Hill team.

His adversary did a merciless ninth-grade equivalent of Muhammad Ali's victory dance. *I am the greatest.* His facial expression wasn't visible, what with the mask, but it wasn't hard to imagine.

"That's your son?"

She nodded.

"I'm Jenny Boylan?" I said.

"Grenadine Phelps?"* she said. It would have been nice to be able to say that this was the first time I'd met a woman named after a liquor, but in Maine, there's a long-standing tradition of naming people after bottles of alcohol. I'd known a Brandy, a Bacardi, and a couple of Sherrys. Brandy had once cornered me in the ladies' room at a blues bar where my band was playing and tried to get me to make out with her. Things like that happened to me more than you'd expect, which at first I'd thought was just my own rotten luck but which lately I'd begun to worry was my fault. On another occasion, for example, I'd accidentally wound up at a convention of ventriloquists, in Kentucky. There'd been this whole scene with this one guy who kept coming on to me using his "muffle voice."

The boys began to fence again, the gigantic Ethan and the tiny, terrified Chandler. Once again, Ethan charged at him, yelling as he advanced like one of the riders of Rohan: "Deaath!" He whacked Chandler's sword and it flew out of the boy's hand and skittered away on the gym floor.

"Flèched him again," said Grenadine wearily, as if irritated that Chandler had not learned that her son only had one trick, and that this was it.

"I'm sorry, what's flèching? You mean that charging thing?"

"Yeah," said Grenadine. "You extend the arm and pounce. Ethan's known for his flèche."

Yeah, well, I thought, Chandler's known for going to the bathroom in his actual pants.

The coach was now out talking to Chandler, who had his mask off. He was sniffing back the tears.

Another boy, an elegant and graceful young thing, picked up the fallen sword and returned it to Chandler with a small bow. He had hair halfway down his back, a huge cascade of blond curls tied in a braid.

---

* This name, along with some other identifying information, has been changed.

He patted Chandler on the shoulder, whispered something encouraging to him. Buck up.

"Jeez, look at the hair on that kid," said Grenadine.

"He's got hair all right," I said. My son Zach was admired for his hair in the same way her son Ethan was known for stabbing people.

But before I could explain this, Grenadine said, "My husband would never allow Ethan to have hair like that. He'd send him to military school first."

I shrugged. I didn't feel like defending Zach to a stranger. Was that really what I was here for, a conversation about hair?

Chandler had his mask on again and was back in the ring—more properly known as the *piste,* or strip. Zach stood to one side, watching the boy. He was the team co-captain.

"Kid looks like a girl," said Grenadine. The way she said it, it didn't sound like a compliment.

Zach looked like a lot of things, but a girl was not one of them, unless you were the kind of person who believed *long hair woman, short hair man.* He was tall and broad shouldered, my boy. The hair had made Zach very popular. There were a number of girls—some of them on the fencing team, in fact—who liked to do the braid. It was fairly obvious how much they all adored Zach. It wasn't obvious to him though.

Below us, Ethan extended his arm and went charging down upon little Chandler again. But this time, Chandler parried and then seized right-of-way. He came forward with the riposte and scored a hit off Ethan.

The dads below me shouted their approval. "Atta boy, Chandler!" they yelled. "Push back on him! Slay him!"

"Oh, honestly," said Grenadine.

The boys were now eyeing each other warily. They moved first one way, then the other, looking for an opening. You could feel the tension between them, Ethan looking for another chance to use his trick, Chandler emboldened by the hit he'd scored. There wasn't much chance that Chandler was going to win this match, but you had to give him credit for staying in the game. Very quietly, I began to hope some not-particularly-terrible thing might happen to Ethan, like the roof collapsing, or the boy's having a tiny nonlethal coronary.

At the edge of the strip, my son Zach stood there watching his teammate's progress. The men below me shouted again.

"It's a good thing my husband's not here," she said, listening to the hecklers.

"How come?" I asked.

She sighed. "There'd be trouble."

"Does he come to a lot of the matches? Your husband?"

"Oh, no." There was a slight pause. Then she said, "He's in Iraq."

Ethan got another touch on Chandler, and the dads below me moaned. One of them—was it Chandler's father?—held his head in his hands, as if he'd been called upon to witness his own son's execution for crimes against the state.

"That must be hard," I said.

She pulled into herself and did not respond. For a second it seemed almost as if the stranger were trying to hold back tears.

"It's better with him gone," she said, in a voice that was almost a whisper.

"Seriously?"

She nodded, and a tear brimmed over one of her lashes.

"Sometimes I hope he never comes back," she said. "Sometimes I wish he'd get—"

Gazing upon the gigantic, merciless Ethan below me, I wondered if I could begin to imagine Grenadine's married life. I pictured a menacing Ethan Senior bearing down upon the tiny, birdlike Grenadine Phelps, and winced. Junior had learned that pouncing trick from somewhere, and it wasn't his mom.

She eyed the wedding ring on my finger. "What about you? Where's yours?"

And just like that, I found myself in one of those situations where neither telling the truth nor coming up with a great big lie was going to accomplish anything. What could I say to her? Well, actually, I'm transgender. I used to be a man, but I've been a woman for ten years now. I'm still married to the woman I married twenty-five years ago, back when I was a man. Crazy vorld, huh? Ha! Ha! Ha!

Wow, she'd reply. Isn't your marriage really screwed up then?

I thought about Grenadine's marriage and my own. People looking at my wife, Deedie, and me—two women, not lesbians, legally married to each other—would say we were insane, way out of the mainstream, a threat to traditional American values. And all that. Whereas Grenadine and Ethan Senior were a paragon of all we revere: a heterosexual married couple, a dad serving his country in the war overseas. By almost anyone's measure, Deedie and I are the dangerous outliers, and Grenadine and her husband Mr. and Mrs. Normal. Even though Deedie and I love each other beyond all understanding, and Grenadine's fondest hope was that her husband would be murdered by insurgents.

Sometimes I don't understand the world at all, is my conclusion.

"I don't have a husband right now," I said to Grenadine. I was satisfied by the ambiguity of this, although it had to be admitted that this too was kind of a lie—since it implied that I'd once had one, or that a day would come when I might.

Down on the floor below us, Ethan hollered as he charged toward Chandler for the match point. The enormous creature bearing down upon the tiny, frightened boy was terrible to behold. Chandler dropped his sword again and raised his hands toward his mask. Ethan wonked him on the chest, and the electronic touch detector—which was automatically scoring the event—registered the hit. Ethan had vanquished Chandler. They took off their masks and shook hands.

"Atta boy, Chandler," shouted his dad. "Way to show character!"

Grenadine rolled her eyes. "Character," she muttered sadly, as if this were something she had heard about once.

Ethan searched the stands and saw his mother there, and then he nodded at her. He had a crew cut and an ingrown smirk.

My own son patted Chandler on the back. Looking down at my boy, I had a strange, nostalgic feeling—wishing that, when I'd been a guy, I'd had half the character now exhibited by my own near-grown son. It's common enough, I guess, a thought such as this, demented though it may be. We look to our children as a kind of cosmic mulligan, our own best hope for a second chance. There were plenty of times I had looked at my son Zach as a better version of me, man-wise. He had the same goofy sense of humor, the same habit of wearing his heart right out there on his sleeve where anyone could crush it, the same buoyant hope that somehow love would prevail over all.

If I had failed as a man—and even those people who loved me most would have to admit this, what with the vagina and everything—then maybe Zach was a last chance to get it right. The man that I had once been clearly lived in him, although this time around we seemed to have been spared the melancholic lunacy.

On the other hand, I knew full well that thinking in this way was a surefire path to frustration. Children are here to live their own lives, not ours, and any parent who looks to her son to right the wrongs of her own past probably ought to get out of the parenting business entirely.

"I'm sorry I said that," said the tiny Grenadine. "About my husband. You must think I'm a basket case."

"Of course not," I said. "I knew you didn't mean it."

"But I did mean it," she said, after a pause.

"Seriously?"

"He's just not a nice guy," she said. "The army changed him."

I shrugged. "People change," I said. Coming from me, this was an understatement.

Something throbbed in my left breast. It wasn't sentiment. An odd, pulsing pain had been lurking in me for a month or two. I'd been doing a self-exam in a shower in a hotel in New York back in December when I'd first found the lump. Incredibly, I'd tried to pretend it wasn't there for the first month or so. But every time I felt for it to see if it was still there, I found it, larger. A mammogram was scheduled for the next day, the morning after the fencing tournament.

I'd begun to do some of the math in my head. Having seen my own father, and then my sister-in-law, slain by cancer, suffering through the chemo and the radiation, and the surgery, only to die agonizing deaths, I'd already decided, if it was cancer I wasn't doing any of that. I'd just go to the zoo and jump into the lions' cage instead.

It wasn't that I didn't love my life—the opposite, in fact. As someone who'd lived a full life as a man, then survived the perilous transition and then lived another ten euphoric years as a woman, I had plenty of things to be grateful for. Quite frankly, I couldn't imagine anyone's having had such a lucky life as my own, in spite of all the tears my condition—and the effects that it had had on others—had engendered. I'd been married for almost twenty-five years to a woman I adored, and who still adored me. I'd had what felt—at times—like the best job in the world, teaching English at Colby. I'd written a best-selling book, been a guest of Oprah Winfrey, even been imitated on *Saturday Night Live* by Will Forte, who, according to some people, did a better impression of me than I did.

I had two brilliant and resilient sons, each of them with amazing and fabulous hair.

Quite frankly, there wasn't a whole lot left on my to-do list. Other than sit back in wonder and see what happens next.

"I hate that," said Grenadine softly. "I hate it, that people change."


I WAS A FATHER for six years, a mother for ten, and for a time in between I was both, or neither, like some parental version of the schnoodle, or the cockapoo. Of course, as parents go, I was a rather feminine father; for that matter I suppose I'm a masculine mother. When I was their father I showed my boys how to make a good tomato sauce, how to fold a napkin, how to iron a dress shirt; as their mother I've shown them how to split wood with a maul. Whether this means I've had one parenting style or two, I am not entirely certain. I can assure you I am not a perfect parent and will be glad to review the long list of my mistakes. But in dealing with a parent who subverts a lot of expectations about gender, I hope my sons have learned to be more flexible and openhearted than many of their peers with traditionally gendered parents.

I would like to think that this has been a gift to them and not a curse. It is my hope that having a father who became a woman has made my two remarkable boys, in turn, into better men.

Zach learned to shave when he was two years old, by watching me.

He says that this is one of his primary memories of me as a man—the morning ritual of the razor and the hot steam from the basin. Zach stood upon a stool so that he could see his face in the bathroom mirror. I used to coat his young, pink cheeks with Gillette Foamy, and then give him a razor with the protective shield still on the blade. As I shaved my face, Zach would shave his. He'd mimic the contortions I'd make with my face in order to keep my skin taut. And he'd shave his own face in the same order I shaved mine—cheeks first, then the neck, then the chin, mustache last.

We stood there before the mirror, the two of us. I wiped the steam away from the top half of the mirror so I could see myself; Zach wiped a smaller hole away for himself at the bottom. Our expressions were so serious as we shaved, as men's faces always are as they undertake this business, as if we are not shaving, but staring out across the bridge of our intergalactic star destroyers.

Afterward, we'd towel down our faces, removing the residual froth and smacking our smooth cheeks lightly with an air of manly satisfaction. "There," he'd say. "I'm clean as a whistle!"

Where he got that phrase I can't tell you. He didn't get it from me.

That Christmas, Deedie bought Zach his own pretend shaving kit, complete with a plastic razor. When he opened this gift, though, he immediately burst into tears. "What?" said Deedie, discouraged that what had seemed like the perfect gift had gone so wrong.

"I don't want a baby razor," Zach wept, looking at me for backup. "I want a real one!"

Twelve years later, when Zach began to shave for real, he did it with an electric razor, one of those contraptions with the "floating heads." I didn't show him how to do it, although I tried. But he stopped me as he headed into the bathroom, and said, "Maddy. I got it from here." A moment later, the door closed, and I sat down in the kitchen and listened to the faint buzzing sound coming through the wall.

I didn't learn how to shave from my father either. Which turns out, I think, not to be so strange. One of the things about manhood I learned from my father is that it's a solitary experience, a land of silences and understatements, a place where a lot of important things have to be learned alone. Whereas womanhood, a lot of the time, is a thing you get to share.

I remember going for a bra fitting once and the saleswoman just waltzing right into my changing room in the midst of things to "check the fit." When she entered the room I was flabbergasted. I wasn't prepared for anyone to barge in while—what's the phrase?—my cups runneth over. But in seeing my astonishment, the saleswoman just laughed. Oh, honey, please, she said. We're all women here.

"How was it?" I asked Zach when he emerged from the bathroom, stroking his face. I was all set to have a big conversation about the experience. Shaving for the first time! A huge rite of passage! Do you remember, my sweet boy, when you were two, and we used to stand before the mirror together, staring through the clouds of steam? I imagined the two of us sitting down for a moment, in order to take the measure of our rapidly passing lives.

"It was fine," said Zach, with a hint of annoyance in his voice. I recognized that tone. It said, it was what it was and it wasn't all that interesting, and do we have to talk about it as if it was? Not everything in the world, my son was trying to tell me, is worthy of analysis and sentimentality.

"Okay," I said, trying not to be hurt. Zach shook his head and bent down next to me.

"Really," he said. "It was fine." He gave me a hug, to make up for his silence, and I hugged him back, and my cheek brushed against his.

*Smooth.*

"I DON'T KNOW," Grenadine was saying as we waited for the next round of competition to start. "I don't think everybody has to stay the same forever. I just don't see why I have to stay stuck, when he's not who I married."

This was, of course, the question that obsessed me. The previous week, Deedie and I had sat in the audience at Kents Hill's theater and watched as our younger son Sean stepped into a spotlight and recited sonnet 116.

*Let me not to the marriage of true minds*
*Admit impediments. Love is not love*
*Which alters when it alteration finds,*
*Or bends with the remover to remove:*
*O no! it is an ever-fixed mark,*
*That looks on tempests and is never shaken;*
*It is the star to every wandering bark,*
*Whose worth's unknown, although his height be taken.*

Sitting there in the audience, I admit that tears had rolled down my cheeks. For one thing, surely no other family had found alteration as had ours, nor any wife been so ever-fixed in her adoration for the one she loved as Deedie had been for me. For another, Sean looked so grown-up on the stage, his wild hair lit by stage lights.

Deedie saw me wipe away the tears. "Dear God," she muttered. "Here we go again."

"How did your husband change?" I asked Grenadine, and thought, *I should be charging for this.*

"He's so angry all the time. He comes home all wound up from the war. Then he won't talk about it. He broods and broods. Then he signs up again. While Ethan and I keep on getting older without him."

"I'm sorry," I said.

"How am I supposed to show Ethan how to be a man?" she asked. "How am I supposed to teach him that?"

"You can teach him right from wrong," I said. "You can teach him how to be kind."

Grenadine looked at me as if I were from another planet, as if learning how to be kind wasn't the thing she was worrying about.

"I'm just afraid that Ethan is going to wind up like his father," said Grenadine.

"Like him how?"

"Like, he's going to leave me. And I'll never see him again." She laughed bitterly. "The less his father is around," she said, "the more Ethan winds up like him."

"There are all kinds of men in the world," I said to Grenadine. "You can teach Ethan to be different."

The referee was talking to Zach on the mat below us. Zach had put down *The Lord of the Rings* and was now twisting his long hair behind him and lowering his helmet over his head.

Grenadine turned to me as if I were her last friend on earth. "How?" she said.

Below us, Ethan stepped onto the *piste*. Of course it was Ethan Zach would be facing next. In one corner, a goofy young hippie with his heart on his sleeve; in the other, the young marine, with his deadly flèche and heartrending scream.

Grenadine said it again, more urgently this time: "How?"

It was a good question.

Our sons faced each other and bowed. "En garde," said the ref, and then the young men drew their swords.

# THE PLOVER'S EGG

On a cold February night in 1994, Deedie and I were watching *Brides-head Revisited* on the television in our little house in Maine. She was ab-solutely pregnant, her hands at rest on the vast Matterhorn of her belly. Snow was coming down outside, and our dinner dishes—now mostly empty—were sitting on the coffee table before us. I was a man then. I had made leg of lamb with garlic and rosemary. On the side there had been new potatoes tossed with olive oil and kosher salt and fresh mint.

It is fair to say we had no idea what the world before us might con-tain. We had seen plenty of our friends transform into parents by this time, and to be honest we hadn't been thrilled by most of the meta-morphoses. Not only was it clear that our former companions were a lot more interested in their squirming offspring than they were in Deedie and me—their friends of many years—but they seemed like they'd transformed into people less interesting than the ones we'd first befriended. Our friends—radicals and satirists, the kind of people you could have over for a martini and a model rocket launch—now seemed bland, exhausted, and unforgivably self-involved.

As we lost one set of lifelong friends after another to the state of par-enthood, we joked that they were like the townspeople we frequently saw in science fiction movies, the ones whose minds are taken over by the aliens, who counsel their dwindling still-human friends by saying, *Don't fight it. They're smarter than we are. It's good.*

Deedie and I were determined that we would be different kinds of parents. I think we imagined that having children would be a lit-tle bit like having Labrador retrievers. Sure, we'd train them, teach them to read and drive a car and fetch, but we'd still be unmistakably ourselves—artists, Democrats, rocketeers. After all, we hadn't embarked upon this adventure in order to become strangers. We had embarked upon it as an act of love.

As the snow drifted down outside that night, we were watching the scene in *Brideshead* in which young Charles Ryder first goes over to the rooms of the eccentric Sebastian Flyte. Middle-class Charles has never seen anything in his life like Sebastian or his friends. *But I was in search of love in those days,* Charles says, *and I went full of curiosity and the faint unrecognized apprehension that here at last, I should find that low door in the wall, which others, I knew, had found before me, which opened on an enclosed and enchanted garden, which was somewhere, not overlooked by any window, in the heart of that great city.*

"Uh-oh," said Deedie.

On the screen before us, Charles looked at a large bowl of plover's eggs gathered in a bowl at the center of an ornate table.

"What's 'uh-oh'?" I said. I picked up the remote and hit the pause button.

"I think," said Deedie, "my water just broke."

I still remember the silence in the house that followed these words. Our dog Lucy, half golden retriever, half beagle, raised her head bitterly and gave us a hard look. Outside, the snow was still drifting down quietly.

What possible response can any man give to the woman he loves in the wake of such a phrase?

"Okay," I said. "I guess we should go to the hospital then."

My eyes fell to the screen, and to our paused movie, where Charles Ryder's hand was frozen, inches from the bowl of plover's eggs.

Deedie took my hand. "Is it really happening?" she said. "Is this how it begins?"

I put my arms around her and kissed my love upon on the cheek. Sure, I wanted to say. It begins like this.

But this was not the truth. Whatever was happening to us, whatever journey we were on, had begun a long time ago.

✦

I FIRST LAID eyes on Deedie back in college. She was onstage in a production of David Mamet's *Sexual Perversity in Chicago*. In the play she was dating this other guy who I knew named Boomer Dorsey. Boomer was one of the college's hot young actors. I'd seen him as Gloucester in *Richard III* a few weeks earlier, in a production marred only by the fact that the actor playing Richmond had the unfortunate combination of a speech impediment and an accent from deepest Brooklyn, which transformed the word *lords* into something that sounded like "wawds," thus:

RICHMOND: Cwy mercy wawds and watchful gentlemen,
    That you have tane a tawdy swuggard here!
LORDS: How have you slept, my lord?
RICHMOND: Swept? The sweetest sweep, an faiwest boding dweams!
    That evah entered in a dwowsy head,
    Have I since yaw departchaw had, my wawds!

The Mamet was a lot better. Boomer—who years later opened up his own pretty damned great Irish bar on the Upper West Side—was playing the part of a blowhard named Danny. But I wasn't paying any attention to Boomer Dorsey. My eyes were fixed upon this woman playing the part of Deborah. I could see her green eyes sparkle from the third row. Checked the program. Deirdre Finney, she was called. Named for Derdriu, the Irish Queen of Sorrows.

Would you believe in a love at first sight? Yes, I'm certain that it happens all the time.

Actually, I know that the line between love at first sight and creepy stalker is probably finer than anyone would like to admit. But I can honestly say that from the moment I first saw Deirdre, when I was twenty years old, I felt as if something had changed, as if I'd been living all my life in a dark room and someone had suddenly turned on all the lights.

Late in the play, Boomer and Deirdre—I later learned her nickname was Deedie—were lying in bed together naked. A single sheet covered their bodies.

DEBORAH: What does it feel like to have a penis?
DANNY: Strange. Very strange and wonderful.
DEBORAH: Do you miss having tits?
DANNY: To be completely frank with you, that is the stupidest question I ever heard. What man in his right mind would want tits?
DEBORAH: You're right, of course.

Sitting there in the dark theater, I had to agree. I didn't want tits, not at that moment anyhow. What I wanted at that moment, more than anything else, was to be Deedie's boyfriend.

I GOT MY WISH of course, but it would be nine years before I got it. In the meantime, I had to date—and then run away from—Rose, and Dora, and Felicity, and a host of others. I'd go out with these girls for a while, even live with them in some cases, but at all times the ghost of my female self shadowed me, as it had since childhood, asking me how much longer I intended to deny the truth about the nature of my character.

And at the moment this question arose, as it always did, sooner or later, there was nothing to do but break up. With one girlfriend, Allison, I went home one day and just erased myself. It was the kind thing to do, I thought. I'd been living with her in New York for three years, but we'd been losing steam. Quite frankly, I'd gone off to grad school in Baltimore partly so I could get away from her without having to have some whole big fight about it. The relationship had become like one of those balloons in the Macy's Thanksgiving parade that starts leaking helium and the next thing you know Superman's collapsed on top of the guys holding the strings.

I did love her, though, for a little while anyhow. That was the thing:

I still believed, on some fundamental level, that love would cure me. That if only I were loved deeply enough by someone else, I would be content to stay a man. It wouldn't be my authentic life, but it would be all right. It was better, in any case, than coming out as transsexual, taking hormones, and having some gruesome operation and walking around like Herman Munster. An authentic life wasn't very appealing. And so I allowed myself to be lifted off the ground by the levitating properties of romantic love. It was a nice effect.

Of course, nobody really gets cured by love, but transsexuals are hardly the only people who believe romance will lead them outside of themselves. You can't fault a person for hoping that love will make her into someone else, someone better. The world is full of false hopes, most of them dumber than the hope of being transformed by love.

After my first year at Johns Hopkins, it was clear enough Allison and I weren't getting back together. I spent a lot of time in grad school sitting in my apartment with the door locked and the shades drawn, wearing a wig that made me look like a run-down Joni Mitchell. Thus arrayed, I sat in my leather chair and read Borges and Poe and worked on a novel entitled *The Invisible Woman.* Eventually I told Allison I was coming up to New York to get my stuff and she said, fine, whatever. It wasn't a surprise to her by that time. I drove to Manhattan in my Volkswagen Golf and loaded the last of my things into the hatchback while Allison was at work. There wasn't much—some posters, a box of books, an autoharp. Then I put her apartment back the way it used to look before I'd moved in, three years before. She'd had a print of the painting *Girl with a Pearl Earring* by Vermeer over the fireplace, but I'd taken it down. That girl always gave me the creeps.

After I put Allison's stereo back where it used to be, after I took my books off the shelves, the last thing I did was to put the Vermeer back above the fireplace. The girl in the painting looked at me with her accusing, liquid eyes, and said, *Klootzak!* In Dutch this more or less means "asshole." She said it again as I left the keys on the kitchen table and then closed the door of the apartment for the last time.

*Klootzak!*

✦

IT WAS TEMPTING, of course, to try to put it all into words. Usually people assume that the reason you wanted to change genders was because deep down you hated yourself, or that you were actually gay and just didn't know it, or that you couldn't figure out a way of being feminine in the culture while still being a man. None of that has anything to do with it, though, not that this prevents people who've never suffered from this admittedly peculiar condition from writing jargon-filled books about it. Critic Judith Butler describes my heartache this way: *If there is a sexual domain that is excluded from the Symbolic and can potentially expose the Symbolic as hegemonic rather than totalizing in its reach, it must be possible to locate this excluded domain either within or outside that economy and to strategize its intervention in terms of the placement!*

Man, that is so true!

My transgender brethren and sistren are often not much more helpful. Even now, occasionally I meet trans people who say, Oh, I'm a woman too! I love to make cookies and play with dolls! To which I want to wearily respond: Jeez, if you want to play with dolls, play with dolls. You don't need a vagina for that.

Most of the time I just have to resign myself to the fact that this whole business is beyond comprehension for most straight people. If you're not trans, you're free from thinking about what gender you are in the same way that white people in America are generally free from having to think about what race they are.

Back when I was a man, though, the gender business was something I fought against. The thought of going through transition and coming out, and launching into some sort of subversive identity—well, let's just say it didn't appeal to me. I didn't want to be a revolutionary. A lot of the time, more than anything, I just wanted to be like everybody else.

I still want that, sometimes.

The women I knew in those days liked the fact that I had a feminine streak, that I seemed to be sensitive and caring, that I didn't know the names of any NFL teams, that I could make a nice risotto. A lot of straight women love a female sensibility in a man, an enthusiasm that goes right up to, but unfortunately does not quite include, his being an actual woman.

Until I started going out with Deedie in my late twenties, my romances didn't last. Because, let's face it: I was keeping the basic fact of my identity camouflaged. How was I supposed to fall in love when I was so frequently lying? How was it possible to be vulnerable with someone from whom I was, at that same moment, in hiding?

When it came time to give a lover the slip, the best strategy, as it turned out, was no breakup at all. I'd just stop answering the phone, or I wouldn't hang around my girlfriend's part of town. By the time we did run into each other, on the street, she'd be in the arms of some other guy, and what could I do? Give her a peck on the cheek, wish her well. Think about her earrings, wonder where I could get some like that.

Tell her I was happy.

AND THEN I RAN into Deedie again. The first time was at a funeral. The second, at a wedding. When we fell in love, I felt as if the thing I had always dreamed of had at last come true. Here, after all these years, was the woman who would make me content at last to stay a man.

Is it really happening? Is this how it begins?

A girl with a pearl earring stared at me with her liquid eyes. *Klootzak!* she said.

THE FLAKES SWIRLED down from a dark sky as we made our way through the snows of Maine. I helped Deedie into the Jeep and fired up the engine. As I headed down the driveway I looked in the rearview mirror at the house to which we would not return unchanged. The last thing I'd done before closing the door was to pat Lucy on the head. She knew what was up. The dog made her disappointment abundantly clear. You people, she said. You don't have a clue.

The dog was right of course. We had hoped that she'd come around to the idea of children in time, but she never forgave us. A few years later, after we disassembled Zach's crib and set up the big-boy bed in his room, Lucy christened the thing by climbing into it and taking a dump. She could have done this anywhere in the house, but she did it in the place where her message would not be misconstrued. *You people. You stupid, clueless people. You see this? This is what you get.*

I drove through the storm toward the hospital. We lived then, as now, in the small village of Belgrade Lakes, a small finger of land between Great Pond to the east and Long Pond to the west. There is room on that finger for one small road, old New England houses on either side, and the lakes beyond that. There was a general store, a restaurant, a bar, and a deranged place called Outlaw Pizza that had a half-dozen mannequins in the parking lot. One of the mannequins was named the Woman with Nine Names. If you asked the owner, Dave, what the names were, he'd just shake his head. "I can't tell you."

In the summer we would cruise across Long Pond in a boat, pick up pizzas at Outlaw and a six-pack of Shipyard from the general store, and head back home. Sometimes Deedie would cut the engine halfway back and we'd just float there in the summer sun.

"Hey, Jim," she might inquire. "How about we drink these beers?"

But the lakes were frozen now, covered with ice-fishing shacks and the trails of snowmobiles. We drove past the cemetery with its crumbling brownstone markers crowned with skulls and willows, past the gravel pit, past the fields and farms and the little churches. We didn't talk much in the car. We knew that something was beginning that was beyond our understanding. I turned on the radio. And there was Stealers Wheel, playing "a medley of their hit."

*Clowns to the left of me, jokers to the right.*

It was a good song for labor, "Stuck in the Middle with You." It would have been better, maybe, if I didn't also associate it with the ear-slicing scene from *Reservoir Dogs.*

We arrived at the hospital and I walked my enormous and beautiful wife toward maternity. Nurses lowered her into a wheelchair. For a few steps I followed after, but then one of the nurses gave me a look. It was the same look that I had given Lucy, back when we left the house. *You. You're staying here.* The nurse nodded toward the waiting room.

There were half a dozen dads-to-be in there even at this hour. They were reading copies of *Field & Stream, Men's Health, People*. One man, a big guy in a flannel shirt, looked up at me. Ah, he seemed to say. My brother.

I turned to Deedie and hugged her. "I'll be right here," I said, trying to give her an E.T. voice, reaching forward with my finger.

At this moment a contraction wracked my bride. "Ughhhhh," she moaned as I touched her heart.

"Seriously," I said. "I'll be right here."

"Ughhhhh."

"We should go," said the nurse.

I kissed her again, then watched her disappear behind the double doors. Then I walked into the waiting room and joined my newfound brethren.

In the distance, I heard the voice of Deedie Finney, the girl I had first seen onstage beneath a sheet discussing breasts and penises with Boomer Dorsey. "Ugghhhh," she said. "Uggghhh."

The big guy in the flannel handed me a copy of *Sports Illustrated*.

"Magazine?" he said.

HAD I TOLD Deedie about my history, you ask? Mentioned the whole run-down Joni Mitchell business? I had not.

At the time I felt that this self had vanished at last, just as I had prayed it would, year after year. I'm cured of that, I thought, if I thought about it at all. The divided, screwed-up person that I used to be doesn't matter. All that matters is the healed, whole man that I have become with her at last.

Sometimes I thought about trying to tell her. But then I had never told anyone, outside of a couple of therapists. I hardly had the language to describe the things I had felt, the person I had been.

And in short, I was afraid.

If you ask Deedie about all this now, she says, "My marriage with Jenny was the luckiest thing that ever happened to me." I know what you're thinking, and please. Sometimes I don't get it either. But whenever I start up with the *I suck* business, she heaves a weary sigh and suggests I take up with a different line of thought. And maybe it's worth noting that after almost twenty-five years, our marriage has lasted longer than that of anyone else we know whose husband didn't have a sex change. Who knows? Maybe if more husbands became women, the divorce rate might be lower.

Still, the burden of the secret that I did not disclose remains with me. It's a hard thing to live with, the weight of having so profoundly hurt the person whom I love.

I think when I was a man, I felt that I was protecting Deedie with my silence. I think this is something men do; they carry the weight of the world on their back and strive to complain about it as little as possible. There are ways in which I wish I still had that kind of silent courage. It's about the only thing from my male life I'm nostalgic for—the ability to protect the ones I love simply by keeping my mouth shut.

The nurse reappeared in the waiting room after an hour or so, pushing Deedie in the wheelchair. "We're sending you home," she said. "She's only two centimeters."

"That's bad?" I said, trying to remember the details of the dilation process from our Lamaze class. It was all a jumble.

"You come back tomorrow," said the nurse. "You got a long way to go still."

What could I do, except stand up and push Deedie's wheelchair back toward the exit? We felt a little embarrassed, Deirdre and I, like a pair of travelers who'd shown up at the airport a day early. As we drove back through the snow, back through Waterville and Oakland and Belgrade, she looked out the window.

The world was silent and still.

When we got home, Lucy was waiting for us. She wasn't surprised we'd come home without a baby. She made no effort to hide her contempt. *You,* she said to me. *You spent your twenties walking around Baltimore in a dress. And now you think you're going to be a father?* The dog shook her head. *Unbelievable.*

Deedie settled herself into a rocking chair in our bedroom. Once this chair had belonged to her own mother. Now Deedie sat in it, rocking back and forth, reading a book as her labor progressed.

"I'll stay up with you," I said.

"It's okay, Jim," she said. "You should get your sleep."

"If you don't get to sleep," I said, "I don't get to sleep."

Deedie smiled gently. "That's nice," she said.

I walked toward the bathroom. On my way there I peeked into the room I had prepared as a nursery. In January I had stripped off the wallpaper in the spare bedroom, painted the walls, built the crib, even assembled the little airplane mobile that dangled from the ceiling. The room was silent, and I tried to imagine the life that would soon fill it, that would soon transform our lives. It was hard to get my mind around.

I came back to the bedroom and got in bed, propped myself up with pillows. Unbelievably, I was reading a book by Robert Bly at the time, *Iron John*. A lot of the men I knew were reading it. It was very popular. It was Bly's theory that men were an "experimental species." Me, I thought the whole thing was kind of half-crazy, but then that didn't make it untrue. From time to time I looked over at my wife. Her hand was on her belly, and she was looking out the window at the falling snow, illuminated by a light that shone on our back porch.

Hours later, when I woke up with *Iron John* still open beside me on the bed, I found Deedie in the same position, as if she had not moved in all that time. She didn't look like my wife, though; while I slept she seemed to have transformed into something celestial and otherworldly. One hand lay on her belly, the place where Zachary waited for us both. Deedie looked out at the snow, and then over at me, and then out at the world again, beautiful, gentle, eternal. The sun was rising in the meadow behind our house, casting dim light upon the unknown world.

THERE WAS AN EPIDURAL, a cesarean. I stood by Deedie's side as the operation proceeded, gazing upon the innards of my dear. Fallopian tubes! Ovaries! The uterus! Adipose tissue! I stroked Deedie's hair, observed the freckles on her nose. There was a slice with a scalpel, and there was Zach, wearing the same expression he wears now when he has to do precalculus.

He thought the world over, compared it to the place he had been. Then he began to weep.

Deedie, hearing the sound of her newborn, said, "That's amazing."

They had me clip the umbilical, a wholly symbolic act, since they'd already snipped it themselves.

The nurses cleaned up the boy and brought him over to his mother. Deedie held Zach in her arms. She looked at him, then she looked at me.

"Oh my goodness," she said. "Look at what we've gone and done. Just look."

LATER, WE COULDN'T believe they just let us leave the hospital with the baby. We walked past the nurses' station as if we were getting away with something, as if we'd pulled off a bank job. We went out to the Jeep and locked the car seat containing the newborn in its bracket. Then we started up the car and drove toward home.

When we got there, we found my old friend Zero making macaroni and cheese. He'd opened up the convertible couch on the first floor for Deedie to sleep in; the cesarean she'd endured had made climbing stairs unpleasant.

"Look, Deedie," said Zero. "I made you a whelping box."

Deedie laughed, but she was weak. Zachary started to cry. Before she even had her coat off, Deedie was on the couch, propped up by pillows, the baby at her breast. We turned on the television. The 1994 Winter Olympics were on—there was some whole scandal about one skater's boyfriend clubbing another skater with a steel pipe. The name of the boyfriend was Gillooly.

Zero looked at Deedie and then at me. "So," he said. "How does it feel to be a daddy?"

✦

ACTUALLY, WHAT IT felt like most of the time was tired. Of the many conflicting emotions that define early parenthood, probably nothing is as all-encompassing as that sense of exhaustion. For a couple who had always enjoyed slow mornings and late nights, the biggest transition—at first, anyway—turned out not to be going from nonparents to parents, but going from sleepers to nonsleepers. The baby was up. The baby was down. Sometimes, when the baby was down, we'd start to worry. Had he been fed? Was he wet? Sometimes we'd wake him up when he was asleep, although now, years later, I can't for the life of me imagine why we thought this was a good idea. The house was full of baby monitors, amplifying the breathing of the small creature in the upstairs nursery. As he slept, Deedie and I would nod off in our chairs or on the couch, or at our desks, until the first sound of discontent. Then it was like living in a firehouse with the alarm going off and all of the firemen sliding down the pole and leaping into their boots. If this happened during the night I'd be the one to drop into the nursery and fetch my sobbing heir, and bring him to Deedie. Then the boy would—as the saying goes—muckle on.

Hours later, sometimes well past dawn, I'd wake up to find all three of us curled up in the bed together. Zachary lay on his back, snoozing contentedly; Deedie lay on her side, her leaking breasts falling abundantly onto the pillows, a blanket encircling us. I would reach over softly and put my arm around my wife and son. Protecting us, I believed, from whatever the world might hold.

WAS I JEALOUS, you ask, of Deedie's superhuman powers, now that she was a mother? As someone who had always identified as female—up until the moment I fell in love with her—did I feel left out, now that my love had experienced what may well be the defining moment in a woman's life? Did I feel like Pete Best, you wonder, after the Beatles became the Beatles? Or like Art Garfunkel, perhaps, after Paul Simon released *Graceland*?

I did not. Mostly, what I felt—besides sleepy—was incredibly lucky. The baby was healthy, and Deedie recovered from the trauma of birth fairly swiftly. If there were times when my sense of myself as female was slowly returning to me, I dismissed these thoughts by reminding myself that I had now made a promise, both to Deedie as well as to this newly minted son, and that it was up to me to stand between the ones I loved and the turmoil of the world. If that meant that there were times I felt a little disembodied, or haunted by some sort of cosmic melancholy, well, that was just too bad. There were all sorts of burdens to carry in the world, and if this one was mine there was more than a little solace in knowing how lucky I was nonetheless, how lucky we all were.

I thought now and again of that character in *Slaughterhouse-Five*, the guy who kept saying, *You think this is bad? This is nothing. There's a lot worse than this.*

Anyway, it wasn't maternity that I had yearned for. It was a sense of womanhood. Does that make me a hypocrite or a halfwit, to admit that I had dreamed of a woman's body, and a woman's life, and even the incredible gift of parenthood, without having any particular desire for pregnancy and menstrual cycles and breast-feeding? I am nervous about admitting this, for fear of suggesting that my quest for identity was opportunistic. Surely it does seem more than a little facile to want all of the perks of womanhood without having to experience the drawbacks—the tedium of a period, the endless come-ons from boys, the swelling dreariness of pregnancy, which, the sisterhood notwithstanding, most women will tell you gets more than a little old after a while. I am fairly certain that admitting this exposes me as a fundamentally shallow person, someone who talks the talk but won't walk the walk.

And yet, I'll say—with more than a little defensiveness—surely a woman cannot be defined solely as a person who has borne children, or who has a menstrual cycle, or who has nursed a child. As the years have gone on, I've come to accept that *womanhood*—like *manhood*—is a strangely flexible term. I've met "genetic" women who have a Y chromosome, who have a condition called androgen insensitivity syndrome that makes their bodies unable to absorb the information that that Y chromosome contains. I've met women who were born without a uterus; I've met women who have exactly zero interest in babies or children, or, for that matter, Brad Pitt. All of these women, however, are unmistakably women, and were anyone to suggest otherwise it would seem ridiculous.

And so I hope that if there is room in the wide spectrum of women's experience for all of these different lives, surely there is room in it—somewhere—for me.

That is, until I remember my Irish grandmother—"Gammie"—watching some television show with transsexuals on it, possibly *Donahue,* or *The Dinah Shore Show.* This was back in the seventies. "Oh for God's sake," she said, sucking on her Kent filter king, "those people aren't women."

"They're not?" I said. She, of course, had no idea that I was a woman just like the ones she was dismissing.

"Of course not," she said.

"They have breasts," I pointed out. "They have—you know. Vaginas."

She shot me a look. Ladies of her generation didn't say *vagina* or vote for Democrats.

"That's not what makes someone a woman," she said authoritatively.

"Really?" I asked. "What does make someone a woman then?"

Gammie took a long drag on her cigarette, then blew all the smoke into the air.

"Suffering," she said.


WHEN ZACH WAS about six months old, I met my former student Veronica Gerhardf in a Portland bar called Gritty McDuff's one Friday afternoon. She'd spent the years since graduation working in Vice President Gore's office. But she was ready for a change, she said.

"Seriously?" I replied. "Because if you want you could come back to Maine and work as our nanny. That would be awesome."

Veronica lifted her pint and drained it. Then she put the glass down on the bar. "Okay," she said.

❖

FEMINIST SCHOLAR Sara Ruddick, a pioneer in the field of motherhood studies, writes that mothering is about nurture and protection—her trinity is "preservation, growth, and social acceptability." To Ruddick, motherhood focuses on the ways moms protect their children from the world even as they slowly move them into it. More interesting—to me at least—is her suggestion that it's not a job limited to women. According to Ruddick, men, too, are capable of "mothering," when they act to shield and educate their young.

This makes plenty of sense. Still, if someone had shared this theory with me when I was a father—and I identified as a feminist even then—it would surely have hurt my feelings. At the heart of this theory seems to be an assumption that caring for children is something women do. If you're a man and you're trying to nurture and protect your kids, it seems to me as if you're being called an honorary woman.

There are lots of men who don't feel that expressing love makes them honorary women. One would think it makes them fathers.

Of the two of us, Deedie was more protective of our son, more conservative, more worried that he was going to, for instance, poke his eyes out with that thing. Whereas I was more likely to show my son—just to pick an example at random—how to put spray cheese on the dog's head. Was it the experience of having carried Zach in her womb for nine months that made her more cautious than I? Was the fecklessness of my fatherhood the direct consequence of not having had the physical experience of labor? I have my doubts about this, although it's also true that I don't think I ever worried about anyone poking his eyes out with that thing when I was a dad, and I never cautioned Zach, upon finding him cross-eyed, that they might stick that way.

On the whole, I think, I was more liberal when it came to encouraging Zach to take risks, or to do something out of the sheer goofiness of it. I pause here to remember Jerry Garcia's actual advice to his daughters, and I quote: "Hey! You guys should do more drugs!"

But any sweeping insights about what fathers do, as opposed to mothers, seems to me fundamentally bound not only by issues of gender, but by issues of class as well. I don't think it'd be too radical to suggest that mothers and fathers of the American upper middle class may well have more in common with each other than any father from this group does with a blue-collar dad. But even this observation may be suspect. I know plenty of blue-collar dads who are all about the spray cheese.

It doesn't take too long to see that any particular father's or mother's parenting strategy is a complex set of behaviors resulting not only from gender and class but from the individual web of history and character, and—above all—the agreements, spoken and unspoken, at the center of their relationship with their partner.

Sue Shellenbarger, writing in the *Wall Street Journal,* says that father figures "tend to challenge crying or whining children to use words to express themselves. Men are more likely to startle their offspring, making faces or sneaking up on them to play." And while "the average behavioral differences between large samples of moms and dads are small, in statistical terms," fathers spend about 6 percent more time in play with their children than mothers do.

I have found this to be sort of true, both in the hetero parents I know as well as the same-sex ones. In some ways, it's only common sense—even among families with two moms, or two dads, there's usually one parent who's more rambunctious than the other.

That said, goofiness—a kind of joyful foolishness—still feels to me like one of the more dependably gendered character traits that I know. There are plenty of funny women in my life; it was Deedie's levity of spirit that surely attracted me to her in the first place. But it is only with a man that I could imagine hanging a giant stuffed rabbit from a tree with a noose and taping a sign to it that read, HERE IS A LETTUCE-RUSTLIN' CARROT-THIEVIN' NO GOOD SON OF A BITCH, as I did on one memorable occasion with the cartoonist Timothy Kreider. This occurred at the end of a very long day, one that had in fact begun with our taking a giant stuffed dog, attaching a cinder block on a rope to its leg, and throwing it off a bridge. Afterward, in our fake mobster voices, we allowed as how "Mr. Whiskers sleeps with the fishes."

I don't do stuff like that anymore, although there are plenty of times my boys wish that I would. Is this because hanging stuffed animals from trees is an inherently masculine activity? Or is it because that was a long time ago, when I had considerably more time on my hands? Have I grown less ridiculous over time because womanhood feels less absurd to me than manhood? Or is it that, now that I'm in my fifties, the whole wide world just seems a lot less funny?

When I was seventeen, my friend Zero and I once drove a car through Atlantic City, New Jersey, throwing hot pancakes at people through the Volkswagen's open window.

It would be nice, I suppose, to do that sort of thing again, to take on the character of "rear bombardier" and fling those cakes like Frisbees out at the citizens of the unknown world. But I can already hear the voice of reason interceding. Oh, Jenny, says the voice. That's the dumbest thing I've ever heard of. Throwing hot pancakes, at total strangers. What if you get syrup on people? You could wreck someone's clothes! You could get arrested! It would wind up in the papers: PROFESSOR, AUTHOR, JAILED FOR ASSAULT WITH BREAKFAST ITEMS.

"I THOUGHT IT WOULD BE FUNNY," SAYS SEX-CHANGE SCRIBE.


ONE AFTERNOON IN late spring, Zach and I lay around on the kitchen floor, building towers out of blocks and knocking them to the ground again. I'm not sure how this came about, but somehow I had a can of whipped cream that I was squirting into the dog's mouth. Zach was laughing so hard he fell over. Falling over struck him as even funnier. I righted him again and squirted some more whipped cream into Lucy's mouth. She lapped it off her lips with her big pink tongue as Zachary laughed and laughed and fell over once more. It seems as if we spent the better part of a day doing this, although more likely it was just a few minutes. I remember how remarkable I found the sound of my son's laughter. Somehow children arrive on the planet knowing how to suck on a breast, knowing how to crawl, and knowing how to laugh. They know how to laugh before they know how to talk, as if joy itself is a more important survival skill than language.

The power was out that day. Living in a place as remote as Belgrade Lakes, having the electricity go out now and again wasn't all that unusual. But with a baby, it surely complicated my life. For instance, I couldn't heat up the breast milk Deedie had expressed and left in the refrigerator. I couldn't play music or turn on *Sesame Street* or warm up Zach's lunch. Maybe that's why we were on the floor playing with the can of whipped cream and the dog: It was desperation wrought from powerlessness.

The child and I laughed our heads off while the dog looked on with suspicion and contempt. Sunlight streamed through the window and reflected off our wooden floors. You people, said the dog. Imbeciles. The wind blew through a set of chimes that hung down outside the kitchen.

Then Zach looked at me with a curious, knowing expression. He hadn't spoken yet, at least not with words, but it seemed as if he had something he wanted to say.

"Hey, Zachary," I said. "Can you talk?"

The child smiled mischievously.

"Hi, Daddy," he said.

WHEN YOU'RE A father of a very small child, right in the heart of that experience, time passes with the speed of a glacier. Now, in retrospect, those years appear to have passed in a heartbeat. This strikes me as the fundamental irony of fatherhood—the odd disconnect between the speed of time passing and the speed of time remembered. Sitting here in the twenty-first century, with my boys now on the verge of college, the days of toddlerhood seem to have vanished in an instant, to have disappeared—as Captain Beefheart once noted—"like breath on a mirror." But back then, time had never seemed so slow. If, at seven A.M. for instance, I had read a book to Zachary, gotten out the Duplo blocks afterward, made and fed him his morning meal of rice cereal and apple juice, hauled out the easel and the watercolor set for a little creative time, then read him another book, and after that bundled him into the stroller and wheeled him along the dirt roads of my town, and then returned to the house and made him a snack, and finally settled onto the couch together to read another book—after all of this, were I to glance up at the kitchen clock I would note that exactly fifteen minutes had passed. Before the clock struck eight, I would have long since exhausted every possible means within my imagination of passing the time. It's no wonder parents suspend their children in bouncy-wouncy harnesses from door frames or lock them into swings. I remember on a least one occasion reading Zach the entire JCPenney catalog, in part because I hoped it would lull him to sleep, and in part because I was just plain out of ideas.

On another occasion, I told Zach to go hide in the house somewhere, and slowly counted down from a hundred before "seeking" him. When I reached the "ready or not here I come" moment, I closed my eyes, just in order to get a few blessed seconds of sleep. After ten minutes, I felt a small hand tugging on my shirt, and I opened my eyes to see my son's hopeful, excited face. "Come on, Daddy," he'd say. "Let's do it again."

Okay, Zach. One hundred! Ninety-nine! Ninety-eight! . . .

And so the days passed, hurtling and dragging. Each minute seemed like hours and hours. But then the years passed by like days.

AT THAT TIME I worked in the English department at Colby College with a number of other teachers who also had young children. There was an eccentric medievalist named Russell Potter who had had four children with his wife one after the other, producing babies just like Khrushchev had once sworn the USSR would produce nuclear bombs: "like we are making sausages in a sausage factory." There was a Victorianist named David Suchoff with two girls in elementary school, and a Shakespearean named Laurie Osborne who had a boy and a girl. We used to have lunch together, all these teachers and I, and we'd talk about the joyful misery of our lives. None of these people had been among my closest friends when they first arrived at Colby, but the shared experience of parenthood had immediately promoted all of them to the inner circle, in the same way that you might wind up forever bonded to someone you shared a room with at the burn ward. (In a similar fashion, people who'd been my bosom companions since adolescence—who had not had children—slowly fell out of the rotation, and while my love for them remained undiminished, we found less and less common ground to talk about as the days drew on. I could sense what they were feeling about me—that I had become another one of those young parents unable to talk about anything other than diapers and roseola. I'd become, in spite of myself, one of the zombies. *Don't fight it. It's good. They're smarter than we are.*

During this time the professors and I frequently talked about the advantages and the disadvantages of having children close together. Deirdre and I were already talking about Science Experiment Number Two. Was it better, I asked, to have two kids close together—what some of my friends called "Irish twins"? Or was it better to spread them out, waiting two or three or four years between Entings?

The Potters recommended having them all at once, of course. That way "they could all be friends." Which was funny, considering the way the Potter kids were always threatening to kill each other. The Osbornes, on the other hand, said it was prudent to wait. You had to think ahead to things like college. If you waited four years between the pregnancies, you wouldn't wind up having to pay two college tuitions at the same time.

It was hard to make sense of this advice. My sister and I were a little more than a year apart, and we hadn't been friends until we were each in our teens and realized that we had a common enemy in our parents. Before that, though, my sister had spent a fair amount of time pounding my head into the cement floor of the basement. On another happy occasion, I remember she had laid me down on my back, pried open my mouth with her fingers, and poured the entire sugar bowl down my throat.

I turned to David Suchoff and asked him for his opinion. Suchoff just shrugged. "What can I tell you, Boylan," he said, "whatever you do, no matter what choice you make, you will suffer."

THE PHONE RANG EARLY. I could tell it was trouble just from the sound of it. It was Deedie, and she was weeping. "Something's wrong with

Sean," she said. He'd just been born the night before. "They're mede-vacing him off to Portland."

"What?" I said. "What's wrong with him?"

"It's his heart," she said.

By the time I got to the hospital, Sean was already gone. They'd bundled him up, his tiny body surrounded by tubes and wires, and rushed him to the Maine Medical Center, leaving Deedie weeping and bereft in the maternity ward. She'd had another cesarean, a spinal headache, mastitis, a failed epidural, and a head cold. And after all of that, her son had been taken away in an ambulance.

Her doctor was there, an obstetrician somewhat lacking in bedside manner. "Is he going to be all right?" I asked. "Doctor? Is he?"

She shrugged. "I don't know," said the doc. "His heart is out of control. If we can't get his pulse down . . . your son might not make it."

"Jim," said Deedie. She couldn't leave her room. "Go to him. Please. Someone should be with him if . . ."

I drove to Portland. My friend Rick Russo was waiting for me at the hospital; he'd flown back from some book tour he'd been on (for *Nobody's Fool,* I think) to help us through whatever terrible time was now beginning. I was led through the infant ICU to an incubation chamber, kind of like the device you'd use to hatch chicken eggs in elementary school. There, wrapped in every imaginable wire, was Sean Finney Boylan, age: one day. His heart rate was 250 beats a minute. Doctors and nurses surrounded him. As I entered the ICU they all looked over at me with grave expressions.

I emerged from the room a little later. As I took off my mask and sterile gloves, Rick gave me an agonized look. He had two daughters of his own. "What's going on, Jim? Is he going to be all right?"

"I don't know," I said to my friend. "I don't know."


A WEEK LATER we came through the door holding the baby. They'd discharged us after a week of trauma, a week in which the doctors thought they had Sean's heart rate under control, only to find it skyrocketing again. He'd been born with a condition called supraventricular tachycardia, which more or less consisted of an extra nerve between his heart and his brain that caused that connection to short-circuit. One night, after his pulse hit the roof again, I had held the child in my arms looking into his tiny face, as the tears rolled down my cheeks. I thought to myself, *There is never going to come a time in my life when I'm not worried about this child. I'm going to spend the rest of my life in constant fear I'm going to lose him.*

His accelerated heartbeat made sweat course down his week-old temples. "Seannie," I whispered. "Please. Stay with us. Don't go away. You're just getting started."

When I was a newborn, I too had suffered a trauma at birth. I'd been born three months premature, which in the 1950s—like now—meant that the odds were against me. My mother had been discharged from the hospital without me, and she went back to my family's small row home in Upper Darby, Pennsylvania, to wonder what was happening to her child. Every day after work, my father took the trolley to Sixty-ninth Street in Philadelphia, and walked to the hospital and stared down into an incubator at his unwell son.

One day, his mother—Gammie—had asked him if she should visit me in the hospital too.

"I don't think so," said my father. "He's not much."

THIRTY-SEVEN YEARS LATER, when Deedie and I came through the door holding our son, we got a different reaction. Zachary and his aunt Katie—Deedie's sister—had decorated the house to celebrate Sean's arrival and rescue. There were signs that said, GOOD JOB SEAN! And CONGRATULATIONS MOM AND DAD!

Zach, two years and two months old, didn't know how much trouble Sean had been in, or how much trouble he continued to be in, for the first year of his life. Throughout 1996 and '97, we had to dose the baby with a syringe of digitalis, morning and evening, to keep the tachycardia at bay.

All Zach knew was that his brother had at last arrived, and that we had gone from a family of three to a family of four. We laid the sleeping

Sean in his bassinet. Zach stood there, looking in wonder at his new companion.

He turned to us. "Mommy, Daddy?" he asked. "Do you think Baby Sean is proud?"

WE SURVIVED those days. Sean did not die, and instead grew slowly round on breast milk. Zach took his painting seriously. "I call this one *Crazy Town*," he said, showing us a canvas with a series of swirling rectangles. There was paint all over his face. Our house filled with blocks, and books, and stuffed animals, and syringes of digitalis, and tiny pairs of shoes.

We'd sit on the couch, Deedie and I, our children in our laps, reading *Go, Dog. Go!*

"What a party! What a dog party!"

We'd done it. The days raced by, at the speed of molasses.

Sometimes I'd look at the boys and wonder, *How on earth are you going to teach them how to be men? You, of all people, Boylan?*

But then, this is one of the fundamental contradictions of parenthood—the unending necessity to teach your children lessons that you yourself still have not learned.

YEARS LATER, it finally occurred to me to watch *Brideshead Revisited* again. I couldn't remember why we'd never finished it. I put the tape in the machine and hit play. The film picked up right where I'd stopped it on a snowy night long ago.

A young man's hand reached out and picked a plover's egg from a bowl and raised it into the air.

Charles Ryder looked at his new friend Sebastian, with whom he was already in love: *He was magically beautiful,* Charles says, *with that epicene quality which in extreme youth sings aloud for love. And withers at the first cold wind.*

# I'M AWAKE. I'M AWAKE.

I opened my eyes. The game was afoot. I gazed around the dark hotel room, immediately sensing a situation in progress. Deedie drowsed to my left, her chest softly rising and falling. Through the screen door that led to the balcony I could hear the ocean crashing on the beach.

A voice cut through the darkness. "What now?" it said. "What now!"

Through the murk I could just make out Zachary's silhouette. He got up on his feet, and his head peeked over the edge of the portable playpen. I checked the clock. Four A.M.

*Oh God please no,* I thought. *Sweet weeping Jesus.*

One of Zach's legs went up and over the rail, followed a moment later by the other. There was a clunk as he hit the floor. Then he stood again. "What now?" he asked. "What now!"

Then he began to run around the condo. The little feet pattered against the floor. As he ran, Zach shouted, "I'm awake! I'm awake! I'm awake!"

We were on vacation. Sanibel, Florida. Sean wiggled in his crib. He sat up, took a look around, and began to weep.

"Waah," he said. "Waah. Waah. Waah."

"I'm awake! I'm awake! I'm awake!"

Deedie opened one eye. I understood in a glance. "Go get 'em, Daddy. It's your turn."

"Waah, waah, waah."

❖

I PUSHED THE STROLLER down the beach. The sun had not yet risen. The breeze blew in off the ocean and whipped my hair around. I was wearing blue jeans and a white T-shirt, a battered sweatshirt that said WESLEYAN.

Zach sat in the front of the double stroller, holding a juice box. He pointed out a group of sleeping seagulls. "Birds are dreaming," he said.

Sean had fallen asleep again, bottle in his mouth. I remembered what this was like. Something similar had happened to me a couple of times during my sophomore year of college.

At two years old, we no longer had to give Sean a syringe of digitalis twice a day. Although he was still a pale, thin thing, like an orphaned waif in Dickens, he was partial to a good bottle. He was one of those hair-of-the-dog boys.

The stroller wasn't really made for the beach. The rubber wheels sank into the soft sand. In a compartment between the wheels was a backpack full of all the things I'd need in case of an emergency. Extra diapers. Wipes. Baby bibs. Vitamin D ointment. Band-Aids. Baby rice. Juice boxes. Crayons. Books by Eric Carle and Dr. Seuss. Cheese sticks. In the event of a nuclear emergency, the boys and I could probably hold out for days.

Zach and Sean and I rolled by the dark ocean, our wheels crushing the shards of clamshells and conches, slipping on slicks of seaweed and the egg sacs of sea creatures. There was no one else for miles, it seemed. The hotels and condos and beach houses to my right were virtually all dark, except for an occasional blue glow coming from a high room in which a television had been left on. I pictured a dad like me, passed out in a big chair, a child in his lap, the television screen crackling with snow. But then, the era when stations shut down for the night, after playing the national anthem, had come to an end right around the same time my sons were born, hadn't it? Time was passing. I'd been a college student, then I was a married man, and now I was a father. I still didn't quite feel lifelike though. The ocean roared all around.

"Wake up!" shouted Zach, and waved his arms. He was wearing a tiny blue jean jacket from OshKosh. "Wake up, birds!"

The seagulls, irritated by youth, spread their wings and rose. One remained behind, beak-first in the sand.

"Daddy," said Zach. "Why isn't that one waking up?"

The bird's eyes were missing. "Oh," I said. "Maybe his dreams are too wonderful to wake up from?"

I smiled inwardly. *Well played, Daddy!*

But Zachary looked at me sternly. "Daddy," he said. "You tell me the truth."

How was it, I wondered, that at age four, he could already tell the difference between the truth and a lie? Did he have some special sense that I'd either lost or never had to begin with?

"The truth," I said mournfully. I looked at Sean, still clutching his bottle. There was milk on his chin. What is it that children dream about, before they know what the world is? Are they remembering the place they came from?

"Okay, Zach. The truth is that bird is dead. I think he can't wake up, as much as he'd like to."

Zach thought about this. "We should bury him," he said.

I looked at my watch, as if I were in a hurry to get somewhere. But where was it I was so certain I needed to go at four thirty in the morning?

"Okay," I said.

Zach raised his arms, and I lifted him out of the stroller. He reached into the storage compartment between its front wheels and extracted a plastic shovel. Then he looked up at me. "It's the right thing to do," he said. He began to dig a hole.

I watched as my son dug the grave. In addition to his jean jacket he was wearing a pair of overalls and a red T-shirt and a small Boston Red Sox hat.

He looked up at me with an expression that suggested he was irritated I wasn't of more use.

"Daddy," he said, "you get things for the headstone."

I walked toward the shore and began to gather shells. I was barefoot, and the cold ocean encircled my feet up to the ankles. Sanibel is famous for its seashells. There were scallops and mussels, a broken nautilus. I returned to the site of the interment. Zach stood somberly by the hole like a New England minister.

"You should take off your hat, Zach," I said. He thought about it, then took off the Red Sox cap and held it in one hand. He didn't ask why, which was good because I couldn't have told him.

"Okay," he said. "We are ready to go."

I realized that this was my cue to lower the gull into its tomb. I wasn't crazy about the idea of touching the dead bird, not least because whatever had killed it might well have been contagious. In the worst-case scenario, Zach and Sean and Deedie could all have been back there later that afternoon, digging a hole for me.

So I borrowed Zach's shovel and used it to lift the corpse. Then I lowered the gull into the hole. Zach nodded. I was just about to cover the bird up with sand again when he said, "Daddy. We should say a few words first."

I looked at the boy. It's worth noting that he wasn't a particularly morose character. But he did have a very strongly developed sense of right and wrong. At preschool, he'd once made one of his instructors cross when she'd asked him to pretend to be a character from a story. Zach's face had grown red and angry. "I'm not a character from a story," he said tearfully. "I'm me. I'm Zach Boylan!"

"Okay," I said. "What should we say?"

"I'm going to say a poem," said Zach. I nodded and thought, *Okay. Is this one of those moments you always remember because it's so adorable? Or because it was the first clue you had that your child would someday grow up to shoot the president?*

"Little seagull," said Zach. "I'm sorry you're dead. Even though you woke me up with your squawking. Although you are gone now, I can still hear your song."

Then he looked down into the grave, with melancholy and wonder, and folded his hands before him. While I thought, *You have got to be fucking kidding me.*

Zach lifted his head and said, "Okay, we can cover him up now." He put his hat back on.

I glanced toward the stroller, where Sean was still asleep. "Shouldn't we wake up your brother?" I said. "Don't you think he should be part of this?"

Zach shook his head. "No, Daddy," he said, a little surprised I'd suggested such a thing. "This is just for you and me."

The sky in the east was growing brighter now, a faint wash of blue and gray above the horizon. I got the shovel down into the sand and covered the bird. Afterward, we marked the spot with a stick and decorated the tomb with shells and seaweed. I thought of Shelley's grave in Rome, where I'd once stood alone and fought off tears. The poet's epitaph quoted *The Tempest: Nothing of him doth remain, but doth suffer a sea-change, into something rich and strange.*

Then, having done the right thing by the gull, Zach climbed back into the stroller, and I took up my place once more at the bridge. "Forward!" said my son, and using my superhuman strength, I once again began to push my children across the face of the broad earth.

AFTER SUNRISE, I returned to our condo and traded the stroller for a bicycle, locking the boys into some sort of New Age yuppie rickshaw that I dragged behind a rented ten-speed. I heard the boys talking to each other as we pedaled down the boulevard. Zach was reading *The Very Hungry Caterpillar* to Sean. He was up to the caterpillar's sixth day: Our hero was eating through a chocolate cake, a Swiss cheese, salami, a lollipop, a cherry pie, a sausage, a cupcake, and a slice of watermelon. To my right was the endless ocean, the skies turning pink and blue now. There were joggers and shell seekers and loner dudes with metal detectors.

We pulled up at a diner. I picked up the boys and carried them, one on each arm, into the restaurant. There was no one else in the place. A waitress looked at me with a grin. "You can sit anywhere," she said. I bore my sons to a booth by a window. I sat Zach down on a cushion, then buckled Sean into a high chair. I opened up my backpack and handed out juice boxes and crayons. My sons set to work.

We ordered scrambled eggs for Sean, pancakes for Zach, a bagel with lox for me. From the kitchen I could hear people speaking Spanish. The ceiling of the diner was hung with old nets into which seashells had been placed. On the walls were giant plastic marlins and paintings of the Sanibel lighthouse. Someone turned on the stereo, and a local radio station played Paul McCartney and Wings. *We're so sorry, Uncle Albert.*

Sean pointed at me and said, "Man."

I looked up at the clock on the wall. It was five fifteen. I took off my glasses and rubbed my eyes, felt the stubble against my palm.

Zach said, "Daddy, do birds go to heaven?"

"I don't know, Zach. What do you think?"

He looked thoughtful. "I don't know much about heaven," he said.

"Well, it's a mystery," I said.

He thought about it some more. "I think there should be birds in heaven."

I agreed. "So do I."

Sean pointed at me again and said, "Man. Man. Man."

"What do you think God is?" I asked my son.

He answered this question without hesitation, as if he'd been working on his answer for some time. "I think God might be an invisible sparkling wind that talks." Thanks for asking.

Sean looked at a large conch shell suspended in the net above us. "Shell," he said.

Zach considered his brother. "Baby Sean is learning a lot of words," he said.

"Pretty soon he'll be talking up a storm, won't he?"

"He'll be talking a word storm!" Zach agreed.

The waitress brought our breakfasts. She poured more coffee into my cup. "Anything else?" she said.

"We are having a special breakfast," said Zach.

"Is that right?" said the waitress. She had a name tag that said DESTYNEE.

"It's just boys," said Zach.

"Special," said Destynee. She looked at me and, incredibly, her eyes were shining, as if she were on the edge of tears.

"Negg," said Sean, raising a fistful of scrambled eggs to his mouth with his bare hands.


I HAULED THE BOYS in their New Age rickshaw back beneath the brightening skies. More people were out now, more members of the dawn patrol. A dad threw a kite into the air and shouted to his daughter: *Run, now run!* Zach was reading *The Very Hungry Caterpillar* to his brother again. On day seven, the caterpillar ate a single leaf. He'd had a stomachache, but he was feeling better now.

I rode along the bike path, which now cut through dunes and areas of tropical forest. Now and again I'd traverse wooden bridges that crossed over murky-looking swamps and canals. There was the rumor of alligators. We stayed on the path.

At length we found ourselves at the Sanibel Island light. I locked the bike and lifted my sons once more, and carried them toward the lighthouse.

The light at Point Ybel is not much more than a high pyramid-shaped scaffold capped with a glass dome. Zach and Sean didn't seem particularly impressed by it, but I didn't expect them to be. One thing I'd learned as a parent was that views are largely wasted on anyone below the age of sixteen. Still, the boys were glad to be placed down upon the sand, and they began to run toward the ocean crashing endlessly before them. I sat down on the beach and watched as Zach combed the point for shells and Seannie immediately set to work digging in the sand. A flock of tough-looking seagulls looked over at the boys impassively.

I rubbed my eyes again, watching my sons, watching the sunrise bathe everything in blinding light.

A woman about my age ran up the beach, huffing and puffing in her workout clothes. She ran toward the lighthouse, touched the scaffold, and then turned around and ran away in the other direction. I watched as she receded. What if I had been that girl now running down the beach, the wind in my hair, and she had been the father, sitting here at the base of the Sanibel Light? Whose life would have been more altered?

Zach came back up from the shoreline and sat down next to me. "Hi, Daddy," he said.

I gathered the boy into my arms and gave him a huge hug. He hugged me back, and as we held each other it occurred to me, not for the last time, that so much of the love we offer our children comes not because we are such warmhearted beings, but because we so desperately, thirstily, crave love in return.

I let him go, and Zach sat down next to me. Looking at his brother, happily digging by the water, he observed, with the air of a much older person, "Baby Sean's really growing up, isn't he?"

"He is," I said.

Zach looked down at the sand. "Daddy," he said, "I keep thinking about that bird."

I looked over at him. He was still wearing his Boston Red Sox hat. The ocean wind rustled the blond curls beneath the brim.

"What are you thinking about?"

"How he was here, and now he's gone."

"I know," I said. "It's sad."

He curled one of his arms around my elbow.

"Why did Grampapa die?" he said.

My father had died eight years before Zach was born. I didn't know that my father was even on Zach's radar.

"He had cancer," I said. "Melanoma."

"Are you going to get cancer?"

"No, Zach. I hope not, anyway."

"How do you know?"

"Because," I said. "I use sunscreen."

We sat together for a moment, watching the ocean.

"What was he like?" Zach asked.

"My dad?" Sean was still studiously digging in the sand. "He was quiet. Thoughtful."

"Was he silly like you?"

"No," I said. "He wasn't silly like me. Although if you squeezed his nose, he'd say, 'Honk.'"

Zach's whole face brightened. He reached out to me and squeezed my nose. I said, "Honk."

"Like that?"

I nodded. "Like that."

Zach looked pleased. He knew his grandfather now.

"What did he do?"

I thought about it. It was such an odd question to answer about a man. What did he do?

"He played the piano," I said. "He raised orchids. He liked to go to the hardware store."

"What's a hardware store?"

"It's a store where they sell paint and tools and help you learn how to fix your house."

I traveled to a day in 1965. Dad was showing me how to use a soldering iron, fixing a toy of mine—a battery-operated flying saucer, in fact. I remembered his workbench, with its vise, and its pegboard, and an array of tiny drawers, each one containing screws and nails of different sizes. It was like his altar.

My father pressed the solder against the hot point of the iron, and a big silvery drop of the stuff dripped against the contact point on the saucer, where a wire was loose. My nose had filled with the smell of melting tin and lead. I watched as my father moved the curled end of the loose wire into the gooshy metal drop. Then my hand was burning, and I cried out loud. My father, realizing he'd accidentally allowed the tip of the soldering iron to brush against my wrist, dropped what he was doing and clapped me to his chest. *I'm so sorry, son. I'm so sorry.* He held me for a long time. *I didn't mean to hurt you. I'd never hurt you, Jim. I'm so sorry.*

"Did you bury him? Like that bird?" asked Zach.

"No," I said, uncertain how to explain cremation to a four-year-old. "After he died, his body was turned into ashes."

"Ashes?" said Zach, uncertain.

I picked up some of the sand at our feet. "Ashes. It's like white sand. We put it in the ground, under a tree."

Zach considered this. As he thought, I remembered being held by my father, heard him tell me he was sorry. I smelled the smell of burning lead.

"Do you miss him?" asked Zach. "Grampapa?"

IN THE LAST YEARS of my father's life he started to sleepwalk. He'd done this off and on when he was younger, but toward the end he made a regular habit of roaming the halls of our house at night. I'd hear his heavy footsteps on the creaking stairs, coming up to the third floor, where I lived in a room sealed most of the time with a heavy deadbolt. I heard him creep through the hallway and open the door to the spare room, diagonally across the hall from mine, and lay himself down in the guest bed. After a while he'd start to snore, and I'd know he was okay, at least until morning.

When the dawn slanted through the small dormer window in the spare room, though, he'd sit up, confused and angry. "Goddamn it," he'd say. "Where am I? What is this? What the hell am I doing here?"

HE HADN'T KNOWN I was transsexual, or if he did, he never said anything about it. I'm not even sure he knew the word *transsexual,* or *transgender,* and almost surely he could not have explained the difference between the two. But that's all right. For a long time I couldn't figure it all out, either.

Once, though, when I was in high school, Dad and my mother were watching television, clicking through the channels, and for a moment they rested on a Movie of the Week presentation of *The Rocky Horror Picture Show.* It was the scene when Frank-N-Furter waltzes around in fishnets singing, "Well you got caught with a flat. Well how about that?"

My father raised an eyebrow and said, "There he is, Jim. Your biggest fan."

For a single, terrified second, I feared that he knew exactly what was going on in my room, up on the third floor, when the deadbolt was drawn. Was it possible, I wondered, as Frank-N-Furter danced before us, that from the very beginning my father had understood the thing that had lain in my heart, and that I had apparently so completely failed to conceal? But just as quickly, I realized this was impossible. The truth about my identity was so completely improbable that my father could make a joke about it, as if the very idea was funny.

My mother picked up the remote and we moved on to another movie. Kirk Douglas was standing in a sea of men in gladiator costumes. "I'm Spartacus!" the men shouted, one after the other. "I'm Spartacus!"

My mother put the remote down. They loved movies about the ancient world, and I could understand why. My mother was Spartacus. My father was Spartacus. My drunken grandmother was Spartacus. Even Sausage, our gelatinous, overweight Dalmatian, was Spartacus.

In our house, sometimes, it seemed like just about everybody was Spartacus. Except me.


ON HIS FIFTIETH BIRTHDAY, we gave my father an inflatable rubber boat. He spent the rest of that day in it, floating around the pool, with a cigarette in one hand and a martini in the other. I'd spent the morning in my third-floor room with the door locked, wearing my hippie girl clothes and reading Betty Friedan. Then, when it was time for the party, I changed back into boy clothes and helped carry the hibachi grill and the beef patties and the charcoal and the cheese out to the pool, and I made my father a cheeseburger.

By the time he turned fifty, he'd been cancer-free for years, but a year later, in '79, he had a second mole removed, beet red in color. Then he was healthy for another six years, until the last one. That time, they had to follow through with radiation, and interferon, and cisplatin. Too late, though.

After his funeral, on Easter Sunday 1986, as we followed the hearse through the rain, I thought back to the happy, sun-soaked occasion of his fiftieth birthday, just eight years before. We'd set up a stereo outside and played his favorite music for him. A couple of Beethoven symphonies, and the Toccata and Fugue in D Minor by Bach. It was the first time in his life that my father seemed to understand the joys of a kick-ass stereo. He lay back in his boat with a look of complete peace as he listened to the Bach.

You could see a place on his leg where they'd taken off the mole, and another on his back where they'd taken the skin to do the graft.

When the fugue was over, Dad opened his eyes and said, sweetly, "Can we play it again? Louder?"


MY FATHER'S MOTHER, Gammie, was married four times, although there were times when she dismissed marriage number one as "a trial balloon." The first husband she actually counted was my grandfather, James, whose nickname for her was "Stardust." My father was her only child, but she lost interest in him after James dropped dead of a brain hemorrhage, just after my father's ninth birthday. By the time my father was sixteen, he was living virtually all the time at a friend's house, on a cot out in the hallway. Now and again he'd show up at his mother's house to find smashed bottles on the floor, dishes in the sink. A wild party began at Stardust's house sometime in 1938 and didn't really finish until 1946.

My grandfather had left her a fair amount of money, but by the time my father hit high school, the cash was gone. What happened to it? As Gammie herself later explained it, "I like men. And I like money. And men who like money, like me."


MY FATHER'S HOBBIES, in childhood, had been collecting baseball cards and playing marbles. So it was a surprise when he introduced me to model rockets on my twelfth birthday, with the gift of a kit from Estes. The name of the rocket was BIG DADDY.

Our launchpad was an abandoned horse-racing track on a farm a few miles from our house. The grass had grown thick and snarly in the center oval of the track, and in the distance we could see the burned-out remains of what had once been the farmhouse. The farmer's windmill had survived the fire, somehow, and it spun in the breeze not far from the ruins. I set up the launchpad and unwound the wires with the alligator clips that connected the rocket's igniter fuses to a battery-powered launch controller. After checking the wind, I adjusted the angle of the launch rod so that the rocket would fly in the windward direction at first, because I knew that once the parachute opened, and the breeze filled it, BIG DADDY would begin to drift.

My father stood at some remove, watching as I ran through my prelaunch checklist. I was very thorough, applying the proper amount of chute wadding into the fuselage (so that the detonator charge, which caused the nose cone to eject, thus activating the parachute at apogee, would not cause the chute's plastic to melt). I secured the igniter fuses with masking tape. I double-checked the wind speed and the angle of the launch rod. Then I looked at my father.

"Are we go for launch?" I asked dramatically.

He replied, with as little enthusiasm as it is possible to imagine, "We are go."

Then I started counting down. "Ten . . . nine . . . eight . . . seven— ignition sequence start!—six . . . five . . . four . . . three . . . two . . . one! *Liftoff!*"

For a moment BIG DADDY sat there on the pad. There was a sizzling sound. I was afraid, for a moment, that it was a dud, that, as they said at Mission Control, we'd have to "scrub the launch." Then, all at once, there was a vast, silvery swooshing sound, and BIG DADDY raced into the sky, leaving only a vaporous trail behind.

We stood there watching the rocket rise out of sight. It neared the sun, and I shaded my eyes with my hand, like I was saluting. A moment later, I felt a hand on my shoulder, and when I looked over, it was my father, who'd placed his hand on my back, probably without even thinking about it. I remember that his other hand was shielding his eyes from the sun as well. I saw the look on his face, a look of surprise and wonder, not only at the miracle of space flight—which was wondrous enough—but also, I imagined, at me. I was a boy of whom nothing might have been expected—*I don't think so. He's not much.* At times I must have seemed like a strange creature to him, delicate and frail. But I'd done this: I'd made the homely creation fly.

I looked back up at the sky. The far-off speck of the rocket passed directly in front of the sun. For a moment I lost sight of it.

Then we saw a bright flash. A moment later there was a fiery popping sound. I felt my father's hand grip my shoulder blade a little harder. Then there was smoke, as the pieces of the rocket fell to earth. We stood there in silence as the ruins rained down around us, some of them still smoking.

I looked down at the ground. "I'm sorry, son," my father said. Then he got out a cigarette—an L&M King—and lit it with a butane lighter. As he blew the smoke into the air, he gave me a weary look that suggested that this was exactly what the world was like, that in the years that lay before us both, it should be expected that all sorts of things would explode and scatter.

"Stupid thing," I said angrily. "Stupid BIG DADDY."


WHEN I FINALLY saw *Cat on a Hot Tin Roof,* years later, I didn't know that Big Daddy was the name for anything other than a rocket. But there was Burl Ives, embodying the man himself. "They say nature hates a vacuum," says Brick, his son.

"That's what they say," replies Big Daddy. "But sometimes I think that a vacuum is a hell of a lot better than some of the stuff that nature replaces it with."


ONE NIGHT BACK in 1973, I was up late in my room with the deadbolt drawn. I was wearing a green paisley skirt and a halter top filled with grapefruits, and I was reading *Tonio Kröger* in German. On the stereo, Jerry Garcia was singing: "Saint Stephen will remain, all he's lost he shall regain." Your typical Friday night. From a long way off, I heard a glass break, down in the kitchen.

*That was weird.*

So I lifted the needle off the record. Then I took off my girl clothes, stuck them back in the secret panel that swung out from my wall, and put on my boy pajamas and a bathrobe and went downstairs. It was almost midnight.

There in the kitchen was my father. He was sweeping glass off the floor. "What happened?" I asked. "Are you okay?"

"Gotta clean up after Mom," he said in a sleepy, mumbly voice.

"Dad?" I said. "What's happening?"

"Daddy died," he said sadly.

This is when I realized that my father was sleepwalking, and that he was playing out some crazy scene from his childhood, from the days after the death of his own father, when Stardust, along with her many suitors, was drinking the money at the endless party. I could see my father's boyhood self, trying to straighten up the house while his mother lay passed out on the sofa.

He was being very methodical, putting the shards of glass in the dustpan. I held the pan still for him as he swept, again and again and again. Then I poured the glass pieces into the trash, and I said, "All done." He stood there with the broom, deep in his trance.

"Who—?" said my father, in a voice that sounded like wind rushing through a tunnel. "Who are you?"

I looked at my father's face—and even though he was forty-five, and asleep, it struck me that, perhaps for the only time in my life, I was seeing what he'd looked like when he was a boy.

"It's time for bed," I said.

"Who are you?" said my father.

I considered telling him the truth in reply to this question, but instead I took him by the hand, led him up the creaking stairs, and tucked him into bed. And kissed my boy good night.

THE YEAR I turned forty, Deedie and the boys gave me a rubber chair that floats in the water for my birthday. Since it was raining, though, I didn't get to repeat the ritual of my father, twenty years earlier, listening to Bach at top volume. I was still a man then, although I wouldn't remain one for much longer.

We had a bottle of dandelion wine that my friend Tim Kreider had made on his porch, and I drank it. The wine instantly made me nuts, in the most pleasant way imaginable. I placed the rubber chair on the wooden floor of our house and put *Peter and the Wolf* on the stereo, and as I listened to the Prokofiev I happily floated around the room as my family waved from the couch. *And if one would listen very carefully, he could hear the duck quacking inside the wolf, because the wolf, in his hurry, had swallowed her alive.*

As I FLOATED around the living room, I thought about my dad. I wondered if he had felt as uncertain of what the job of father entailed as I did. Like most of the men I know, he was an interesting mix of the masculine and feminine. Sure, he'd been an athlete in high school and college, and yes, his favorite place in the world other than our own house was the hardware store. He loved to spend hours stripping wallpaper and sanding windowsills and building walls with a sledgehammer and a chisel. At the same time, his hobby was raising orchids in a greenhouse that he and my mother built off the kitchen.

There were times I couldn't figure him out—he spent all morning swinging a sledgehammer around, making walls out of fieldstone, and then in the afternoon would meticulously divide a phalaenopsis and water his flowers with a misting wand. Still, if there were masculine and feminine things about my father, he never seemed at war with himself about it; he seemed, above all, a man at peace.

I was not a man at peace, I thought as I floated on my raft from the kitchen to the porch. I was restless and uncertain. A will-o'-the-wisp, a flibbertigibbet, a clown. Still, I know a lot of men who meet that description, and it's that very quality in them that I suspect is responsible for their inventiveness and their charm.

I had been lucky in having Dick Boylan for a father. As a dad myself, I wasn't going to be anything like him. But in his kindness and his humor, his curiosity and his love, he taught me everything I knew about being a man.

And from whom, I wondered, had he learned this? He'd lost his father when he was still a child. Just as my own children, in years to come, would lose theirs.

ON THE BEACH in Florida, Seannie was hunting for jellyfish. Before us was the Point Ybel lighthouse. "Do you miss him?" asked Zach. "Grampapa?"

I watched as another woman my age loped toward us in her shorts and running bra. This one looked so much like a female version of me that I had to stare. She had the same blond hair, the little wire-rimmed glasses, the birdlike nose. I wondered whether the father of this stranger loved his daughter.

The woman reached out to touch the lighthouse with her fingertips. Then she turned around and ran back in the direction from which she'd come.

I nodded. "Yes," I said, although my voice had fallen to a whisper. "I miss him."

Sean came running toward us. He had something in his hand, something globular and dead and tentacled.

"Yellyfish," he said. He dropped it in the sand.

"Hey, Baby Sean," said Zach. "Watch!" He leaned over and squeezed my nose. "Honk," I said sadly.

Baby Sean thought this was the most wondrous thing he had ever seen. He looked at me, and then his brother, and then at me again.

"Can Baby Sean honk your nose, Daddy?" said Zach.

I nodded. I really didn't see what difference it could possibly make now.

Sean reached out tentatively and clasped my nose. I felt his tiny fingers encircling my nostrils.

"Honk," I said. "Honk. Honk. Honk."

ON THE WAY back to the condo, Zach read the end of the book to his brother. The sun was shining all around us now, burning off the mist. I was still thinking of that woman I'd seen. If I'd been her, instead of myself, what would my life have been like? How was it possible, at this point, to imagine a life for me that did not include Zach, and Sean, and Deedie?

"What happens," Zach explained, "is that in the end of the story, the very hungry caterpillar turns into a butterfly. He builds a little house, and climbs inside it, and then he changes."

"Then?" said Baby Sean. "Then?"

"Then nothing, Baby Sean," said Zach. "He changes, and becomes a butterfly. And has to fly away."

TIME OUT I

▼

# CONVERSATIONS with FATHERS and SONS

Richard Russo

Ralph James Savarese

Trey Ellis

Augusten Burroughs

# RICHARD RUSSO

*I didn't care about you at all.*
*There was a poker game to go to.*
*The track was there.*

© *Elena Seibert*

Richard Russo—known to his friends as Rick—is the author of seven novels, including *Empire Falls,* which won the 2002 Pulitzer Prize for Fiction. He and I shared an office at Colby College in the early 1990s, when we were both professors of creative writing there. The friendship quickly grew to include Rick's wife, Barb, and their two daughters, Emily and Kate; in our will, the Russos are appointed the legal guardians of Zach and Sean, should anything happen to Deedie and me. Our friendship has weathered many transitions—not only mine from male to female, but Rick and Barb's, from parents to grandparents. In June of 2011, Rick and I sat on the sun porch of the Russos' house in Camden, Maine, to talk about parenthood and fiction.

▼

JENNIFER FINNEY BOYLAN: Rick, a lot of your readers probably think they know your father because your novels frequently have a kind of brilliant but feckless middle-aged man at its center. And whether it's *The Risk Pool* or *Nobody's Fool* or *Empire Falls,* I think there is a certain "Russo Man."

RICHARD RUSSO: Right. The rogue male.

JFB: How close is that to your father?

RR: My father was a man of just enormous charm. He had the ability to walk into a room and make everybody happy, just by his presence.

Women in particular, he had a way of making . . . especially women who maybe once had been beautiful but weren't anymore . . . he just had a way of making older women, sometimes elderly women . . . he would compliment them and charm them and just make them feel . . . you could just see their faces light up, you know, when Jimmy was around. He had that ability to just charm everybody. He was an incredibly generous man, too. Whenever he was around. But the problem with him was always not being around.

JFB: Why was he not around? I mean, he married your mother. How long had they been married when you came into the picture?

RR: Well, he married just before he shipped overseas. And he came home a different man. You don't land on the beaches in Normandy and make it all the way through France and on all the way to Berlin and come back the person you were when you left. I think that my mother and father, before he left, were kind of on the same page about what they might have wanted the shape of their marriage [to] be. But by the time he came back, he had changed and she hadn't. My mother, to another extent, would never change. She was, even deep into her eighties, a woman who looked at the world in essentially the same way. Whereas my father came home with very little tolerance for any manner of bullshit. He was celebrating the fact that he was alive.

So the last thing in the world he wanted was any kind of responsibility. When other soldiers came back and took advantage of the GI Bill, or put a down payment on a house, or started having kids and settling down, he just wanted no part of any of that, and my mother's point with him always was that it's time. She said, "Can't you see? Look around you. Everybody else is growing up. Everybody else is coming into parenthood, everybody else has at least some ambitions as to what the rest of their lives are going to be like. Time for us to just do what everybody else is doing." And my father just wasn't in it, and he never would be.

He said, "I didn't care about you at all. There was a poker game to go to. The track was there."

JFB: How old were you when he said that?

RR: Well, I was probably in my late twenties, early thirties. I was going back [to Gloversville, New York] summers to work construction and save money for the next year of college.

JFB: It doesn't sound like he was saying it particularly apologetically.

RR: No! No. I mean, there was an element of apology in it, in the sense that he said, you know, if I had to do things all over again I wouldn't have done it exactly that way, but he'd come to the conclusion that my mother was just batshit. "I wasn't going to live with your mother!"

He said, "I knew you were around and I knew I had responsibilities, but it was just easy on a day-to-day basis to forget, just easy to forget. There was always something going on."

JFB: What did you learn from your father when he was around? Your novels lead me to suspect that now and again he would show up and take you off on an adventure of some kind, whether you're fishing, or . . .

RR: Well, I mean, part of it was negative, and some of it was very, very positive indeed. On the negative side, [what] I came to realize—and it's only become crystal clear in the last few years when I've thought about it more—was that my father was also really afraid of me. When he did turn up, it was almost always with someone else. He'd have a friend of his, or if he picked me up, we would go to New York City maybe and catch a Giants football game or a Yankees game, but it was always with my uncle Chuck, and they'd always meet a couple of other guys there. Later on, when I got to be a little older, we'd go someplace where he could always count on knowing people when he arrived. So even then the burden of what slender parenting he was doing he could share with a half a dozen other drunks.

I always thought when I was younger that it was just disinterest, and I didn't recognize it as fear until much later. Or inadequacy.

JFB: What was he afraid of? Was it that you were the ghost of responsibility? That he shirked?

RR: Yeah! Or feelings of inadequacy from just not doing your job. If you don't do your job ninety-nine percent of the time, you're not going to have a really strong feeling of competence that other one percent of the time. And I was not an easy kid, in the sense that I think he thought of me as someone who as soon as he got home would be reporting back.

JFB: You were your mother's spy.

RR: Her instructions to him whenever I left the house with him was always just a series of don'ts. I always had a sense of him as a very dangerous man, which, of course, at times he was. There were times when you did not want to be standing next to my father. Because something would come flying at him and it wouldn't hit him, it'd hit you.

So it made me an alert child, but it also made me a vigilant child. When I was with him, I was always trying to figure out his absence. Always trying to figure out if he was the man that my mother portrayed for me. So he must have seen me as a kid that was always taking notes. Always disapproving. And I always had the sense that by the time he dropped me off again at my grandfather's house that he had just about as much of me as he could stand.

The powerful and positive things I learned from my father had an awful lot to do with work. Because he did such hard physical work and he played so hard. I would watch him when we were working road construction together in the summers. I would watch him, absolutely slack-jawed at how hard that man could work. And he was then in his fifties and he could outwork and outdrink everybody. I mean, he would limp in the first couple of hours in the morning, but once he burned off the alcohol he was simply amazing. The amount of what I could only consider punishment that man could endure. And when he began to get older and have some physical illness and injuries that just come from a life of hard work, his ability to manage pain left me just amazed. And also, as he became ill—the first barb of lung cancer, then he went into remission for a while, and then he went into a second bout of lung cancer—he had an ability to absorb not only physical pain but psychological pain, of just knowing what was happening to him, and going through those radiation treatments without ever complaining, without ever showing any . . . he had to be afraid, but he never showed the slightest weakness. At all.

JFB: So do you think you got that as a son, a certain fearlessness, a certain dedication to work? As your friend, I've rarely seen you afraid, and when I have, you've been afraid for other people. I've seen you afraid for me, I've seen you afraid for Deedie when I was midtransition. I saw you afraid for our son Sean when he was born. But I've never seen you afraid for yourself.

RR: Well, I am a person who puts one foot in front of the other. I'm never afraid of something not working. I'm not afraid of failure in the traditional sense, because it's just not part of the way I go about things. In the sense that I have seen other writers, I've seen students, I've seen people absolutely paralyzed, afraid of making a mistake and the mistake leading to failure. It's something about my makeup that comes from watching my father work and seeing my grandfather also, through various deprivations in his life, put one foot in front of the other. That's kind of what I do. And if I'm not afraid, it's because I always have a kind of attitude about these things that, if this doesn't work, we'll throw it out and try something that does, and if that doesn't work . . . That's just how you do it, you put one foot in front of the other.

JFB: Rick, I think if I had been your father's son—or daughter—I would have resented his absence. I would have been mad. I would have been hurt. And yet in your fiction, at least, these Russo Fathers, these Russo Males, you're always very forgiving of them. Do you think that's surprising? I think you have every reason to be damaged and angry. Instead, there's a tremendous amount of love for him, for this man who said to you, "I never thought about you." Why is that?

RR: I don't know. [*Laughs*] I don't know.

JFB: That's not a very good answer, Rick.

RR: If I could sum up the way I felt about him as a child, he was simply wrong. As I got older, he was just a lot of fun. He was just an enormous amount of fun. He was wonderful, he was so full of shit.

I mean, I would just watch him in such amazement, the way he believed at times, in a kind of deep, almost philosophical way, that inanimate objects were alive. And I would see him try to fix something. He was not a gifted man with his hands. He was always buying tools.

He'd go over to somebody's house and work on a truck or something like that, but he was such an impatient man. If something didn't come apart, the wrench that he was using that didn't fit and he couldn't get it in there, he'd resort to whacking the shit out of it with the wrench, you know? And [he'd get] angrier and angrier, and then he'd begin to talk to the tools. He'd say, "Ah, there, how do you like that, you cocksucker?" And at some point, he would take the entire set of tools out of the garage, and toss them, one crescent wrench after another, out into the woods. Screaming at each one of them as he threw them. "How do you like that, you asshole?" And he'd throw another wrench out into the woods. And then later in the afternoon he'd go buy another set of tools.

The pure entertainment value of the man was just astonishing to me. I had more fun when I got old enough and the longing was replaced; there's some part of me that just said, you know, you can either take what he's offering—maybe he should be offering more—but you can either enjoy it and let the rest go, or you can be bitter and resentful and all of those things. For me, [it was] just an easy choice. It was always an easy choice. Just to have fun with him. For pure entertainment value, the man could not be beat. He was endlessly, endlessly entertaining.

He was always trying to, or was frequently trying . . . gosh . . . he'd frequently try to shame his enemies. And he had a fair number of enemies. He was always sending drinks, if you were at a bar or a restaurant, and there was somebody there he knew he hated, he would always send them a drink.

And these were often people who had a lot more money than he did and a lot more social standing, so in terms of both class and all the materials in the wake of that, with money issues, I've seen him when he didn't have money, sometimes he'd borrow money, he'd borrow money from someone, to send a drink to someone he despised, because the message in that is, okay, you're a judge or you're a lawyer, or you're whatever, but we're in the same restaurant, and I'm going to buy you a drink, because I want you to know that I'm here, motherfucker. And the next time you look up, you're going to see me, and you'll see me in your rearview mirror, and I'm always going to be there. And he had a lot of class rage a lot of the time, but that's the snapshot. That's the kind of quixotic gesture that he was famous for. And in its own way too, entertaining.

JFB: Yeah, of course.

RR: Because the payback for him was the moment at which the waitress came over with the drink and set it down and said, "This is compliments of Jimmy Russo," and she'd point and my father would be there with the glass and raise his glass to this guy . . . and sometimes, later, they'd have a shouting match out in the parking lot afterwards. He'd try to time it so they left the restaurant at the same time. You know, a shoving match, a shouting match. But there again, that's the guy who didn't do the GI Bill, who had no interest in getting ahead, but that, years later, was still at war. He was still at war, I think. A very ill-defined conflict. But he knew what it was about! And that was all that was necessary.

JFB: As a father, have you made quixotic gestures? Even though your philosophy is, to some degree, the opposite of his, are there things you've done as a father that you think you can feel the ghost of Jimmy Russo lingering there?

RR: Not so much as a father. I have been guilty of theatrical, quixotic gestures from time to time, although the kids are not usually involved in that. Although Kate did tell a story at Emily's wedding about the day I couldn't get my push mower going. I couldn't get the lawn mower started, pulling on that rip cord, and I couldn't get it to start. It would get up and then die, and I was swearing at it as much as my father used to swear at inanimate objects, and I finally picked it up and threw it over the fence. [*Both laugh.*] That had a profound effect on Kate, she remembered that and told the story. If Steve [Emily's husband] was going to be a Russo, he had to understand that inanimate objects have life, that things cannot be fixed. You have to understand that things can't be fixed. You swear at it, and you throw it over the fence.

JFB: I'm thinking back to the commencement speech you gave at Colby years ago, and one of the pieces of advice you gave to the happy graduates was "Have children."

RR: I felt deeply that our lives changed with Emily and Kate, in ways that were quite extraordinary and quite profound. Certain things you anticipate about having children and certain things you don't; one of the things you don't realize is that you really don't understand the meaning of fear until you have children. So in part I was saying to these Colby graduates, "You're really going to like the fear."

JFB: But what's the fear? What's that fear about?

RR: Of something happening to them. You now have something that you cannot afford to lose, and you can't afford to lose it in a way that's certainly more profound than your fear of losing your own life. And I think it's more profound even than the fear of having your spouse fall ill or losing your spouse to a cardiac. I think that with children, for so many years they are so dependent. They depend on you for everything, and so for me it was just a new level of terror that came with having these little people and finding yourself completely won over by them. The terror that comes with knowing that you might not be there when they need you. And for me, of course, just the notion of being there was very, very important because my own father was largely not there.

And so for me I set the bar rather low as a parent. There was rule one and no rule two, but rule one was to be there. And I think that you're not a father for very long before you realize that even with the bar set that low, you can still screw up.

JFB: I guess I'm curious if you think, looking at this now, another generation ahead: What has your daughter Emily learned from you [now that she is a mother herself], and what of yourself do you see in your one-year-old granddaughter?

RR: It's had a more profound effect on me than I imagined it would. One of the best reasons to have children, of course, is because that's when you become fully invested in the world, in a way that you have something more important than you.

JFB: What would Jimmy Russo do if he was around to look into the eyes and able to spend time with his great-granddaughter?

RR: He would tickle her till she wet her pants.

My father was a man who never knew how to stop anything. And he was wonderful with children. He was really good with old women and children, and he would be over the moon with that child.

And then he'd leave.

# RALPH JAMES SAVARESE

*The first time I met my son, [DJ,] he grabbed the pointer finger on my right hand, took me to the couch, and started banging his head against my head— not hard, but not soft either. . . . We performed this bighorn ritual for twenty or thirty minutes. Years later, when he was literate, DJ explained, "Dad, I was trying to say hello."*

Ralph James Savarese is the author of *Reasonable People: A Memoir of Autism and Adoption.* He lives in Grinnell, Iowa, where he is associate professor of English at Grinnell College.

▼

JENNIFER FINNEY BOYLAN: Your son is one of the first nonspeaking autistic people to go to college—Oberlin, in fact. Tell me the story of how he took the SATs.

RALPH JAMES SAVARESE: It was the ACTs, actually. Because he's a nonspeaking person with autism whose senses are poorly integrated, a person who can't always locate his body in space and who has great difficulty with fine motor activities, we had to negotiate with the testing service to have each multiple-choice answer bank enlarged so that he could point independently and unambiguously at the answer.

He consumed two-thirds of the extended test time besieged by anxiety; he knew that the test would have a great impact on his future. When at last he stopped fidgeting and compulsively sharpening pencils, he moved through the questions rapidly. By February of the following year, he was accepted early decision at Oberlin College.

JFB: So let's back up ten or twelve years. How did DJ come into your family? How did you come to adopt him?

RJS: My wife, Emily, was the assistant director of the Center for Autism and Related Disabilities at the University of Florida. In that capacity, she had begun to work with DJ. One night he and his sister were found on the street looking for food. DJ was about three and a half years old, his sister four and a half. The kids were taken from their mother, who had serious drug and alcohol issues. The sister went to live with their mother's sister, and DJ, who was already in a five-day residency program at the hospital, went to live with a foster parent on the weekends.

A few weeks into his foster placement, Emily asked if I would play with him. He really wasn't doing well, she said.

The first time I met my son, he grabbed the pointer finger of my right hand, took me to the couch, and started banging his head against my head—not hard, but not soft either. In the background Emily was mouthing, "Go with it," because she'd never seen him reach out to somebody.

We performed this bighorn ritual for twenty or thirty minutes.

Years later, when he was literate, DJ explained, "Dad, I was trying to say hello." The pressure of his head on my forehead had allowed him to take me in.

The sensory stuff in his kind of autism is just overwhelming. After the adoption, I remember trying to wash his hair. He screamed at the top of his lungs. His scalp was incredibly hypersensitive. And yet he could swallow Tabasco sauce as if it were water.

JFB: So how did you go from a moment where you're first encountering this child to thinking, We should make DJ part of our lives; we should be his parents?

RJS: One night—it was Emily's birthday—we received a call from the Department of Children and Families saying that DJ had been terribly injured. DJ's caseworker asked if we could come to the hospital because they weren't legally allowed to ask the birth mother to the hospital, and the foster mother was under investigation.

I should say that Emily and I had just taught DJ his first communicative gesture: the American Sign Language sign for *more*. I would tickle him, make the sign for *more* by bringing the first three fingers on each hand together, and wait to see if he could copy me. One day, after much repetition, he did. He thought it was hilarious that by putting his fingers together he could get me to tickle him.

So we went to the emergency room and there's this little boy, unbelievably bruised. His ear had been kicked inside his head; his ribs were black and blue. Somebody had savagely attacked him.

He looked up—he was making high-pitched gerbil sounds that I don't ever want to hear again—and, seeing me, he made the sign for *more*. He wanted to be tickled. He wanted, I think, some kind of normalcy in the midst of his horror, and he wouldn't calm down until I tickled him. Later, I realized that he wanted more of us, indeed more from us.

A month shy of his sixth birthday, DJ came to live with Emily and me.

JFB: Now I know this is a painful question, but could you talk about what DJ's life was like before the age of three?

RJS: His birth mom was very poor. Her husband had left her. She had very serious drug and alcohol problems, was perpetually homeless or living in very, very subpar housing, and was working on and off as a prostitute. I mean, it's difficult to speak about because—when DJ was attacked in foster care, it later became apparent that he had been sexually abused as well.

JFB: Had you always wanted to be a father? Or had you decided—long before that moment when DJ banged his forehead against yours—that being a parent was not for you?

RJS: I had, and still have, a terrible relationship with my own father. I was pretty convinced that I didn't want to have children. The notion that I would father an autistic child, I mean, *fatherhood*? Are you kidding me?

JFB: And yet suddenly you're the father of a severely autistic boy. How did you figure out what to do?

RJS: First of all, my wife is absolutely amazing. She knows a ton about autism, but more than that, she's got a kind of Buddhist, still-water-runs-deep kind of calm. Having her model a way to act with DJ was really, really important.

Let me be clear: This is the hardest thing I have ever done. It's been incredibly demanding; it's involved enormous sacrifices. But it's also been the richest thing.

DJ has had a life, and that life sustains us.

JFB: He's had a life because of you.

RJS: I don't want to sound like some sort of super-good person; I'm radically imperfect. But sometimes I think about where DJ would be now if we hadn't adopted him. I think about all of the kids our society writes off as having no potential or as being unworthy of love.

Last June my son graduated with highest honors from Grinnell High School and is now off to Oberlin; at six he had been labeled profoundly retarded.

JFB: How did you teach him language?

RJS: Imagine a sentence in which every word has Velcro on the back and a word bank to the right of the sentence. Emily would start very, very simply with a picture of a car—a yellow car—whose caption read, "The man got into the _____ car." The word bank would contain the words *yellow, red,* and *green.* Emily would pick up the word *yellow* and place it in the blank, pointing at the photograph and model-ing both the cognitive and motor actions. She would then have DJ do this. Every object in our house had a photograph, a computer icon, an American Sign Language sign, and a word attached to it. We wanted to immerse DJ in a signifying universe. To say that it was slow going would be an understatement.

But when he finally cracked the code of reading in the third grade, he moved like lightning. Later, he said that the feeling of picking up the Velcro-backed word and palpably putting it into the sentence helped him.

JFB: Could you tell the story of the trampoline?

RJS: We began to sense the degree to which DJ seemed to learn more quickly if he was in motion. I convinced Emily to buy a fourteen-foot trampoline with a netted enclosure. First and foremost, it was a way to wordlessly bond with him and, frankly, to tire him out so that he would sleep at night. Later, we would tie words to the netted enclosure and really make the jumping an affect-laden, cognitive learning activity.

I ended up building an indoor trampoline house after we moved to Iowa, where the trampoline is level with the floor. It's a six-hundred-square-foot building heated by a woodstove. We jumped every single day, all through the winter.

There's a karaoke machine, which of course has words on it, and we would sing the songs while jumping and try to get DJ at least to hum them. To this day, he talks of how important that was.

Something about the regular rhythmic bouncing, the proprioceptive input the trampoline gives his body, stabilizes or calms the sensory distortion. It's as if he were catching a performance-enhancing ride—a taxi with rhythm.

JFB: So tell me about when DJ began to use the computer to type out words and to express himself that way.

RJS: The first real breakthrough came when he was reading *Jack and the Beanstalk* at school. DJ had a label-making machine that he used for worksheets, and on this worksheet he encountered an open-ended question about the story's conclusion: "What are Jack and his mother thinking?" To our everlasting shock, he typed, *Where a Dad?*

He was clearly using the story to ask a profound question about his birth family. And then he started getting the hang of grammar, of word choice—all of those things.

I remember DJ's answer to the question "What is a pyramid?" *A sand triangle,* he typed. "What is a mausoleum?" *Dead people live there.*

Later, text-to-speech software gave him a sense of empowerment. He could now contribute to class discussions. It empowered him to say, "Maybe I *can* learn to speak."

JFB: And he did it simply by typing with one finger, right?

RJS: One finger. Interestingly enough, I typed the book that I wrote about DJ, *Reasonable People,* with one finger—all 496 pages of it! I just sensed that I'd be closer to his way of seeing the world.

JFB: One of DJ's favorite expressions is *easy breathing*, which reminds me of a line from Keats, from that poem "A thing of beauty is a joy forever." That phrase came out of a stressful situation, if I remember right?

RJS: He loves the phrase *easy breathing* because he has lots and lots of anxiety—in part from his autism and in part from his childhood trauma. And, I must say, in part from living in a terribly stigmatizing world. It's a big deal to try to stay calm.

His philosophy of life can be summed up by a memorable line from the sixth grade: "Reasonable people promote very, very easy breathing." He's sort of like an anxiety seismograph.

I remember at one point he was having some dental work done, and he had been anesthetized. He seemed to wake up very, very slowly and it was making me nervous. When he was half or three-quarters awake, he typed out on the labeler, "Easy breathing forever." It took being anesthetized for this boy to feel at peace!

JFB: How will your life change when DJ goes to college?

RJS: I don't think I fully appreciated until now how much I enjoy hanging out with him, conversing with him, hearing his little autistic chorus in the background. I am going to miss him terribly. We're very close.

DJ loved the fact that Oberlin admitted the first female and African-American students in the U.S. He wanted to be its first nonspeaking student—and the first nonspeaking student *anywhere* to live in the dorms. He worked like crazy to get into this school, and so we said, Let's figure out how to do it.

Look at what this kid has shown is possible.

When Dr. Sanjay Gupta asked him in an interview on CNN, "Should autism be treated?" DJ had the presence of mind, and media savvy, to type out, "Yes, treated with respect."

JFB: What advice would you give to dads out there in the broad world? What do you know now that you wish you had known before?

RJS: Love your kid for who he or she is. Build self-esteem.

It's pretty common for the parents of newly diagnosed autistic kids to go through a grieving process. I tell them: Don't waste time. Your culture has taught you to believe that autism is devastating and that you'll never get the love you want as a parent.

For Father's Day some ten years ago—I still have the card on my desk—DJ typed:

*Dear Dad,*

*You are the dad I awesomely try to be loved by. Please don't hear my years of hurt. Until you yearned to be my dad, playing was treated as too hard. Until you loved me, I loved only myself. You taught me how to play. You taught me how to love. I love you.*

*Your Son, DJ Savarese*

If I had remained attached to normalcy, I would have missed the richness that comes in another form. So love your kid. Make it a little bit less about you, and you'll be able to relax about who he or she is.

And have easy breathing forever.

*Courtesy of Trey Ellis*

# TREY ELLIS

*How can a woman compete for the oceanic love I feel for my two soft miniatures?*

Trey Ellis is the author of three novels, including *Platitudes* and *Right Here, Right Now,* which received an American Book Award. A professor at Columbia University, for years he wrote the *Father of the Year* blog, about his experiences as an African-American single father. We first met in 1981, when we were both young writers working on *American Bystander* magazine. Thirty years later, on the night before Ellis's forty-ninth birthday, we met in the Columbia Student Union, two old friends surrounded by young people.

▼

JENNIFER FINNEY BOYLAN: Do you remember *American Bystander,* you and me and all those young writers, the early eighties in New York? The magazine that was supposed to make us all rich?

TREY ELLIS: It was funded by the original cast of *Saturday Night Live.*

JFB: Although we never saw them. I met John Belushi one time. I remember I went to the editor's house, and Belushi was there. And he threw me up in the air, and he caught me. And he said, "There you go, kid," and then he left. That's my whole memory of John Belushi, being thrown in the air.

TE: Well, at least he caught you.

JFB: Our friendship was the friendship of young men in their feckless twenties; there was so much we didn't know about the world. Back then, were children on the radar for you? Did you always think to yourself, "Someday, I'm going to be that guy who's going to have a great family"?

TE: No, I didn't. My own parents fought all the time. The house was just a sad, crazy, dysfunctional marriage. I never saw them once kiss.

So, I never had a real relationship to observe and model after when I was a kid. I just invented relationships, these perfect things, in my imagination.

JFB: Is that how you became a romantic?

TE: I'm a sap.

JFB: Did that make it harder to find a relationship, after your wife left you, and you found yourself a single dad with two tiny children?

TE: Yeah, because, in some ways, there's something infantile about sappiness. I started dating so late that everything was all virtual for me. The romantic has blinders to the complications of life and thinks, Yeah, I should be able to find a woman who is just perfect and everything is uncomplicated. She's a great mom, and she's great in bed, and she's a great cook.

But life isn't like that. That's part of growing up. With my new wife, it's like the Grace Jones line, "I'm not perfect, but I'm perfect for you."

JFB: In your memoir *Bedtime Stories,* you write about the loss of your first marriage and about your time as a single father after the divorce. But there's a fairly long stretch in the middle when the marriage seems doomed—at least to your readers—and you're still trying to make it work. You make room for her new Rasta boyfriend; you try to have an "open relationship." I thought of the line in Thurber, "Sometimes it is better to fall flat on your face than bend over too far backwards."

TE: My friends resented her much more than I did, or do. She would tell the kids, "I still love your father." She wanted to have this kind of open, polyamorous thing where she could just sort of float in and out.

JFB: So it was like what? Divorce with benefits?

TE: Yeah. But everything I've read suggests that children of divorce do just as well as any other kids if the parents don't fight each other. So

I said, "I'm not going to fight. I'm not going to tell them their mom is crazy."

JFB: Later, after you did divorce, you entered a vulnerable, painful, hopeful period when you were mourning that loss, but also trying to find a new relationship.

TE: It was really tragic. I cried a lot. When it got better, I was looking like an African chief. Or a Mormon polygamist. I had all these different facets of women around my life.

JFB: And all of them were trouble.

TE: Yeah, because I made a lot of terrible mistakes. Making mistakes when you're single is different than when you make them when you're a parent.

JFB: Was it like there were like two Treys? There was the one who was the hound, looking for these beautiful women that you could make love to? And the other Trey who was trying to protect your children, was trying to be a good dad?

TE: It wasn't like being a hound. It was more like I really wanted to be in love again. I didn't just want to get laid indiscriminately. I idealized my old family, my old nuclear family. I was looking for someone to put in that piece.

Often, if the women I was meeting had children before, I didn't date them because I was really specific—and really opinionated—about how I raise kids. I thought bringing a woman into our family with her own kids and her own parenting style would be too much.

There was a woman I liked, before meeting Amanda, that was really nice. I think part of my appeal to her was that I was real authoritative with her boy. He was a little troubled, maybe ADHD or something, and about the same age as my son. I didn't know if I wanted to raise a family with that boy in the house with my perfect son and daughter.

What I really wanted was someone to come in and be the nanny. Someone who would just do what I say in terms of raising children.

In the end, none of that worked. And now, years later, I'm remarried to a woman, Amanda, who had her own very young child. So all the stuff I ran away from, I realize now it didn't make any sense.

Now that I'm married again, and I'm a stepfather with a five-year-old, it's hard for her to say, "Dad." She'll say, "Trey," and kicks me and fights with me all the time. She won't say, "I love you."

JFB: Did you feel like you had to win her over? You won her mother, but now you have to win over the daughter as well?

TE: Yeah. I keep trying that. And when she plays hard to get it makes me try harder. It makes her kick me more and be meaner to me.

Then, when I pull back, she climbs up in my lap and hugs me. I should realize that I've already won her over.

JFB: You have a son, Chet, and a daughter, Ava, from your first marriage. One of the things that you wonder in *Bedtime Stories* is "How can a woman compete for the oceanic love I feel for my two soft miniatures?"

And I would think that that's kind of the central problem for a dad who is also dating. You're looking for a particular romantic love at a time when to some degree, your heart's already full.

TE: There was a woman I dated—a countess!—who wanted to be the center of attention. She wanted a man that would just do anything for her. And I would do a lot of things for her. But I also had to do things for my children.

There's such a difference between the sexual romantic love and the unconditional love for your kids. There's no sense, especially after you've been divorced, that you can divorce your kids.

JFB: Although lots of men do something like that. I was talking to Richard Russo about his father, and at a certain point, he was just gone. He told Rick, "I never really cared about you at all. The track was there." I think lots of men divorce their kids.

TE: That was not a possibility for me. Being chained to them forever, in some ways, means you just accept them in sickness and in health, until death do you part, in a way that marriage really isn't.

JFB: There's a moment early in your memoir when Chet calls you "Mommy Daddy." And it was a moment that, of course, made me think. You were Daddy, but you were Mommy too? How did your role change when you became a single father?

TE: It did, and it didn't. As a relatively modern and progressive dad, it wasn't just that I was the car seat and my ex-wife was the breast-feeding. I was changing diapers and massaging and bathing and a lot of stuff that men a generation ago didn't do.

We were very conscious about these gender roles. But it also was an excuse for my ex-wife to do less work, frankly. Before she left I was doing sixty percent; eventually I ended up doing ninety percent.

JFB: When you were dating, did women find the fact that you were this caring, awesome father a turn-on? Or was it, "Oh, he's got kids. Forget it."

TE: There's a thing called mommy porn. I used to—

JFB: What did you call it?

TE: Mommy porn.

JFB: Which is?

TE: You know, when they see a guy holding a kid in a Snugli or something. Or, like, a guy with a drill that was going to do all this stuff around the house.

JFB: Did it ever work the other way? Was there some kind of racist condescension where people would say, "Oh, good for you for staying with them," as if it was just assumed, well, of course, the expected thing would be to leave? You write that African-American men of your generation "are better known for their absence than their presence."

TE: Chris Rock has this line: "Hey, I take care of my kids." But you're *supposed* to take care of your kids. What do you want? A cookie? There are such low expectations for black fathers. On Mother's Day, I used to walk down the street, just me and the two kids, and people would look at me and say, "Hey, happy Mother's Day." I would get that a lot.

Sometimes, I dated women in their thirties. And some of them were like, "You've got an instant family. You're a good dad. Let's get married." Just like boom. "I'll take care of your kids." They were sick of the younger guys who hadn't settled down yet. Other women I dated had their own kids. They wanted to blend families in ways I wasn't ready for.

Then I met Amanda, and I just thought she was fantastic. And she had this very young child. And just the way we all came together was really nice.

JFB: If you knew, when you were a young man, that this is the thing that you would find, that this life is the one you'd be given—do you think you'd have been happy? Or did it take the experience of living your life before you knew that this is what would make you full?

TE: I think that there are many different paths that I could have taken that would lead me to happiness. I love being a parent. But I also see friends without kids, who kayak together and travel the world together. They have a very different kind of best-friend, sexual adventurous relationship together.

If I hadn't had kids, that wouldn't be a terrible way to live either. You know, I think that you get what you get, and it keeps changing. What I have now is magnificent. It's wonderful, but I don't think it's the only way that would have gotten me to this place.

JFB: When you think of the best moments of being a dad, what comes to mind?

TE: Having a kid under each arm watching TV. You know, or even just waking up in the morning, in the bed, and having both of them crawl into the bed and snuggle. Having them under my arm.

I like feeling protective of them. It makes me feel like a red-tailed hawk, and there's two baby hawks under my wing in the rain.

# AUGUSTEN BURROUGHS

*We break free, but just because*
*we leave our parents doesn't mean*
*they leave us.*

Augusten Burroughs is the author of, among other works, *Running with Scissors,* a memoir about his relationship with his mother, and *A Wolf at the Table,* about his father. On the twenty-seventh of July 2011, we sat on a rooftop at Eighty-first and Columbus in New York City, talking about parents and insanity. Just across the street, fifteen floors below us, was the sphere of the Hayden Planetarium, surrounded by moons and planets. As we talked, the temperature rose into the nineties. By the end of our conversation we felt like a pair of melted candles.

▼

JENNIFER FINNEY BOYLAN: For those who came in late, could you describe a little bit what your experience was of your mother and of your father?

AUGUSTEN BURROUGHS: My parents met when they were young. They had an unhappy marriage. My father was an alcoholic whose disease progressed rapidly after their first child was born. My mother was—it's sort of a long complicated story—

JFB: You can say that again.

AB: She'd always wanted to be an artist and was now married with a young son. Seven years after they had that young son, I was born. My mother was bipolar, but it was not diagnosed back then. My father was a very heavy drinker. It was a very verbally combative household. My mother had a degree in the arts, had an MFA. My father was a professor of philosophy at the University of Massachusetts, Amherst. My brother was, for most of my childhood, out of the house.

They sought the help of a psychiatrist to save their marriage. He was a very untraditional psychiatrist, but it didn't work and they divorced. My mother became closer and closer to this psychiatrist, whose practice was, again, absolutely out of the norm. He would eventually lose his license to practice medicine. My mother would have psychotic breaks every year, in the fall, usually. At a certain point, she just could not raise me. You know, I was like, thirteen. So she sent me to live with this psychiatrist and his family. He had a large family of biological children. Not all of them lived at home, but [he had] long-term psychiatric patients [living there too]. The house was always filled with people, and it was very busy. I grew up in that environment, and the doctor believed that when you were thirteen, you became an adult, free to make all your own choices. So it was a life with very little supervision, and it was a life with a lot of chaos.

JFB: In your memoir *Running with Scissors,* I feel a lot of readers responded to the unlikely combination of your tragic circumstances as well as a kind of comic response, a sense of the absurd, to that experience.

AB: At the time it seemed so hideous that it had to be funny. I mean, there were definitely lots of comical stuff that went on, but it was all sort of set within some pretty awful stuff. The thing about terrible circumstances, when you're in them, is that they're not survivable if you focus on just how bad they are, for one thing. . . . There was just so much of it that it was ridiculous.

JFB: So in *Running with Scissors,* it seems like you were able to make some measure of peace through humor. Whereas with *A Wolf at the Table,* the story you wrote about your father, it seemed much more raw and more angry, as if the emotions were still very volatile. Is that a fair observation?

AB: Oh, no, they were very different. *A Wolf at the Table* is a much angrier and more unresolved book. [When I was very young] I had not yet developed the defense mechanism of perspective, and being able to look at my circumstances with humor, which is like a life raft.

In that book, my father [comes off as] a monster, because [to me,] at that age he was a monster.

JFB: Do you think the job of fathers in raising sons is fundamentally harder than the job of the mother? I think that's one of the things I was struggling with as I went from a father to a mother. Wondering, okay, well, is this a different job than I signed up for? Or is it the same job with a different accent? And I'm still struggling with the answer to that.

AB: I know a man who works with his hands for a living, very rugged guy. Single father of a daughter. And he's the best mom you could ever want, because what's a mom? A mom is the word we use to describe nurturing, and, you know, unconditional acceptance and love, so what's a dad? My mother, when my parents divorced, used to say to me, "Don't call me your mother, call me your parent." I've been thinking about that since I was a kid—What is a mom? What is a mother?

JFB: Early in transition, I was very afraid for my boys not having a father, and that this was something I'd taken from them.

AB: They didn't, and you did, and that's fine. It's not like you abandoned them on the street. You did take away the father, if a father is the man. It's gone! Poof! You took it away, that role, that briefcase and that hat and that suit, as surely as if you stepped on it with your foot like a cockroach.

But what's a father? What did you really take away from them? You took the ability for them to call you Dad, or Deedie to call you her husband.

JFB: Or to look at one of their parents and say, "I'm going to be like him."

AB: Well, they still can say exactly the same thing, and I'm sure they do. Why wouldn't they?

JFB: The things I was going to teach them, I think, are the things that I'm still teaching them—human kindness, generosity. As a result of having me as a father, I think my boys are forgiving of people who are different. I think they're funny. I hope those are all the things they would have had anyway.

AB: I would hope it would be even more than forgiveness. I would hope they would feel proud to have a parent—I would feel safe. If I had a parent who went against the grain of society to protect themselves, to do what was right and sane, versus festering and writhing and becoming who knows how unstable. There's a great deal of safety, from a kid's point of view, to having a parent know exactly what they want. "This is going to be different here, guys, okay, but we're doing it." There's something about that that is only honorable.

JFB: Is that what your father didn't have? Did your father somehow not know what he wanted and who he was?

AB: My father was completely disconnected.

JFB: It seems like, in your writing at least, that your parents were almost perfectly matched for bringing out the worst in each other.

AB: They really were.

JFB: Each of them seems three-quarters of the way sane when they're away from each other, but both of them seem all the way crazy when they're together.

AB: They formed an unstable chemical when they were together. It was a relief when they were apart. My father was never sophisticated enough to grasp the notion of "I'm not your mother. I'm your parent." That distinction he would never think to make.

JFB: What did your mother mean by that?

AB: She was saying to me, this is not about losing your father, but I do not want you to think of me as your mother. Don't come to me asking me to make your lunches.

JFB: Why did she not want to be your mother?

AB: Because my mother did not want to participate in the tasks that are associated so heavily with the word *mother*. In the context of someone who's twelve, thirteen, fourteen, my mother was not the kind of person to make lunch for you.

JFB: She wanted to be seen as an artist, not as someone who makes your peanut butter and Fluff.

AB: Exactly. She sort of felt she had better things to do. And she did, I'm sure, she did, that's fine, that was never my . . . I admired that.

JFB: What about now? Do you feel free of them, your parents? Do people ever break free of them?

AB: We break free, but just because we leave our parents doesn't mean they leave us. The things that our parents taught us from the moment of our arrival in the bassinet, until whatever age it is that we leave, that is a part of our weave and weft.

JFB: Is there anything in you that has ever yearned to be a father? I know for gay men, that can be a more complicated question than to a straight couple. But is there?

AB: Oh yeah, definitely. I've always wanted kids; I've always wanted a large family.

JFB: What would their names be? Have you figured out their names?

AB: I'd have funny names for them. I don't know . . . Gunther?

JFB: Sons or daughters?

AB: Both, all of them. Like a litter.

JFB: What do you think your father thought he was going to be when he set out on this [journey]?

AB: I don't know. I never really knew my family very well.

JFB: When we're kids, we think our parents have this plan. Like this guidebook somewhere.

AB: I never found that. I thought my parents were insane and I couldn't wait to get out. Even when I was lonely, I thought they were completely fucking insane.

JFB: And you knew they were just winging it?

AB: Yeah, because it was just a chaotic mess.

JFB: I think that's one of the things that makes your experience, in addition to the many other things, so different, because I think for a lot of people that I know who were raised in two-parent homes, there's a certain point at which they realize their parents don't know what they're doing. It's a great shock. In a way, for me, it wasn't really until I had my own kids that I understood. It made me forgive my parents a little bit. Of course, my parents never did anything to me like your parents did to you, and on the whole it was a very stable family. It was years before they found out how unstable it was, because of what I was hiding from them.

I don't know about you, but I'm really getting hot up here.

AB: It's hot up here, man.

JFB: So—was there a shadow family that you imagined belonging to? What was that like? Who were they?

AB: It was derived from different images on TV, I think. I liked the idea of a large family because it seemed, I don't know, part of the pack. Just to be able to relax and not [be] so tense. Worried. I was always worried, so I think I would always like . . .

I would have liked Willy Wonka.

I guess what would have made a difference is to have had happy parents, regardless of anything else. That they'd been happy people. Or happier. Not so angry. It would have nurtured and watered the light-heartedness that I have, that I feel inside but that I don't really express enough, except in writing.

JFB: If you fell in love with some guy who had two sons, seven years apart—like your family—would that be appealing? Or would you run in the other direction?

AB: It would depend on how fucked up they were.

Like, this guy I bought my camera from, he came out and I met his teenagers, you know. And his daughter: She's fifteen and smart as shit, and funny. And the son's smart—I just was like, I wish you were mine! I totally wanted those kids. Oh, I would have loved it.

But then, you know, there are the kids who are, like, little judgmental, petty, dimwitted things. And if I had some—if this person I fell in love with had kids who felt very entitled and were not bright?

I'd feel like I would be compelled to ruin their lives.

# II | MADDY

▼

## "I'LL GIVE YOU SOMETHING TO CRY ABOUT," I SAID.

*Zach, Jenny, and Sean Boylan, fall 2001. Wal-mart.*

# THAT'LL TEACH 'EM A LESSON

We moved to Ireland in 1998. I had a job teaching American literature at University College Cork. The boys went to Montessori School, where they learned to sing in Irish. *D'aois MacDonald bhí feirm, E-I-E-I-O!* Getting them ready in the morning was a challenge, though, especially Sean, who at age three had become rather particular regarding his sartorial choices.

One morning, as I was trying to get him dressed, Seannie resisted the shorts that I had selected for him. They were plaid and had an elastic waistband. He pulled them off, threw them on the floor.

"Okay, you're not doing that," I said. I laid Sean on his back on the floor and held him down with one hand while yanking the shorts back over the child's kicking feet. Then I pulled him into a standing position. "When I put your shorts on, you leave them on," I said.

Sean yelled, "I don't want pants! Oh, I hate pants!" And threw them onto the floor again.

"Goddamn it," I said. "What did I just say?" I clenched my jaw, and the muscles in my temples pulsed.

I'd finally come out to my wife in the months before we left America, told her I had gender issues, that I wasn't sure how deep they went, but that I hoped she could stand it if I cross-dressed once in a while. She'd been strangely sanguine. Sure, why not, she'd replied. Fantasy's a good thing.

Among the other things I'd brought to Ireland was a small suitcase that contained a wig and a pair of heels, size twelve. Every once in a while, when the kids were asleep, I put this stuff on and read the *Irish*

*Times,* did the crossword. Still, this wasn't nearly as satisfying as it might sound.

I got Seannie down on the floor and pulled his shorts on. The child kicked and screamed as if being stabbed with knives. Still firmly holding my son down with my right hand, I pulled a pair of socks onto the boy's feet, and after this stuffed each writhing, kicking foot into a tiny sneaker. "No!" screamed Sean. "I don't want them! I don't want them!"

"I don't care what you want," I explained, raising the child into the air and walking with him out into the hall.

"What's going on?" asked Deedie.

"Just trying to go out the fucking door is all," I replied.

"I hate you, Daddy," said Sean. "I hate you!"

"Jim," said Deedie. "Stop."

"I'm just going out the door with my son wearing his actual goddamned pants," I explained.

"I hate you, Daddy! I hate you!"

"Jim, please," said Deedie. She reached for the child.

"I've got him," I said, and walked out the front door still carrying the screaming boy. I opened the back door of the Opel and stuffed Sean into his car seat. Then I lowered the restraining straps over the child's head and shoulders and clicked the buckle between Sean's kicking legs. He writhed and wriggled like a condemned man in an electric chair. "I'm sorry it's like this," I said. "But you're a bad boy."

"I'm not a bad boy! You're a bad daddy! I hate you!" The tears rolled down Sean's face like rain.

I looked at my son with fury. "I'll give you something to cry about," I said. Then I slammed the car door.

I walked back inside. Zach looked up at me in fear. "What happened? Where is Baby Sean?"

"I locked him in his car seat," I said.

"Why?" said Zach. "Why?"

"Because," I said. "I'm teaching him a lesson."

Maybe it's no surprise that, in the wake of my decision to start sharing my secret with Deedie, I was a more terrible person rather than a more tranquil one. I had hoped that by cross-dressing openly once in a while, I'd be able to shed the burden of secrecy and to obtain a kind of equilibrium between my various selves. But instead, sitting there after-hours by the peat fire in our living room in Cork, wearing a Coldwater Creek skirt and a wig that still made me look like Joni Mitchell, I only felt stupid and embarrassed. I was mortified by the strangeness of it all, even as Deedie sat by my side. I wondered what possible explanation I could offer if the boys woke up. *Who's Joni Mitchell, Daddy?* Worst of all, I knew that the thing I felt inside could not be expressed with clothes. To be honest, clothes weren't really all that interesting to me; they're still not. All they were was a means of making the thing I felt on the inside visible. But it was the thing inside that haunted me.

By the time we got to school that day, the tears were rolling down my face as well as Sean's. I pulled into the Montessori parking lot and I unbuckled Sean from his car seat and I held him in my arms. "I'm so sorry, Sean," I said. "You're not a bad boy. You're a very good boy, and I love you."

I remembered the time my father had accidentally burned me with the soldering iron while trying to fix my flying saucer. *I'd never hurt you, Jim. I'm so sorry.*

ON WEDNESDAY NIGHTS, Deedie and I would head down to the Gables pub on Douglas Street and listen to the session. We sat on stools, drinking our pints of Murphy's and Beamish, as some of the finest musicians in the world sat in the corner, waving their fiddle bows around, playing banjos and guitars and bouzoukis and the Irish box. We befriended a guy named Johnny Neville, who played in a band called North Cregg. During the break he'd talk to us about his family. Johnny had two boys about the same age as our sons.

"Who's taking care of the kids while you're out here playing?" Deedie asked.

Johnny nodded. "That would be," he said, "my good wife."

He and his friend Christy Leahy played a wide range of old tunes, a lot of it in the Sliabh Luachra tradition, but there were a few original songs as well. There was one of Johnny's that always made my throat close up, a ballad about his abusive, alcoholic father. It was called "The Wobblin' Man."

> *You'd wind him up and let him go,*
> *And watch him wobble to and fro.*

As I listened to this tune, my eyes shone with tears. But they did not fall. Deedie reached out and clasped my hand. "Are you all right, Jim?" she asked.

I said that I was fine.

ONE DAY, WHEN I picked Zach up at the Montessori School, I found him sobbing uncontrollably. "What happened?" I asked his teacher.

"Ah well, you know," she said. "He's had a bit of a disappointment."

As we drove back to the apartment, through the crazy narrow streets of Cork, I tried to get the details from him. Apparently there'd been some sort of race. Which he'd lost.

"I'm sorry about that," I said to the six-year-old.

"Whenever I race you or Mommy, I always win," he said, deep in his misery.

"Well," I said, "maybe we're not as fast as the Irish."

"I thought I was as fast as a cheetah!" he said.

"You are fast," I noted. "You just weren't the fastest!"

He sobbed some more.

"You don't have to keep doing that," I said.

He looked up at me. He had no idea what I was talking about.

"The weeping. You lost a race, but it's not the end of the world."

"It is for me," he said.

"Maybe you think that now," I said. "But there's worse things in the world than losing a race. You should save your tears."

"Why?" asked Zach. "Am I going to run out?"

There were a couple of things I wanted to explain to my son. One of them was that, no, you'll never run out of tears. At the same time, tears weren't something you let fall indiscriminately. You wanted to save them for when you needed them. That was my theory at the time, anyhow.

"No, Zach," I said. "You won't run out of tears. It's just that there are times when it's good to hold things in."

"Why would I hold things in?" he asked. "That doesn't make any sense."

"Because that's how you protect people," I said. "It's one of the ways boys protect girls. It's like you put that sadness in a box, and you bury it in the ground."

Zach looked out the window. His tears had stopped. "I should protect Mommy, you mean?" he said. "By putting my tears in the ground?"

We were almost home. Through the open windows of the Opel I could hear the bells of St. Anne's ringing through the air. "Yes," I said. "That's exactly what I mean."

THAT NIGHT, a scream rent the air. Zach and Sean both came running into the living room. "What happened?" said Deedie, leaping to her feet.

Zach held up his hand. Deep tooth marks were sunk into the meat of his thumb.

"Sean bit me!" he said. He was sobbing.

"I didn't!" said Sean.

"Seannie," said Deedie. "Look at Zach's hand! Look at what you did!"

"I didn't bite him!" said Sean. He was holding his friend Big Pig in one hand. Sean had a council of porcine advisers, including Big Pig, Little Pig, and Irish Pig.

"Everyone makes a mistake once in a while," said Deedie, casting a glance in my direction. "But we don't lie to each other in our family."

Now Sean was crying. "I'm not a liar!" he shouted. Deedie picked him up and walked down the hall to his room. Seannie had kind of a grim room in the apartment, a damp, mildewy chamber just shy of growing mushrooms.

"Time out for you," said Deedie.

I picked up Zach and held him in my lap. "I'm sorry I'm crying," he said. "I wanted to protect Mommy. But it hurts too much."

"It's all right, son," I said. From down the hall, I heard the sound of Seannie wailing. His door closed as Deedie left him in there to consider his recent mistakes.

Ten years later, Zach confessed to me that Sean had been telling the truth in this encounter. What had happened, in fact, was that in order to frame his brother, Zach had bitten himself.


DEEDIE AND I were having dinner at the table in our apartment in Cork. She'd taken a leave from her job as a social worker for the year and spent her days working out at the Brookfield Health Club and shopping at the city's English Market, a "farmers' market" several blocks long. There were loaves of Irish soda bread, pink salmon laid out on ice, bottles of sweet cream and honey.

She poured out a bottle of Pouilly-Fuissé, and we clinked glasses. The boys were asleep.

"Are ye all right then?" I said. This was a phrase we heard each day at the English Market, the Irish equivalent of "Can I help you?"

"Brilliant," said Deedie. She'd made salmon and green beans. It had been raining outside, but now the sun was out. Everything shone with rain.

"Seriously," I said. "Are we having a good year?"

Deedie nodded. "I think I'm as happy as I've ever been," she said.

"Me too," I said. "I thought I'd be homesick, but I'm not. Not much, anyhow."

Deedie sipped her wine. "Home will be there when we get back," she said. "In the meantime, there's all this salmon."

I looked at my wife. After ten years of marriage, she was as beautiful as when we married. I was not sure the same could be said of me.

"And you don't mind—the gender stuff?" I said restlessly.

"That," said Deedie. "Whatever. I'm not crazy about it, but you're happy, right?"

"Pretty much."

"Well, all right then," she said.

She ate some salmon. From outside, the sound of tires on the wet road made a sound like a shush.

The doorbell rang.

I put my glass down, but I missed the edge of the table. The goblet shattered on the floor.

As I walked toward the front door, I stepped on a small sliver of glass. I felt it disappear deep into the flesh of my heel.

I opened the door. There stood a deliveryman, holding a huge bouquet of roses. They were from my mother. *I'm sending these for no reason at all,* read the card. *Except to remind you both that you are loved.*


A WEEK LATER, I went to Amsterdam by myself. I brought a suitcase of female gear, checked into the American Hotel on the Leidseplein, and did the presto change-o. After a few hours I stepped out onto the streets of the city, in a black skirt and a light blue top. No one looked at me twice. Was this because I was so undetectable as a female? Or because, when all was said and done, what I looked like turned out to be of far less consequence to the world than I had anticipated?

I walked around Vondelpark and considered the swans, visited the Rijksmuseum and stared at paintings by Rembrandt and Vermeer. They didn't have *Girl with a Pearl Earring,* but it was just as well. I didn't need to be called *klootzak* anymore. I knew how to say this in English.

As I walked around the city, I was aware that my foot hurt. That tiny sliver of glass in my heel appeared to be sinking deeper and deeper. I pretended that I couldn't feel it. When I failed at this, I simply hoped the sliver would work its way out on its own in time, although I'm not sure anything else in the world had ever behaved in that fashion, at least not in my experience.

At the end of the day I found myself in the Anne Frank house on the Prinsengracht.

I climbed the small staircase up to the hidden annex, walked through the passageway hidden by the bookcase, crept through those tiny rooms full of such longing and horror. There weren't a lot of other tourists in the house that day. And so it was that I found myself dressed in drag, alone in Anne Frank's bedroom.

There was her tiny bed, the photographs of Hollywood movie stars from sixty years ago still pasted to the wall. A sheet of Plexiglas protected the photographs from the fingers of tourists.

I stood there frozen, imagining the young girl passing her days here, waiting to be set free. There was a window on one wall. Birds were singing.

In spite of the room's aching sadness, it was still a teenager's room. It made me think, for a second, of the room I had lived in when I was sixteen, a chamber with two different secret panels—one for my bong, one for my bras and earrings and my copy of *The Feminine Mystique*. Next to my bed, instead of a photograph of Joan Crawford, there had been a photograph of the surface of Mars. I used to lie in bed and look at the planet, imagine what it would be like to live there.

I thought about Anne Frank, driven into hiding by Nazis. The glass in my heel ached.

*What about you, Jenny?* I asked myself. *Is this really how you're going to live?*

I fled from the girl's bedroom, went down the stairs, and fought my way in a blind panic out into the streets of Amsterdam. I rushed in my heels to the Prinsengracht canal and stood there in self-loathing and despair, looking down at the dank green water.

*I have made up my mind,* Anne Frank wrote, *to lead a different life from other girls and, later on, different from ordinary housewives. My start has been so very full of interest, and that is the sole reason why I have to laugh at the humorous side of the most dangerous moments.*

I saw two hippies coming down the street, American college boys with backpacks. I remembered the first time I had come to Amsterdam, back with my friend Doober, the summer between high school and college. I remembered asking him one morning, "Don't you want to see the Anne Frank house?"

"I don't know, man," said Doober. "Sounds like kind of a bummer."

The hippies passed me by. One of them cast a curious look in my direction, as if embarrassed just to walk by this strange distraught woman. It had to be admitted that he looked not unlike myself, when I was a young thing, with his long hair and leering eyes. I wondered if he was thinking the thing that I had thought at the lighthouse in Sanibel, that time I'd looked at the jogging woman who so strangely resembled me. Did he see, as he gazed upon me, how we all resemble each other? How any of us could be brother and sister? Or both?

"*Entschuldigen, Fraulein,*" he said, pausing. "*Sie sind verletzt?*"

Excuse me, miss. Are you hurt?

"*Mir geht es gut,*" I said. I wondered if he could tell the truth about me from my voice. "*Es ist ganz nichts.*" I'm fine. It's nothing.

The boys loped onward. A few meters farther down the street, they laughed. I wasn't sure about what exactly, but I had a guess.

The burden of shame fell even more heavily upon me. There I was, in my twinset and skirt, standing in the very shadow of the Anne Frank house. Where boys had looked upon me. And concluded I was German.

WHEN I GOT back to Cork, the boys were waiting for me at the door. They rushed forward, their arms spread, and I gathered my sons to me. They were still so small I could pick up one with each arm.

"Daddy's back!" they shouted.

THE NEXT DAY, I went to the hospital to have someone take a look at the piece of glass in my foot. Ireland, while enjoying what turned out to be its all-too-brief period as the "Celtic Tiger," had not poured a lot of its newfound wealth into its health care system, and as a result, the wait at the ER at the Cork hospital turned into an ordeal the likes of which I'd have been more likely to expect from a hospital in, say, Libya. I waited in a decaying chair next to a guy with an open head wound for about five hours, until at last I was ushered into an examining room and a doctor sat me down. On the floor in front of me was a bright red pool of blood.

"Mind the puddle," said the doc.

An hour later I was in an operating room, as surgeons used knives and tweezers to feel around for the elusive splinter. It took them a while. The anesthetic didn't work. I spent some of the time screaming my brains out.

At long last, the doctor came up to me with the piece of bloodied glass held triumphantly in his tweezers. "You see?" he said. "There we have it at last!"

I looked at it, thought things over, and screamed some more.

When I came out of surgery, Deedie was waiting for me. "What happened to you?" she said.

"Glass in my foot," I said.

We limped out to the car. "How long has there been glass in your foot?" she asked.

"A couple weeks," I said. "Remember that goblet I broke when that guy delivered the flowers?"

She sat me down in the car, went around to her side to slide behind the wheel. "So you've just been walking around with a piece of glass in your foot for two weeks?"

I nodded. She was angry with me. "What's wrong with you?" she said. "Why didn't you say anything?"

"I don't know," I said. "I didn't want to be annoying. I figured it would work its way out."

She drove me to the pharmacy to pick up my prescription for pain-killers. "He didn't want to be annoying!" she declared, as if making some sort of argument to an invisible third party.

"Kind of stupid, I guess," I said.

She glanced over at me. "Did you have that glass in your foot the whole time you were in Amsterdam?"

I nodded.

She shook her head. "Why don't you tell me when you hurt?" she asked. "Why do you have to keep it all inside?"

Deedie parked at the apothecary to get my drugs. As I waited for her, I thought about my friend Johnny Neville, singing about his father.

*You wind him up and let him go,*
*And watch him wobble, to and fro.*


Deedie came back to the car ten minutes later, drugs in hand, to find me wracked with tears.

"Jimmy? Oh, my sweet Jimmy-pie," she said, and held her husband in her arms. I lay my head upon her shoulder and shook.

She had seen me weep, now and again, over the ten years of our marriage. But Deedie had never seen me weep like this.


WHEN WE GOT HOME, the children were waiting for us. As Deedie ushered their babysitter, Liz, toward the car, the boys hugged me tight.

"Daddy, you were crying," said Sean.

"I was," I said. My face was all red, and my cheeks were still wet.

Seannie pointed at me and grinned, as if he'd figured something out.

"Daddy," he said. "You were a bad boy."

I nodded. He had that right.

"Why were you crying?" said Zach. "What's wrong?"

I gathered my sons into my arms again, wondering how on earth I could protect them, how I could save us all from the doom that was suddenly drawing near.

"I don't want pants," I whispered. "Oh, I hate pants."

# THE ORPHAN GIRL

Zach was sitting at the lunch table with his friend Emma, eating a peanut butter and Fluff sandwich. On his napkin I had drawn a cartoon of our dog Lucy. From Lucy's mouth came a word balloon, and in the middle of the balloon was a cartoon heart. This of course was ironic, given the fact that the dog loathed all sentient creatures, my sons not least, as mentioned earlier.

"I saw your daddy," said Emma. They were in second grade. "He looks like a girl."

Zach looked at the cartoon dog, then back at Emma. "Can I tell you a secret, Emma?" he said.

"Yes." By this, she didn't mean that she would keep the secret, only that he could tell it to her. Emma had asked Zach to be the vice president of the Drama Club a few weeks before this, a post that seemed prestigious to Zach at first. Later, he learned that all the Drama Club did was appoint officers. They didn't actually put on any plays.

"My daddy's turning into a girl," said Zach.

Emma's eyes flickered. She put down her Ring Ding.

"That," she said, "is the saddest thing I have ever heard."

"It's okay," said Zach. "She's still the same person."

Emma shook her head, as if Zach somehow had failed to grasp the gravity of her words. "That," she said again, "is the saddest thing I have ever heard."

Zach didn't understand what was so sad about it, but it was hard to disagree with Emma, once she'd decided something. In the years to come, he'd find this was true of lots of people.

✦

IN THE YEARS since "transition" we've often been asked how it was our family survived the whole miserable business. Looking back on it all now, it seems inevitable that the love our family shared was bound to triumph, that the things that bound us all together were fated to prevail over the things that were tearing us apart. But it didn't feel inevitable at the time. What felt inevitable was the complete loss of everything we had ever known or loved.

For one thing, the vast majority of our friends and relatives seemed to be subtly, or not so subtly, rooting for divorce. This was true not only among Deedie's supporters, who just thought the whole idea of staying with a transsexual "husband" the height of absurdity; it was true among mine as well. "You're never going to really be a woman until you get away from the life you created as a man," one friend told me. "You need to move away somewhere and start over." According to these well-wishers, staying with Deedie and the boys, continuing on as a professor at Colby and living in the town in which we had made our home, would be like trailing my male life behind me, no matter what sex I became. I might change my name to Jennifer and switch over to diet from regular Coke, but as long as I stayed put, I would still be casting James's shadow.

People rooting for us to split weren't necessarily mean-spirited, of course; splitting up and each of us "moving on" seemed like an obvious and generous way to do well by each other. Surely Deedie deserved what she had signed on for—a husband—and surely I deserved a chance to find the thing everyone presumed that I would now desire as well: a husband of my own. This solution—divorce for both of us, and a second marriage for us each to a decent, loving man—was the cleanest all around, it was felt. If the danger for me in staying with my family was that I would always still be casting James's shadow, then the danger for Deedie was even more severe. If she stayed with me, she would be casting a shadow of her own, living the life of a woman who had never quite accepted the fact that the man she loved no longer existed. She would be like some twenty-first-century nether-version of

Miss Havisham, frozen in time, still going through the rituals of a life that had long since gone on without her.

In short, what our friends and family hoped was the well-intended hope of men and women in a culture riddled with homophobia—not to mention transphobia, a word most people had never even heard of. They hoped that Deedie and I, severed from each other, would henceforward be redeemed by the love of some nice man.

That we would want to stay together, that we would want to continue our marriage as quas-bians, wasn't just a hope that had not yet occurred to our friends. It was also one that had not yet occurred to us.

IF THERE WAS a single person in the world who thought that my changing genders was a brilliant idea, it was Deedie's sister Katie. Twelve years older than my wife, Katie was a United Church of Christ minister who had recently come out as a lesbian. It was Katie who had married the two of us at the National Cathedral in Washington back in 1988; it was Katie who had come to sit at Deedie's bedside when the children were born. She had a mercurial, passionate, intense personality, and she was as quick to laugh as she was to dissolve in fits of bereaved, self-pitying tears. She had always been a big fan of mine, though; I think she saw in me an example of what she hoped a man could be—sensitive, emotional, and involved with his sons.

Katie knew that something was up with her sister and me in the months following our return from Ireland in late 1999. She heard the strain in Deedie's voice; she could tell that we were holding something back. When at last I spilled the beans, her first reaction was one of relief. "Oh thank goodness it's only that you're a woman," she said. "I was afraid it was something serious."

Oddly—or perhaps not so oddly—Katie's support for my transition (you really had to call it enthusiasm) wasn't exactly what Deedie needed. (Quite frankly, at that point in her life, I think Katie thought it would be great if everybody became a woman.) But talking to a sister who thought that her husband's transformation was an occasion for celebration wasn't of much help when what Deedie needed most was sympathy and support. And so, fairly soon in the process, Deedie turned to her oldest sister, Susie, for support. Susie, fourteen years Deedie's senior, lived in Oklahoma, and while no one could consider her a conservative (all the Finneys had inherited the progressivism of their father, Tom, a major Democratic consigliere to Kennedy, Johnson, and Clark Clifford), she was certainly less thrilled for her sister at the prospect of her finding herself suddenly legally married to another woman than sister Katie was. Susie's favorite expression was "Wellll . . . ," drawn out in a loving Southwestern twang. Susie's "Wellll . . ." was a soothing, loving sound, an expression of both hope and humor, kind of the Oklahoman version of Tony Soprano's "Whaddya gonna do." It was this phrase, more than anything else, that helped Deedie negotiate the awkward, heartbreaking early months of her husband's transition from male to female.

DEEDIE: Susie, what am I going to do? The man that I love is a beautiful woman.
SUSIE: Wellll . . .

And so each of us got our own Finney sister—Katie for me, Susie for Deedie. The fourth Finney sibling, Todd, was kept in the dark for now. Why was it that I failed to share our secret with him, a man who, in the long run, turned out to be as loving as a brother could be? Was it that, given the death of Deedie's father, he was the closest thing to a father-in-law I had? He had given his sister away at our wedding; he had given the toast at our reception. Was it that, even as I exchanged my citizenship papers from the land of men for those from the land of women, I still felt the tug of the patriarchy?

Or maybe I was just afraid he'd drive over to our house from Vermont (where he lived in a cabin he had built himself) and beat the crap out of me. Todd Finney, a pacifist and a forgiver by nature, had—so far as I knew—never taken a swing at another living soul. But the way I figured, there was probably a first time for everything.

In the months that followed, Katie acted as my Sherpa to the world of women. She took me to Northampton, Massachusetts, for a long weekend—about as trans-friendly a town as can be imagined—where we stayed at an inn and I got some heels-on-the-ground experience in walking around in the world. She was endlessly patient with me, serving as my chaperone as I got my hair done, and we went shopping in hippie boutiques for clothes and earrings. We had plans to go out to dinner, but she was plagued by a stomachache that had been bugging her off and on for months. On the last day, minister Katie held my hand and said a prayer. I was a man again, just about to get in the car and drive back to Maine.

*Make us servants,* she said, her eyes closed, *unto thy will.*


I STARTED THERAPY just after New Year's Day 2000. By that summer I was taking hormones and going through electrolysis. I tried to share the transition with Deedie, as best I could, and told myself that we were considering its various milestones together, as a couple. And yet transition was not something we could easily share; it was, almost by definition, a process that was taking the man Deedie loved away from her. I tried to get us to have conversations about it all, to ask her just how far down this road she imagined I could go without losing her, and yet the only thing she really wanted was not to have to have this conversation at all.

"What do you want?" I would ask her. "What can I do for you?"

Deedie sat at the dinner table, tears coursing down her face. The boys were in the next room, watching *Rugrats.*

"No matter what happens from here," she said, "I lose. Either I stay with you, and I lose the man I love most in the world, or I leave you, and I turn my back on the person I love right at the moment she most needs me."

"Maybe," I said. "Maybe there's some kind of middle ground?"

"Where?" she said, slapping her hand on the table. "Where's this middle ground, between the man I know and the woman you need to be? Where?" She looked at me with fury.

"I don't know," I said.

❖

TEN YEARS LATER, the thing my son Sean remembers most clearly about this time is that I began to smell different. It didn't frighten him—at age five—that my hair was growing longer or that I had gotten my ears pierced. "Those things weren't deep-down," Sean told me later. "What really made me know you were changing was your smell. That's what I remember that made me think that something was happening way down deep."

"What did I smell like?" I asked him. "How would you describe it?"

Sean, who grew up to be a wry, brilliant man, reminiscent of my own father in his fondness for understatement and irony, just smiled elusively.

"Different," he said.

I WENT DOWN to the post office in our little town and mailed my "transition letter" to my colleagues at work, a delicately worded document that told the other professors at Colby what was up with Professor Boylan and begged somewhat piteously for compassion and understanding. (It also announced that I was working on a book about the journey, a text that at the time I was calling "Same Monkeys Different Barrel.") When I got back from the post office, I found Deedie on the phone, talking to Katie. Her face was ashen.

She hung up and ran to me, putting her arms around me and beginning to cry. Katie had been diagnosed with ovarian cancer.

When she died, less than a year later, Deedie and I were standing at her bed in the hospice in Ithaca, New York, along with her lover, Mary Jo. We took petals from all of the flowers that had gathered in the room and covered her body with them. She looked beautiful lying there, at peace at last, surrounded by flowers. But of course, we would rather have had her alive.

During the year between the diagnosis and her loss, Katie's illness was by far the greater of the two traumas our family faced. My gender transition seemed a whole lot less important compared to Katie's mortal illness. As it turns out, there is actually a big difference between changing genders and dying.

I read a poem by Galway Kinnell at Katie's funeral. The last line was, "Maybe a life is just an interlude. Before, and after, all that singing."

After the funeral one of Katie's parishioners came up to me. "Now remind me," she said. "Which sister are you?"

I HAVE WRITTEN elsewhere about the details of the transition from male to female—the electrolysis and the therapy and the surgery and the trips to the large-size shoe store—and I am truly sorry to disappoint readers who are hoping to hear about all of those thrilling details one more time. My reluctance to revisit that aspect of things stems not only from having told that story before; it's also that, at this late date, I grow weary of stories of transsexuals always being stories about a trip to a hospital; it's as if every story about Jews in America always had to be a story about a bris. The surgery is not the most important thing about any transgender person's story, dramatic and astonishing as it might be. The surgery is just one day, and the key player is a doctor whom in most cases the patient barely knows. That's not what being trans is all about. Being trans—and sustaining a family—is about everything that comes before that moment, and everything after. That's where the story lies.*

My own memories of the trip to the hospital are of being given re- markable drugs that made everything feel safe and warm. And, more important, of being surrounded on all sides by people who loved me— Tim Kreider, and Russo, and Deedie. Mostly, I felt happy, and adored. I went to sleep singing "I'm Gonna Wash That Man Right Out of My Hair." A few hours later I woke up, and there I was, finally home at last. More than anything else, what I felt was relief.

I blinked in and out of the painkillers. At one point I woke to hear Deirdre talking to our friend Liz on the phone. Liz, the maid of honor

---

* For the curious—as well as to serve as a guide for others with the same con- dition—a short list of available resources, both online and upon the shelves of libraries, is appended at the end of this memoir. You can also e-mail me directly at jb@jenniferboylan.net and I will try to help you as best I can.

at our wedding, and one of our best friends, was one of the people who had initially suggested that the best step for Deedie, in the wake of my news, was to phone up a lawyer and find a new boyfriend. She's changed her heart about this in the years since, but at the time, the idea of her friend Deedie's husband becoming a woman didn't seem to her like a great development in our relationship.

"No," Deedie said. "She's still asleep." Bright sunlight filtered through the curtains. I looked over at the bed of my roommate, Melanie, whose experience could not have been more different than my own. Melanie had come here alone, and had nearly died after her procedure. Her bed was empty now.*

"I tell you what, Liz," she said, "the thing is, I was approaching this whole thing like it was 'part two' of this horrible year, like first Katie dying and then my husband having a sex change. But the thing is, I guess this experience is actually totally different. I mean, it makes me want to talk to Jenny's sister, who's totally cut her off, who won't even have a conversation with her. I want to explain to her that having your sibling die is actually a *lot* different than having a sibling change genders. I mean, for God's sake, Jenny's not dead, she's still here, and whatever anyone thinks, she is a remarkable person and you have to be glad she's alive. Just sitting here with her, it's impossible not to see how happy she is, and to be grateful she's here.

"She keeps forgetting what we're talking about, and it frustrates her; she wants to be part of every conversation. I don't know, I'm afraid when the anesthesia wears off she's going to be in real pain. But I don't know. I wish her sister could see her.

---

* I'm aware that my own story as a trans person is unique, at least in part because many things that could have gone wrong failed to do so, and I have worried over the years about the many ways in which my tale may have given false hope to some readers; my story is surely only that, and is almost certainly the particular result of circumstances unique to my life. The story of my roommate Melanie, which formed the centerpiece of Richard Russo's afterword to my book *She's Not There: A Life in Two Genders,* provided an important counterweight to my own narrative. The tenth-anniversary edition of that memoir provides, among other things, an update on Melanie, at whose wedding, years later, I served as matron of honor.

"No matter what else you say about my husband, she's an amazing woman."

IT WAS THE loss of Katie, the sister we both loved, that, more than anything else, returned Deedie and me to each other. It wasn't that she was suddenly thrilled about being married to a woman, and it wasn't that I, for my part, was sanguine about being married to someone who had mixed feelings about me. But as we weathered that hard time together, we were reminded that there are a lot of things that entwine lovers together. If in the end we lost physical intimacy—at least the kind we had enjoyed as husband and wife—it also occurred to us that physical intimacy may not be the most important kind. And if it's true that Deedie's love helped me traverse the ocean between men and women, then it's also true that my love for her helped her traverse a sea of her own—the one between mourning and solace.

The night after Katie's funeral, I had gone to sleep in a lake house near Aurora, New York. The sounds of the wind whipping across Cayuga Lake permeated my dreams.

I saw Deedie's sister Susie standing on the porch of the cottage. The wind screamed across Cayuga, shaking the rafters, filling the house with unceasing moans and sighs that built to a crescendo and died away and rose again. Susie had a music stand in front of her, and the wind tore the pages from her book and they blew away toward Lansing and Ithaca. In one hand she held a baton. She was conducting the howling winds like an orchestra. Susie turned and looked at me over her shoulder.

"The howling augments the grief," she said.

ONE DAY I came home to find Sean patting Lucy on the head. He looked thoughtful. "Are you all right?" I asked.

"Yeah," said Sean. He was playing with Thomas the Tank Engine. His favorite engine was number five, red James.

"What are you thinking?"

"Daddy," he said. "It used to be you and me and Zach, the three boys, on one side, and Mommy and Lucy-dog on the other. We were, like, a team."

"I know," I said, feeling my heart clench.

"Now it's Zach and me on one side, and you and Mommy and Lucy-dog over there."

"I'm sorry, Sean," I said. My voice was barely a whisper. "I'm so sorry."

"It's okay," said Sean. "The boys are just outnumbered."

# THE GRIFFIN

We were sitting around the kitchen table, the four of us, eating dinner. Zach gave me a look.

"What?" I said.

"We can't keep calling you 'Daddy,'" he said, shaking his head. "If you're going to be a girl. It's too weird."

"Well," I said to my sons, "my new name is Jenny. You could call me Jenny if you want."

Zach laughed derisively. "Jenny? That's the name you'd give a lady mule."

I tried not to be hurt. "Okay, fine," I said. "What do you want to call me?"

"The important thing, boys," said Deedie, "is that you pick something you're comfortable with."

Zach thought this over. He was pretty good at naming things. For a while we'd had a hermit crab named Grabber. Later on, we'd briefly owned a snake named Biter.

"I know," he said. "Let's call you 'Maddy.' That's like, half Mommy, and half Daddy. And anyhow, I know a girl at school named Maddy. She's pretty nice."

Sean considered this. "Or 'Dommy,'" he added.

Then we all laughed at Dommy. Even Seannie laughed. Dommy! What a dumb name for a transsexual parent! After the hilarity died down, I nodded.

"Maddy might work," I said.

✦

IT TOOK LESS time than we had feared for our family to begin to seem normal to us again. I was in charge of waking everyone up and making breakfast and straightening the house and getting the boys to practice their instruments: Seannie on French horn, Zach on the three-quarter-size tuba. Deedie was in charge of dinner and shepherding the boys through their homework and coaching Seannie's soccer travel team. After a time, Deedie and I even began to seem familiar to each other again, and the things that had changed in me seemed, incredibly, less important to Deedie than the things that had remained the same.

In the fall we picked apples. In the winter we skied and sat around the fireplace in our living room afterward, drinking hot chocolate. In summer we fished on Long Pond, and Zach landed one giant large-mouth bass after another. Most of the time we forgot that there was anything extraordinary about our family. Were we really so strange?

Even though we seemed to have made the leap across the inscrutable chasm of gender in one piece, a nagging, unsettling question would return to me, usually at night when I found myself awake in the wee hours. What kind of men would my children become, I wondered, having been raised by a father who became a woman?

I'd hear the sound of the grandmother clock ticking downstairs as I lay awake in the dark. I'd think about my own precarious boyhood and wonder how I was going to help my sons become themselves. I'd hear a voice in my heart demanding an answer to the same question my harshest critics had asked of me: What about the children? the voice said. What about the boys?

ON A SUMMER afternoon in 1967—the Summer of Love—I drove a Sears riding mower back to my parents' garage in Newtown Square, Pennsylvania, and parked it between the blue and white '64 Pontiac on the one side and the green '58 Buick on the other. Then I pulled the throttle to the off position, and the engine slowly died. I sat there on the tractor for a moment, still feeling the inertia of the blades spinning beneath me. The garage was full of the smell of gasoline, of freshly mown grass. Then I walked into the house and opened the refrigerator and stood there for a while feeling the cold air drifting around my neck and my bare grass-stained legs. I reached in and pulled out a tall green bottle of Wink, poured it into a glass my father got at the Esso station, the same one that promised to put a tiger in your tank. On my way back outside, I grabbed a Ring Ding. It went well with Wink.

Nick Strachman and his older brother were playing baseball in the block beyond our house. The ball made a sharp socking sound as it landed in Nick's mitt. Years later, Lou opened up a clothing store for men, out on West Chester Pike, but it didn't stay open long. As for Nick, he wound up as a purveyor of frozen steaks. Thirty-five years after we'd been in elementary school together, he called me up one Sunday out of the blue, from Nebraska, wanting to know if I'd be interested in buying a side of beef.

From my mother's bedroom I heard the soft tinkling of a music box. There was a small ballerina figurine in her jewelry box that pirouetted and danced to the music when the box was opened. When no one was home, sometimes I went into my parents' bedroom, and wound up the music box, and watched that ballerina dance to the weird, sad music. That distant music now meant that my mother had opened her jewelry box, that she was taking off her earrings and laying them next to her necklaces and pins.

Beyond a line of trees Dr. DeWees was running his mower in his backyard, and the sound of the blades echoed in the hollow. Suddenly, there was a sharp crashing sound, and a moment after that the tractor's engine died; and then there was the sound of Dr. DeWees cussing out the rock that had gotten jammed in the blades. The cussing continued for a while, as Dr. DeWees addressed himself to the rock and then the tractor.

I was drinking Wink.

A copy of Harper Lee's *To Kill a Mockingbird* was lying facedown on the back step. I'd had to write a theme about it for school, on what Atticus Finch meant when he said, "You never really know a man until you walk around in his heels." His shoes, I mean. At school we'd kept talking about Atticus, but that wasn't the character I was interested in; I was much more concerned with Boo Radley. More than anything else I wanted, like Scout, to let him out, even though I knew it was impossible. Hey, I'd say to him. Hey, Boo.

My father was building a wall in the side yard. There was a *chunk* as he hit the slate with his hammer. Then he pulled the stone over to the wall and found the right place for it. There was a soft flinty snick as he struck his butane lighter and lit up an L&M Filter. On his transistor radio was the sound of the Phillies game, the boys playing over in old Connie Mack Stadium, the sound of the distant crowd roaring as Jim Bunning hit a grounder to second.

It was a boyhood, and it was mine, and it was typical, with the exception of the business inside my heart.

My mother stood on the threshold of the front door and rang a copper cowbell. The sound of that bell—clanky and slightly obnoxious— had the ability to reach my sister and me, wherever we were, and get us to drop whatever it was we were doing and run toward home. On this day, I simply stood up and walked around from the back porch to the front yard, where my mother stood. My sister, who'd been out in the woods, walked up the driveway toward us, in no particular hurry.

My boyhood, like others, ended over a period of years. Even the melodramatic and salacious event of gender reassignment didn't represent the moment it all finally ceased, assuming that there even was such a moment. Sure, you could conjure such a moment up, if you wanted—say, the day I dropped out of Boy Scouts because I was tired of the angry ex-marine scoutmaster lining us up for inspection every Wednesday night and yelling at us, telling us we were all soft, that we were weaklings. Or maybe you could say it all ended when my parents packed up the Oldsmobile Omega and drove me and my Grateful Dead albums the five hours north to Wesleyan, in the fall of 1976. Maybe you could nominate the day of my first kiss, or the day I met Deedie Finney, or the day I got married, or the day my first child was born. There are many such days marking the end of a boyhood, you could argue.

But most of the time I think that the boy that I was is still with me, in spite of the woman's life that is now mine. I hear that boy's voice when I tell a joke or raise my voice to sing some filthy song I picked up in Cork. I feel his loneliness, sometimes, when I hear children in our neighborhood in Maine, calling to each other, as twilight falls at the end of a day in summer. And sometimes, if I hear the clanking, tone-less ringing of a cowbell, I'm still tempted to get up from where I'm sitting and start running through the grass toward home.

THIRTY-FIVE YEARS LATER, in the late afternoon of an October day, I went for a bike ride on the golf course with my boys. At ten, Zach was emotional, buoyant, a child who liked to sneak up behind people and hug them. His brother, Seannie, was the exact opposite—quiet, sturdy, private. Seannie still had his training wheels on but could outpedal both his brother and me. On one occasion he skidded off the path and bounced right off a large boulder. Without a pause, he looked up at me and said, "That was fun. Let's do it again."

I felt proud of my children as they biked on ahead of me, up the gentle slope of the path that circumnavigated the fifteenth green. We'd been out on the course now for almost an hour. With their mops of blond hair, the ten-year-old and the eight-year-old zoomed ahead of me, and as I watched the bikes ascend the hill I could only feel pride and wonder. They were turning out all right, my kids, in spite of everything. Like everyone else, I watched them for signs of trauma, but so far there was nothing that distinguished them from their classmates in the third and fifth grades.

The wind blew in my hair, and I paused for a moment to catch my breath. I thought about Deedie back at the house, making a rub for a slab of barbecued ribs we hoped to be devouring later that day. We had all come so far as a family, and yet in some ways things had not changed at all. My heart, and Deedie's heart—in Russo's phrase—still "inclined toward the other," and for the most part that which made us similar to other families seemed a whole lot more important than that which made us different.

I saw my children ascending the hill, two blond boys on bikes, racing each other to the crest. The sound of their laughter came to me from a distance.

I got back on my bike and followed them up the hill. It took a while for me to catch up with them. They were waiting for me at the water tank by the sixteenth tee. Seannie had leaned his bike against a bench and was filling a cone-shaped cup from one of the water barrels that was stationed around the course. Zach was waiting in line behind his brother, holding a cone cup in his hand.

"You know what I could do with a cup like this?" I said to Zach. "What?"

"Well, if I ran a string of elastic through it, and cut a small hole in the bottom, you could use it as a beak for your costume."

Zach thought this over. "Really?" he said cautiously.

The griffin costume that Zach had settled on for Halloween had been the cause of unending discontent. I had purchased a set of wings in Camden when I went over to see Russo the weekend previous, but Zach wasn't thrilled about them. "They look like angel wings," he'd said grumpily. "Not griffin wings." I understood his dissatisfaction. To be mistaken for an angel when what you are aiming for is griffin is not a small thing.

Then I'd found a lion costume at a local flea market. I figured, you take a lion costume, you put wings on the back of it, you got yourself a griffin. Zach thought otherwise. "It's a baby costume," he said, looking at the lion in dismay. "I'm not wearing it."

"Okay, well, you solve the problem," I said.

"I don't know where to get a griffin costume!" he said. "I'm just a kid, I don't have any money."

But these water cups from the golf course gave me a new idea. I could make a griffin beak out of one and attach it to Zach's nose with elastic. Then I could sew a tail onto a pair of his yellow pants. It might work. At any rate, the important thing to bear in mind about a Maine Halloween is that no matter what kids dress up as, they always wind up buried beneath heavy coats and mittens and hats anyway, since by the end of October, winter is beginning to move in, and sometimes we even have snow.

I stuffed a water cup in my fleece jacket, thinking, *I'm going to make a griffin beak out of a cone-shaped water cup I'm stealing from the golf course!* Zach clicked his helmet back on. "I'm going to go on ahead," he said.

I looked at the steep hill before us. There was a small bridge without a guardrail at the bottom. A ravine filled with boulders and a small stream ran beneath the bridge. Sometimes the boys and I followed the stream from our house, through the woods, and onto the course, and hid beneath the bridge.

"You wait at the bottom of the hill," I said. "Seannie and I will be along in a second."

We would be back at the house in a minute, I thought. I could almost see our house through the trees at the back of the hole on the other side of the ravine. We'd be inside in twenty minutes, and I'd make a fire in the fireplace, and perhaps I'd try to make a griffin beak out of a water cup. I imagined the taste of the ribs Deedie was making, the meat with the vinegar and cumin and molasses and salt.

Zach biked on ahead. Seannie drank from his cup, then snapped on his helmet. His bike with the training wheels was blue. He called it "Shooting Blue Moon."

From the ravine I heard a soft snap, like a tree branch falling.

Seannie and I sailed down the hill. We both kept our brakes on; the rear tire of Seannie's bike locked and smoked against the pavement as we skidded downward. We stopped at the bottom of the hill, halfway across the bridge, and looked up at the ridge before us. Sunlight was sparkling off the trees, and fleetingly I actually thought, *If I could relive a half hour of my life over again, it would be this moment, the boys and me together in this amazing soft light.*

But it was at that moment that I realized that Zach was not waiting for us at the bottom of the hill, as I'd asked.

Neither was he up at the ridge before us. Could he have biked on up the hill and gone home already? It seemed impossible.

From the ravine I heard a soft cry. I looked to my left. Zach's bicycle lay against a rock, mangled, the front half crushed like aluminum foil. The child was nowhere near it.

I dropped my bike to the ground and ran across the bridge, then down into the ravine. There were shoulder-high thistles and brambles I had to crush past in order to get to the stream. "Zach?" I shouted. "Zach?"

The boy was lying on his back a few yards from the stream. His eyes were closed. I called to him, and his eyelids fluttered halfway open, and for just a second he seemed like he recognized me, as if I were someone he had known a long, long time ago.

I lifted him in my arms, and I drove him to the hospital. It was the same hospital in which he had been born. I remembered the night Zach had come into the world—the cold snow coming down all around, the sound of Stealers Wheel on the car stereo, the dads in the waiting room with their copies of *Sports Illustrated*.

It was a whole lifetime ago, by which I mean just a few seconds.

The doctors put Zach on a gurney. As they wheeled him away, he whispered to me, "Don't worry, Maddy. I'm going to be good as new!"

My throat closed up as he disappeared behind a set of swinging doors. *My boy,* I thought. *I've lost my boy.*

A nurse handed me a clipboard filled with forms. "So," she said. "You're his mother?"

TIME OUT II

▼

# CONVERSATIONS with WAIFS and ANGELS

Edward Albee

Barbara Spiegel

Timothy Kreider

# EDWARD ALBEE

*There is no one to tell you
who you are except yourself.*

Edward Albee is an American playwright. A three-time winner of the Pulitzer Prize, as well as a recipient of a lifetime achievement award from the Kennedy Center, he is known for the plays *The Zoo Story, Who's Afraid of Virginia Woolf?, A Delicate Balance, Tiny Alice, Three Tall Women, The Goat,* and my own favorite, *Quotations of Chairman Mao Tse-Tung.*

We first met after he saw a play of mine at Johns Hopkins in 1986, a work titled *Big Baby,* which was a short dramatic piece about a baby that gets really big. After the play, Albee stood up in the audience and asked me, "Mr. Boylan. Could you please explain—why is the baby—so large?"

Edward was adopted at birth by a couple he calls "those people." We met at his loft in New York—a beautiful space filled with modern and impressionist paintings and primitive sculptures—to talk about waifs, orphans, angels, and imagination. Albee being Albee, of course, he started asking me questions the moment I stepped through the door.

▼

EDWARD ALBEE: What is the need to make this distinction between being a father and a mother?

JENNIFER FINNEY BOYLAN: [*Sitting down on couch*] Well, it may be that there is no distinction. That's one of the things I'm exploring, Edward. I know that my sense of the world is different, but it may be less about the difference between male and female than the difference between someone who is bearing a secret and someone who is not.

EA: I guess I'm really asking because it seems to me in some way that you are less different to your sons because you're the same person.

JFB: There's definitely a before and an after in my life. For them, the before is such a long time ago. So their memories of me as a man—

EA: Can you think about being a father? You must remember very specifically their birthing. And your response as a father, yes?

JFB: Yes.

EA: Was it more complicated than that?

JFB: My response was astonishment at the otherworldliness of it. And joy and concern for the woman that I love. I was hoping she was all right.

EA: When they were born, did you have any intimations of what might be going on later?

JFB: I hoped it would not come to that.

EA: So that must have affected your response to being a father.

JFB: My fear that this would come to pass?

EA: Mm. Well, not fear, but concern.

JFB: Well, there are all kinds of dads, including ones like me who were better known for making a good risotto than being able to throw a football.

EA: But when they were born, you were a guy.

JFB: I was.

EA: Therefore, you were their father.

JFB: Am I or was I?

EA: You haven't become their mother.

JFB: Well, I'm their sire.

EA: Yeah. So, you are a parent. I just wonder, aside from all sorts of things, what difference it really makes.

JFB: Well, maybe none. Perhaps none. Perhaps what's more important than us being male or female is the fact that we're human. I'm comfortable with that.

EA: You see, if you're a father it means you've had sex with a woman, your wife or someone else, and impregnated her.

JFB: You think that's what it means? Seriously?

EA: You never birthed those two. Isn't that a different quality of parenthood?

JFB: I think it is. On the other hand, I know gay men who have adopted children and neither father gave birth to the child.

EA: Well, that's very, very complex.

JFB: Well, yeah. Welcome to my world, Edward.

EA: Ten weeks of discussion. My God.

JFB: We don't have ten weeks.

EA: I'm getting awfully concerned about so many of my gay friends who are adopting kids. I'm getting very worried about them. They don't know what they're getting into.

JFB: What are they getting into?

EA: They're getting into a long-term thing, a very long-term thing that I don't think that they ever anticipate.

JFB: Why should they not be able to understand a long-term commitment any more than a straight couple? Straight couples can be just as blind.

EA: Because it has nothing to do with sex. If neither of you is the parent, neither gay guy is the parent, is a parent of the offspring, then all the rules are off.

JFB: But are they not the parents? Does parenthood have to mean biology?

EA: Does it mean making or is it the being?

JFB: I think it's the being.

EA: Yeah. Well, what do we do about the making then? You made two boys. Through your own need and choice, you have become their mother rather than their father, but you're still their father.

JFB: Well, even if that's true—which I'm not sure it is—it makes me a very different kind of mother than most other women I know. And it makes me different from most of the fathers I know. And yet, my experience as their mother, as their parent, has been more universal than—absurd.

EA: Do you find that you think about them differently as a woman than you did as a man?

JFB: Well, I think as a father I was a little bit more feckless. I just wanted to make them laugh. I was very goofy and I would do these ridiculous stunts and things to make them laugh. I loved hearing that.

As a mother, I keep after them a lot more. I nag them more, sometimes—

EA: You're behaving like a woman. [*Laughter*] But do you think about them differently?

JFB: I worry about them more. Because they've had a parent who is so different.

EA: When you look at them now do you ever say to yourself, "I am their father"?

JFB: No.

EA: But you are. You're also their mother.

JFB: It's a long way from Tipperary, but we came from there. It's also the trick of memory. Trying to remember who we have been.

EA: And what we choose to remember, yes.

JFB: I try to remember who was I when I was your student in 1986—that frightened, hopeful scarecrow of a boy.

EA: You were also cute.

JFB: Was I?

EA: Yeah. [*He smiles wistfully.*]

JFB: Well, look who's talking.

Do you remember those long talks we used to have about James Thurber?

EA: I don't know why people don't read Thurber anymore.

JFB: Sometimes I think it's just down to you and me. I was thinking about how, when I was a thirteen-year-old transsexual on the Main Line of Pennsylvania, I wanted to be James Thurber. That's who I dreamed of being, of all of the artists that I could have chosen to be. It seems so strange to me now.

EA: There are so many things that I admire about Thurber's work. I thought he was an extraordinary prose stylist, among other things. I found those few very, very, very serious old-fashioned stories that he wrote quite amazing.

JFB: "The Cane in the Corridor." And "One Is a Wanderer," in which that sad, lonely protagonist walks around singing "Bye, Bye, Blackbird" to himself. I got to play "Bye, Bye, Blackbird" on Thurber's piano at the Thurber House in Columbus. I felt rather cheeky doing it.

EA: Nobody could be funnier than Thurber when he was being funny.

JFB: He was funny, but you also felt this kind of smoldering anger and resentment. Was it the blindness? I think what I related to in Thurber was that as a young transgender person so deeply in the closet, I felt that my problems were fundamentally unresolvable. But that there was a way of getting along in the world and that my sense of humor was going to help me. Writing was going to help me too, but I would never have a sense of resolution in my life, or so I believed back then. As a young man did you feel that your situation in the world was unresolvable?

EA: I had no problem. Look, remember. I didn't belong with those people that adopted me. They had nothing to do with me. I had nothing to do with them. We were together through contract.

JFB: The thing I can't get my mind around is their son was— Edward Albee. How could they not have been grateful?

EA: That wasn't the one they bought. They bought something they could turn into what they could tolerate. And ended up with me instead.

JFB: Well, who did they want?

EA: They wanted somebody who probably would be a businessman, certainly would carry on the family and all that—family name— and give them grandchildren and things like that. The entire family was sterile. The mother of the sister, my father's sister, couldn't have any kids, nor could he. I don't really know who was lacking there. Both of them perhaps. I don't know. But I know that the grandfather, old EF, he wanted a grandson. That's why I turned up.

JFB: Your biological parents were Louise Harvey and an unnamed man. Who do you imagine they might have been?

EA: I don't know. That's the only thing that bothered me about being adopted in the days when you couldn't find out that sort of thing. I would like to know where I got my odd mind from.

JFB: Do you think that your odd mind came from them or do you think that you invented it yourself?

EA: Well, it must have come in part, probably more from him than from her. Maybe not.

JFB: Because oddness of mind is a thing that fathers give us?

EA: No, I just think maybe because I was a guy that I turned out to be so unlike other guys. Must be in my father's personality. But then again I was surrounded by men who were more passive and women who were more—

JFB: Characters.

EA: Yeah, characters. And aggressive. When I was told that I was adopted my feeling was relief. I'm not these people. I don't owe these people anything. I never felt like I belonged there.

JFB: But it's funny, Edward. I was not adopted. I was the son of a Main Line banker and his very sweet wife and yet, I didn't think I was related to them either. I often fantasized who were my real parents. That I must have been adopted somehow.

EA: Maybe the basic difference is, there are some of us who want to find out—create ourselves—and others who wish to be whatever they want us to be.

JFB: And we created ourselves. I guess that's the thing about wondering about your biological father. If it turned out, somehow, that he was actually George M. Cohan—

EA: Then he'd have a lot to apologize for.

JFB: Who would he have been? Have you imagined, given that you are known for invention—?

EA: I just think he would have been interesting. It ties into my great love for that line from "Knoxville" from James Agee's book. "Finally I am put to bed. Sleep, soft smiling, draws me unto her: and those that receive me, who quietly treat me, as one familiar and well-beloved in that home: but will not, oh will not, not now, not ever, but will not ever tell me who I am."

[*There is an unexpected pause here as both Edward's eyes and JFB's mist up.*]

JFB: I think there is—well. [*Clears throat*]

EA: There is no one to tell you who you are except yourself.

JFB: Knowing who your parents are doesn't necessarily provide the answer, Edward.

EA: No. No. Because a lot of people have to abandon all the things that they're supposed to be and their entire upbringing if that's not who they are.

JFB: There was a moment when you said, "All right. I'm leaving." And you packed a bag and you left.

EA: It was a wonderful feeling of liberation that I could get on with the business of being who I was. I knew what I was giving up. I wasn't crazy. I knew I was giving up wealth and comfort and all of that stuff, but I'd gotten my education. I'd gotten what I needed. Enough to spend the next ten years undoing a lot of stuff and finding out totally who I needed to be.

JFB: Did you ever know what your parents' reaction to your work was? The Albees?

EA: The father, no. I never found out anything about his reaction to anything. I know that the mother would refer to me as "my son, the playwright."

But I don't think she was ever sympathetic to the work. No, it was not the kind of theater that she thought one should be seeing. Theater is not to make you happy, but escape. No engagement. All escape.

JFB: What was her idea of a great night on the town?

EA: Oh, a wonderful musical.

JFB: George M. Cohan. [*Laughs*]

EA: Are you completely satisfied with where you are and who you are?

JFB: What? Am I satisfied? You mean completely?

EA: Mm.

JFB: On a good day.

EA: And the bad days?

JFB: The bad days I guess I feel lingering guilt at having made the lives of the people that I love more complicated.

EA: If life is not complex what's the point of living it?

JFB: You were blessed with a long relationship with Jonathan Thomas. What would have happened if you had adopted children?

EA: Never occurred to us.

JFB: Never on the radar?

EA: Never for a second.

JFB: Because?

EA: I thought that I was having kids by writing plays.

JFB: Humor me. If you'd had a child, who would he have been? Or she?

EA: I would have forced them to be as individual as I could possibly have forced them to be.

JFB: How would you have done that?

EA: I'm pretty good at seeing and hearing bullshit. I think I would have been saying, "Come off it. Come off it."

JFB: What would his or her name have been?

EA: I have no idea.

JFB: I know you have no idea. Would it have been Edward Jr.?

EA: I think I would have rather had a son than a daughter.

JFB: Why?

EA: 'Cause I'm gay. I relate much more to guys.

JFB: Other than teaching him not to tolerate bullshit—which, by the way, that was my goal, too, and it's actually a bigger job than it sounds—what else would you have liked to have taught your son?

EA: That when you get to the end of it you should be okay with the fact that you dealt pretty honorably with yourself and other people and didn't compromise too much.

JFB: Is it fair to say that in your plays, couples are frequently dissatisfied with the state of their marriages?

EA: They both change or one of them changes and the other doesn't.

JFB: Don't start with me.

EA: Every relationship has its duration.

JFB: A thing I took from Thurber is that it just seems as if every form of love, heterosexual love anyway, seems at some point to lead to bedlam.

EA: Well, gay relationships rarely go on for a long time untroubled, too, you know.

JFB: I was thinking about your play *The Goat,* which is a play that I saw in the heart of my own transition. [*It's a play about a man who sacrifices his marriage because he falls head over heels in love with a goat named Sylvia.*] When I left the theater, I think you'll be pleased to know, I left the theater that night and I went back to my hotel and I wept—

EA: Good for you.

JFB: No, good for you. I took it very personally.

EA: You wept for me?

JFB: No, I wept for me. I'm not worried about you, Edward.

EA: [*Chuckles*]

JFB: No, I thought, Oh my God, that's me. That I'm someone whose passion is so unseemly that I'm just bringing chaos wherever I go. Although in a way, I guess our story ended differently in that it was as if Deedie in the end said to me, "Okay, we'll make room for the goat."

EA: Don't you have to be ruthless if you're going to become who you need to be? Don't you have to be ruthless?

JFB: Yeah, I think so. I think so. Although I think for me to become who I needed to be also required taking as much of my former self with me as possible.

EA: No, you have to be ruthless in response to other people's reaction.

JFB: I guess. Although maybe I'm less ruthless than you are.

EA: Let me get you some green tea.

JFB: Okay. Shall I follow you in?

[*We walk through the loft, past its paintings and primitive sculptures, into the kitchen, where Edward starts looking through the cupboards.*]

EA: Do I have any green tea? Here's some green tea. Do you like green tea?

JFB: Yes, please.

[*There is a long interval as the water boils and we speak of Easter Island, which we visited within weeks of each other in 2005, and which made a lasting impression on us both. We talk about going back there together for Edward's eighty-fifth birthday in 2013.*]

EA: Do you take anything in your tea?

JFB: No, I think I'll take it just like this. What are you looking for?

EA: I was looking for my sugar substitute. The Equal.

JFB: Edward, you have no equal.

EA: Yes, I do.

JFB: Oh, that's nice of you to say.

EA: A little bit.

[*We walk back into the loft and sit back down on the couch together.*]

EA: How does your older boy handle the problem of you with friends?

JFB: Oddly there has never been a problem with me.

EA: Interesting.

JFB: I say, "Well, how can that be?" He says, "Our generation doesn't worry about the things that your generation worried about. Plus, we don't sit around talking about our parents."

I think that to some degree they are protected by my being so public and by being a visible voice in the country for people like me, like us. Sometimes what kids can taunt each other with is secrets. "Oh, did you know that Zach's father is now a girl?" What can people say, except "Yeah, everybody knows that."

[*A rushing sound comes from outside.*]

EA: Is that rain?

JFB: That is rain. It's quite a rain.

EA: Oh my goodness. I didn't know whether the air-conditioning had suddenly come on. It's rain. Good.

JFB: Edward, I met you two months before my father died in 1986. Much later, I learned that you and he were born about two months apart in 1928. While you didn't have any children with Jonathan or anybody else that I know of, you do have children, in the way that students do become the sons and daughters of their teachers. And one of those students, of course, was me. So the good news is, you do have a son. The bad news is that she's a woman. [*Laughter*]

EA: Oh, I don't know. Not too many guys can claim that.

JFB: So what is the difference between motherhood and fatherhood?

EA: It's two things, of course. What the kids have been instructed to expect. What they understand a mother to be and a father to be. But it's also how really differently you feel having been a male parent and now being a female parent. So much of it has to do with what we are instructed and how we're instructed to behave as certain things.

JFB: There was a time when I thought, I am not only the luckiest but, like Tiresias, the wisest, because I've lived as a man and I've lived as a woman. Now, though, sometimes I think my experience as a man was not like that of any of the men that I know and my experience as a woman is not like that of many other women that I know.

[*We drink our tea, and Edward looks at his collection of paintings and sculpture.*]

JFB: Is there a painting here that makes you think about parents and children?

EA: About parents and children. No. [*Laughter*]

JFB: What about the Chagall?

EA: Well. That's his sister, yeah. But I don't think in those terms.

You're making me think about things that I haven't thought about from your point of view. Do you know one thing I've never thought? What it would be like to be straight. I've never thought about that. I was so accepting of being gay. It was my first awareness of who I was; I never even thought about it.

[*We listen to the rain for a while. Edward speaks about a play he has recently abandoned.*]

JFB: What's the play?

EA: It was called "Laying an Egg." It's about a forty-seven-year-old woman who's been trying to get pregnant for a very, very long time and keeps having miscarriages and her brother's wife keeps dropping kids every three weeks and everyone thinks she's too old to have a kid now. It'd be very dangerous for her and the kid will be damaged and all the rest of it.

So, she finds a Bulgarian doctor who's giving her all sorts of interesting medicines and she gets pregnant. The way the play was going, at a certain point in the pregnancy they could no longer find the fetus because it was encased in something very much like an egg.

JFB: Hm. And at the end of act 1—

EA: Well, that was the end of act 2.

Do you and your wife still live together?

JFB: Do we—? We do.

EA: Who are you to her? Are you still her husband?

JFB: I am her wife.

EA: She made the transfer?

JFB: Yeah. Sometimes I'm her spouse or partner. Less frequently I'm her wife, but I'm never her husband.

EA: Hm. What does that indicate? A loss there of some sort?

JFB: Well, she has lost a husband, but she's got me.

EA: Yeah.

[*A pause*]

JFB: Oh look. The rain has stopped.

EA: Yes, that was huge. Huge and brief. But fun.

# BARBARA SPIEGEL

*I was concerned about her future. If she was going to be a dwarf, then there was no problem. Whereas now she was going to be different than us. I know how society can be.*

© *Barbara Spiegel*

Barbara Spiegel is the director for District 1 of the Little People of America, which encompasses all of New England. I went to visit her at her home in South Portland, Maine, on a beautiful day in September. She is the mother of three children, Alexandra, Irina, and Talia. I knocked on her door and she answered—a four-foot-two-inch-tall woman in a tie-dyed T-shirt. As we spoke, thirteen-month-old Talia (like all of Barbara's children, an achondroplastic dwarf) crawled around merrily on the floor.

▼

JENNIFER FINNEY BOYLAN: Wow. What a beautiful home. Although I guess I thought your furniture was going to be—

BARBARA SPIEGEL: Little?

JFB: Smaller.

BS: I changed my furniture because I knew you were coming. [*Laughs*] Actually it's kind of funny. I've moved nineteen times in my life. So the concept is just crazy. I'm going to customize everything in my house? Seriously? I mean, kids ask me the same question. "Is your house little?" And I'm like, "No. Because then, it's like I've gotta find another dwarf family to buy it."

JFB: So help me understand the dilemma that mothers and fathers with achondroplasia face in terms of deciding to form a family. Dwarves have to spin a kind of genetic roulette wheel when you have a child with someone else who shares the condition. Right?

BS: Right. Goodness, my husband and I both have achondroplasia, so we stand a 50 percent chance of passing it off to our child. We have a twenty-five percent chance of the child being average size, which is all fine and dandy. But then we also have a twenty-five percent chance of the child being double dominant, inheriting the achondroplastic gene, the FGFR3 gene, from both parents. And that's fatal.

JFB: So it's [a] fifty percent chance that your child will be born like you. A twenty-five percent chance that the child will be of average size. And a twenty-five percent chance that the child will be stillborn.

Those are kind of frightening odds. How do little people deal with it?

BS: Well, it's even more complicated than that. Because if you're giving birth, the chances are pretty good it's going to be a C-section. Our pelvis can't do that.

JFB: Wow.

BS: Well, in a way it's awesome. Because you don't have to do labor.

I told my doctor, "I'll let you know when I'm done," and he said, "You should carry till thirty-nine weeks," and I was like, "I'm telling you now, I will not. Just my luck, I'd go that long and the thing would be poppin' out."

JFB: But when you first conceive a child, there's no way of knowing if it's going to be like you, or if it's going to be—what do I say?

BS: We say "average-sized person."

JFB: An average-sized person, or if it's going to be stillborn.

BS: They told us our middle child, Alexandra, was going to be average-size at first. There was a mix-up at the lab.

JFB: Were you feeling disappointed? Or relieved? Or what?

BS: I was concerned about her future. If she was going to be a dwarf, then there was no problem. Whereas now she was going to be different than us.

I know how society can be.

I was also concerned for my own physical capabilities. As a baby, she's going to be all long and lanky. How was I going to manage that?

Then, a week later, I get a phone call from the doctor's office, "Your daughter is not average size. She's going to have achondroplasia," and

I said, "I'm—I'm sorry, what?" They mixed up our genetic stuff with somebody else's and I guess when the diagnosis came back for this average-size couple they probably did the, you know, "What the hell?"

At that point, my husband and I decided we were going to take it to another testing facility, because I didn't want them calling me, in another week, and going, "Oh, you know what, that baby that you've named in your belly now? It's double dominant," because when you have that double-dominant gene and you know ahead of time, there are choices that can be made.

JFB: The double dominant means the child will be stillborn.

BS: Yeah. And so some people would choose not to carry that out.

JFB: Is that a common choice with people with achondroplasia?

BS: If it is it's not talked about.

JFB: But you'd think it would be talked about.

BS: Most people go through with it. Whether it's for religious reasons or "I'm forty years old. I don't think my body's ever going to get pregnant again. I want to be a mother, whether it's for four days or four hours."

JFB: Moms choose that, even knowing that they will lose the baby, because they just want to have the experience of being a mom? Even for such a short time?

BS: Yes. Or they just truly believe that it is a life and it's not their job to take that life. Whenever divine intervention decides the life is over, that's when it is. There are a whole bunch of different reasons people might go through with it.

But a lot of people don't want to roll those dice. One of our children is adopted.

JFB: It's a genetic—

BS: Mutation. Although I hate that word. It makes me sad, like there's something wrong with me. But, whatever. It's a genetic mutation, it's not me, per se.

But I should say that adopting a child is rolling the dice too. Our adopted daughter is from Russia. We had to answer questions like, "Well, you have one child already, why do you want to have another one?"

JFB: What was your answer to that question?

BS: Because we fell in love with her.

JFB: Do you ever feel that people—average-size people—in their experience with you, in some ways, are taught to be more loving, because they see in you another way of being human?

BS: Absolutely not. My friends deal with the same shit as anybody else.

There are some neighbors that—I wouldn't say they're nicer to me, because this is not exactly the warmest and fuzziest neighborhood. At least not for us. One neighbor, when we first moved in, actually we were at a party. In somebody's drunken stupor, they sat next to me, on the stairs, at the club, and were like, "You know, I think it's really cool that you're little."

I looked at them and I was like, "Well, that's good that that's cool because there's not jack I can do about it."

JFB: What was it like for you to fall in love the first time? Did it change the way you saw yourself?

BS: My parents were—messed up. They were average-size people. They divorced when I was three. I lived with my mother for a couple of years and then—due to an unstable household—I then went to live with my father and stepmother.

I would often hear from my stepmom, "If you were average-size, you would have guys knocking down the door for you, but guys aren't going to give you the time of day."

My stepmother would remind me how I wasn't like everyone else. It was a very screwed-up situation. But I grew up confident despite her. Like I was going to prove her wrong.

JFB: For people who believe that no one's going to fall in love with them, that first romance does change who you are. I—I don't know if you've figured this out already, but I'm transgender.

BS: Yeah. I read up about you.

JFB: You did? Okay. So, I've been comparing our experiences in my head. For me, being different was—well, it was invisible for a long time. But I still had that feeling—no one's going to fall in love with me. As for now, well. Invisibility is a luxury which neither you nor I actually get.

BS: When you're a little person, you don't meet people eye to eye.

JFB: Eye to eye?

BS: I'm always having to look up at average-sized people. I remember that's how I met my ex-husband—he's a little person too.

JFB: How did you meet?

BS: I was taking out the garbage. He was walking by. I was cleaning out a dead woman's apartment.

JFB: Wow. Romantic!

BS: I know. Our fairy tale. Right there on the streets of New York, me hauling out the trash.

JFB: Did you date a lot of other little people, back when you were single?

BS: Almost never. We got more attention, the two of us being together, than if it was just me.

JFB: And attention was a bad thing?

BS: It was annoying because it felt condescending. Because it was like, "Oh, how cute!" "Oh, how cute"? I mean, really?! Why is it cute? If a man and woman get married and have children, in the average-size people, it's, "Oh, that's wonderful, congratulations." But with us, it was, "Oh, it's so great that you found each other."

[*Talia crawls over to her mother, and Barbara picks her up. For a moment she looks at the child in her arms.*]

JFB: So what do you imagine for the future? What do you hope for your daughter?

BS: That she can be as well adjusted as her sisters are. And that when she gets older, that she can kick some ass.

# TIMOTHY KREIDER

*She told me that she couldn't really
bear to see pictures of soldiers killed
in Iraq or Afghanistan because, for
all she knew, I might be one of them.*

© *Timothy Kreider*

Tim Kreider and I have been friends for over twenty-five years. For
years he was a political cartoonist before turning to essays; his most recent
book, *We Learn Nothing,* was published by Free Press (Simon & Schuster)
in June 2012 and contained a short essay on the changes in our friendship
in the wake of my gender shift. Kreider, forty-four at the time of this conversation, also wrote about the revelations of finding his biological mother
and his unexpected half sisters in the essay "Sister World." We met in the
lobby of the Algonquin Hotel in October of 2011 to talk about biology
and destiny.

▼

JENNIFER FINNEY BOYLAN: Here we are in the lobby of the lovely
Algonquin, where Tim is eating barbecued pork sliders—
TIMOTHY KREIDER: Just like Dorothy Parker used to eat.
JFB: It was in this lobby that you first met me *en femme.*
TK: You were not only a lady but were drinking a very ladylike
drink. It was something in a secondary color with fruit and a parasol,
and I got a big, honking martini.
JFB: Yeah. Were you disappointed?
TK: Disappointed? What do you mean?

JFB: The fact that I would be the kind of woman who would drink drinks with a parasol.

TK: No. I guess I figured as long as you're going to be a woman, you might as well go whole hog.

I remember sitting in this lobby with you. At moments it was weirdly normal, and at other moments, it felt like the LSD was kicking in.

JFB: Is there any more tea?

TK: I'm sorry. I took it all.

JFB: Oh, we'll get some more hot water from the waiter.

TK: Good luck with that.

JFB: So I remember asking, a long time ago, "Do you ever want to go find your biological parents?"

I remember you kind of looked at me. You said, with what seemed to me like disdain, "I have parents. Why would I want to find some strangers? I have a mom and a dad, and they're good parents."

How did that change?

TK: [*To waiter*] Hi. Could we get another pot of hot water, please? Thank you, sir.

You know, I felt, in many ways, I'd won the parent lottery, and I think I was a little more conscious of that than people who happen to be born to great parents because it had been, at one time, such a crapshoot. I mean, there's a whole room of infants that they had to choose one from.

And it's got to be like going to [a] pound, you know, like, "Oh, this one has a floppy ear. Let's get him." So I lucked out, I felt. They were very smart. They were kind. They were funny in different ways, and they encouraged all my interests even though they weren't all interests that they shared or understood.

You know, maybe this is a big digression and not what you want to talk about, but did you know that my mom and I took part in a very famous study at Johns Hopkins?

JFB: No.

TK: It's called the Strange Situation, and it was a landmark study in attachment theory.

JFB: The Strange Situation.

TK: There would be a mother and infant in a room by themselves. Then the mother would leave, then the mother would come back. Then a stranger would enter the room and then the mother would leave the child with the stranger and then come back again. Something like that. And, by observing the reaction of infants in this situation in a very formal, clinical way, they were able to group people into several different classifications as either securely attached, ambivalently attached, insecurely attached, et cetera. And longitudinal studies show that people stay in those same categories or tend to stay in those same categories by and large for long periods of time, if not for life.

JFB: Do you know what group they classified you in?

TK: It sounds like, based on my mom's description of my behavior, I might have been ambivalently attached, but that's not something I can gauge.

JFB: At what point did you change your mind about your biological mother? Was it like a nagging feeling that came over you, the older you got?

TK: I think that the older you get, the more aware you become that you are, to some extent, a prisoner of your genes and there's certain things about you that are, if not impossible to change, really not very malleable.

Certain aspects of your personality are pretty set, and eventually, you start to wonder, Okay. What's the deal with that? Where did I— where did this come from? And your parentage starts to seem like one possible answer to that.

Also, this was around the time I was forty, and it occurred to me that my birth mother, who was twenty-one when she had me, would now be sixty-one, which isn't old, but it's not young either. And you don't know. Anything could happen.

You don't necessarily have all the time in the world to make these decisions, and also, I'm just usually up for an adventure. And it seemed like something I'd rather do than not.

JFB: Were you afraid of spoiling the mystery?

TK: Yeah, sure. I like mystery. In fact, when they sent me a report from the adoption agency containing a lot of nonidentifying information, which included way more detailed information than I expected, about the circumstances of my birth and adoption—well, really, a whole little like nativity story of me.

JFB: Would you be willing to tell the story?

TK: It's not entirely my story to tell. I would say it was, you know, pretty typical of millions of stories that happened around that time. Let's just say it was youthful recklessness that led to a pregnancy. And this was pre–*Roe v. Wade*.

So she was sent away with a cover story from her father—everyone agreed he would be killed by this—and, you know, went to some home for miserable teen mothers overseen by mean ladies where she waited to have me, give me up for adoption.

I definitely hesitated before reading this because no matter what the story was it would then be one thing instead of another. The mystery would be replaced with just the plain old facts and my life would be like everybody else's life.

JFB: What was your fantasy of who she might be or who your father might be? Wasn't there some story about your horrible toe?

TK: You know, I have yet to confirm this. I have this second toe which is longer than my first toe and crooked at the end. It kind of bends over towards the smaller toes. It's called the Morton toe.

It's an indelicate thing to ask girls to see their feet, but I have yet to ask my birth mother or half sisters whether they have this toe.

JFB: So you knew you had the toe. There was nothing in the birth report—*P.S.: Has hideous toes, same as mother.*

TK: Nobody in my adoptive family has the toe. I've got this Other— this Other toe—"other" capitalized like they do in grad school. This toe that is Other.

JFB: Wasn't there a long delay between getting the first report from the adoption agency and when you decided to actually make contact?

TK: Uh-huh.

JFB: I believe that you said to me, at one point, "Well, my biological mother gave me life and then gave me to a good family, and now, I will do her the favor of leaving her alone."

What did you just put on that slider? What is that? Applesauce?

TK: It's some sort of applesauce but—

JFB: It's applesauce on your burger?

TK: Well, it's not a burger. It's pork.

JFB: Awesome.

TK: That folder sat on my desk for four years, and I don't know why I kept not getting around to it. It was just like any other daunting chore. Like, you know, doing your taxes or filling out insurance forms. Except, obviously, there was something more to it than that. And I don't know why I did it either.

All it involved was filling out kind of a nosy little questionnaire for the state of Maryland and then writing a letter of introduction, which the agency would forward to my birth mother if they could locate her.

But writing a letter of introduction to your unknown birth mother is the sort of task that can take a writer a while.

JFB: So what was that letter like? Did you go through lots of drafts?

TK: Mainly, I wanted, initially, to reassure her that I was not a crazy person who intended to glom onto her in some clingy, desperate way. I wasn't hitting her up for money, didn't want to intrude on her life, because, after all, it's possible that she had her own family who she may never have told about me, and I didn't want to wreck all that for her.

I have another friend, who was adopted, who actually called her birth mother out of nowhere. Like, she did the tracking down herself rather than having an adoption agency. And she had scripted out her whole conversation in a very careful way, you know, in case her mother was not free to talk or didn't want to acknowledge her.

She had planned to say something like, "I was adopted. You know I was born on such and such a date in such and such a city and was adopted through this agency. I've been conducting a search for my biological mother, and that search has led me to you." Not in any way saying, "You are my mother."

So she got through about half a sentence of that, and the woman on the other end of the phone said, "I know who this is." Like she had been waiting for it every second of her life.

JFB: So you wrote this letter to your mother saying, "I'm not a crazy person." Tell me more about the letter.

TK: I told her a little bit about my life now. I told her that my parents had been great parents and my upbringing had been fine. And another reason I'll say that I think I wrote this at the time I did is that life had unexpectedly turned out okay against what might have seemed like the odds.

I had a contract to write a book, and I got to be a writer. And I was living in New York and doing okay, and it seemed like possibly a narrow window in which this would be true.

JFB: So then let's cut, all Quentin Tarantino–style, to your biological mom's house. Your mom finds a letter from you. What was that like for her?

TK: She answered that letter within two weeks, and she told me later she would have answered sooner but she was on vacation in Italy. The night she got back—they'd just gotten off this long transatlantic flight back to the house.

There was a heap of mail on the dining room table that their house-sitter had put there. She wasn't going to deal with any of this. She wanted to have a glass of wine and put her feet up and then go to bed. And, as she tells it, at random, she picked one envelope up off the table, and she saw the return address, and she instantly knew what it was.

She told her husband what it was, and he said, "Well, what are you going to do?" And she said, "What do you think I'm going to do?" You know, as if there was any question in her mind, and so she wrote back.

And her letter, I would say, reciprocated the tone of mine. We were both very cautious and deferential. Wanted to make clear no one here is crazy.

But, clearly, there were great and complicated emotions restrained behind both our letters, and so we exchanged a couple of more letters and then last names and other contact information so that we could write each other directly. Eventually, we talked on the phone and—

JFB: So what was the phone conversation like?

TK: Our first phone conversation lasted about an hour and a half, and it was a little bit like—it's been a long time, I suppose, since you've been on a date. But when you go on a first date, even if the first date goes really well and you have a lot to talk about and you make each other laugh, when you go home, you're completely exhausted because you've been on and evaluating a great deal of information and under a lot of stress. It was a little like that.

JFB: Did she sound like you?

TK: In a way, she seems younger than me now. She seems like me ten years ago. I was much more strident then politically, much more intolerant to the other side. I was just more absolutist in my views, and she seems like that.

Like she seems like she's in her twenties when she talks about politics, for example.

JFB: I think you told me something about how she wanted to apologize for the wildness of her younger self to you.

TK: Well, I wouldn't put it like that. At no time did she apologize for anything, but she did tell me—this was the first time we met in person. She told me pretty much her whole life story, and I felt that she wanted me to understand why this had happened.

She seemed very reproachful of her younger self in a way that you would if you hadn't attained much distance from it yet. Most of us get to grow up gradually, and so, you know, for a while, we're unforgiving of our youthful screwups and then, eventually, we're like, "Eh, I was young."

JFB: We embrace them.

TK: Yes. Though of course, I never had any accidental children. But she felt like she had just made irrevocable, terrible mistakes.

JFB: Had the child that she'd given up haunted her? Was she somebody who had been waiting to hear from you all of her life?

TK: She told me that she couldn't really bear to see pictures of soldiers killed in Iraq or Afghanistan because, for all she knew, I might be one of them.

You know, she just didn't know if I was okay. I took with me all these visual aids the first time I met her, like childhood photos and drawings, because I was panicking a little bit. I felt I needed, you know, diagrams, charts.

Mostly she didn't want to look at that stuff. I suspect it might have been too painful for her, but the one thing that she looked at, that seemed to bring her a great deal of relief, was a photo of my young adoptive mother with me on her lap.

And she just looked so pretty and happy, and she looked like she loved me, and I looked well cared for. I think it was just a load off her mind to see that, "Okay. Decent people, who loved this child, got him. He was okay. I made the right decision after all. It all worked out."

JFB: How did she break the news to your half sisters?

TK: She had often wanted to tell them about me, but she felt like there was no ending to that story yet. And she, I think, felt like she would be at a loss for words if they asked, "Well, what happened to this kid? Where is he?" You know, she had no idea.

That would be a scary thing to tell a kid if they were really young. "Oh, you had a brother, but I gave him away."

But those girls are nobody's fools. They intuited that something was up with her before she told them. In fact, one of them caught her compiling what looked like a family medical history as if for one of them, and their mother acted all sheepish as if she'd been caught at something when she saw her. And that was Emma, my younger sister, and after that episode, she called her older sister on the phone. She said, "So listen. I think we maybe have a secret half sibling."

JFB: You're right. She is nobody's fool.

TK: No, she's not. Very Nancy Drew–like.

JFB: So how did she break the news?

TK: My birth mother sat them down and said, "Okay. Look, girls, I know you know that there's something up. Here's—I have something to tell you." And she told them.

JFB: And their reaction was?

TK: I do not know what their reaction was at that time. I think, in a letter, she described them as being, you know, in a little bit of shock but basically taking it well.

JFB: Shock that there had been such a secret or shocked that their mother had a—

TK: I think shocked that there had been such a secret. Yeah. I mean it would completely revise your little story in your head about what your family was. There's not just the four of you. You're not the oldest child anymore, for example. All that stuff suddenly gets revised. It's weird.

Although, when I met them, about a week after I met her, they were unbelievably kind and warmhearted and open and accepting with me. They were really just nothing but nice about the whole thing, although they could easily have been standoffish or jealous or hostile.

JFB: It seems, in some ways, as if finding out that you had half siblings was at least as powerful as meeting your biological mother. Is that right?

TK: It was very moving.

JFB: In the fantasies of wondering about your biological family, you'd always wondered about your parents. The fantasy did not necessarily include the siblings.

TK: No. I don't think it really occurred to me, and it turned out I had these two half sisters who were twenty years younger than me. And there are all these factors that sort of conspire to arouse this great tenderness in me toward them. Like they're female. They're much younger than me. They're very smart and lovely. They're people I would like anyway.

But I felt totally blindsided by this affection for them. I mean, I adore them horribly. I can't help it.

JFB: One of the things that we had in common, back in the day, when I was a guy, was that we both had the sense of not fitting in, the sense of not being right, and for me, there was always a name for the way in which I didn't fit.

I remember you writing to me, during the flurry of letters we swapped back and forth during the time of my transition, something like, "Well, I never felt like I was at home in a man's body either, but it's not like I want to be a woman. I just wish there was some pill I could take that would make me feel like I fit."

When you met your biological mother and your half sisters, you told me that it was as close to that moment as you're likely to get.

TK: Did I say that?

JFB: Well, yeah. I think you said to me there was a profound sense of feeling less vulnerable.

TK: Most of the good things that have happened to me, in life, have radically cheered me up for about two weeks and then I was pretty much back to complaining about them.

JFB: Well, except when you got stabbed in Greece; you were in a good mood for a whole year.

TK: Yeah, then I went back to complaining.

JFB: I guess you didn't—

TK: I mean, getting stabbed's a big deal.

JFB: It's like Flannery O'Connor. "If only there was someone to shoot you every day."

TK: Exactly right. And, you know, I feel like most people, good or bad things happen to them, and eventually, they just return to their same old emotional baseline and they have to contend with the same bullshit of being a human being in the world.

JFB: We probably need, just for the sake of exposition, to provide a couple of sentences explaining the whole stabbing thing.

TK: Oh, I got stabbed in the throat years ago and nearly died but, instead, did not and was considerably cheered up by that whole experience. There.

JFB: See? That wasn't so hard. The stabbing story is now down to two sentences.

TK: Now, finding this family was not like that, in a sense, because even though, you know, the initial euphoria of meeting those people has somewhat passed, those relationships are human relationships. They're complicated. You know, we have fallings-out. We have stuff we have to figure out together.

The euphoria hasn't completely gone away because they're not going to go away. You know? And it's going to be part of my life forever, and it really is one of those changes that I—I don't know. I haven't thought of an articulate way of putting this, but it ups the plateau a little bit. Instead of just returning to the same old plateau, I think it raises your baseline.

JFB: But is it fair to say you feel more like you fit in the world?

TK: Well, that seems like a two-part question. I mean I think that, to the extent that I feel more like I fit in the world, is mostly because of being in my forties instead of my twenties, which is a miserable time for anybody who's smart. Actually, it's a miserable time for everyone generally. Although incredibly fun.

JFB: Yeah. And when you're in your twenties, you're beset with everyone telling you it's the happiest time of your life.

TK: Yeah. Those people are misremembering. I mean, I long to feel as if I get to belong with these people in a way, and some of that you have to earn by actually living with them and having fights and reconciliations with them. But some of it, you don't have to earn. I am like them. We're like each other.

You know, I just had drinks and dinner with my younger half sister, Emma, last night, and she and I are like, in so many ways, we're the most alike of everyone in that family, I think.

JFB: How are you alike?

TK: We're both really—we're both trouble. You know, we're—that's with a capital T. You know, both have very histrionic breakups and are then devastated months afterwards.

In the midst of one of these, she asked me, through tears, "Has anything like this ever happened to you?"

And I wanted to laugh very loudly in her face for joy. Instead, I looked sympathetic and said, "Why, yes, Emma. In fact, it has," and told her about one of my own many, many histrionic breakups.

JFB: Of all my friends, you were the one who has always had the most contempt for the idea of people having children.

TK: For a long time, it just seemed to me like, at a certain age, everyone in the world wanted to go into the field of tax law, and everyone was like, "Don't you have any interest in tax law? Don't you think you'd find that fulfilling?"

And I was like, "No. That sounds really boring and awful." It just seemed like something everyone else had an inexplicable craving to do that I did not share. I did not get it. Never once entered my head.

It still sort of seems like that, but I would say that meeting my half sisters, in particular, has given me some inkling as to why it might be rewarding for people because, as I may have said, I adore them horribly.

This is embarrassing to admit, but I have a photo of them on my desk, and looking at the photo reliably makes me happy. You know, just the fact that they exist cheers me up.

A few years ago, if you'd asked me what my favorite things were in life, [I] probably would have said fucking and drinking for hours with my friends. And now, pretty much my favorite thing in life is just spending time around my sisters. It's crazy and a little bit humiliating, but there it is.

I would rather just hang out with them than do just about anything else.

JFB: Do you think there's any connection to having been adopted, having gone through the childhood with this mystery somewhere in the back of your mind, and your general disinterest in being a father?

TK: Yeah. I mean, as is true of just about everyone, I don't think my reasons, my conscious reasons for doing what I do, are my real reasons. I mean, I think it's no coincidence that I was given up by my birth mother right after being born and that I've never had any interest in reproducing myself.

And she, also, did not want to have any more children after giving me up for adoption. I think that that was probably traumatic for everyone involved.

JFB: So you've gone through this process, and now, that mystery is now not a mystery. Now it's an answer that you have, and it seems as if the answer has been one that has provided some degree of wholeness to your life and taken away some mystery, although also replaced it with all sorts of new problems, complications.

TK: Yeah, but they're better problems. They're problems that are involved in just being connected with people.

JFB: But somewhere out there, to this day still, is your father. Do we know where your father is now?

TK: No, not for sure. I know what town he was from, and I found one mention of him online on Classmates.com. Just a record that he had, in fact, gone to that high school, and I believe he is still in that same area.

JFB: Your mother is not—hasn't been in touch with him since—

TK: No. He—no. The—their last exchange, forty-four years ago, was not amicable, and she's heard nothing from him since.

JFB: Did he—was he part of the decision to give you up?

TK: He, I believe, had offered to marry her, and she wanted no part of that. And I think he was angry that what he thought of as his gallant gesture had been rebuffed.

JFB: Who was he?

TK: I don't know much of anything about him. He was—

JFB: You know a name?

TK: Yeah, which I don't think I'll state for print. But he was a friend of my birth mother's. And she has not told me much about him, and I don't think she knows much about him anymore.

JFB: So are you curious about him? Are you curious about him in the same way that you were curious about your mother?

TK: Well, somewhat. I mean, half the genes come from him. Although, at this point, I'm honestly hard-pressed to think of any characteristics of mine that can't be attributed either to my birth mother's family or to my adoptive family.

JFB: To some degree, it sounds as if, for many people, searching for a birth parent means searching for a birth mother.

TK: Well, they're easier to find. There's some record of them. Also, and maybe this is a sexist assumption, but it seems safer for me to assume that she would have some interest in getting back in contact with me. A birth father might well be more ambivalent about it.

JFB: Why is that? I mean, I think you're right. But why do we assume fathers would be more ambivalent towards parenthood?

TK: I think there is a chemical bonding process that happens when you're carrying a child, and that's a very real thing, but then there's also just the cultural stereotype of women as more nurturing.

It's perhaps unfair for me to imagine that. Maybe that guy wonders where I am and what happened to me every day. He knows I'm out here.

I've heard from people who have a lot of experience with adoptees searching for their biological parents that there are a lot of women who are ambivalent about getting back in touch with their biological kids. And they first say they don't want to know anything about them. They don't want to hear from them, but almost all of them eventually do.

I guess I find it easier to understand the man being more ambivalent or actively resistant to finding out anything. Seeing it as some sort of unwanted, unwelcomed responsibility.

JFB: Your mother said something to you like, "I've thought about you every day"? Isn't it possible to imagine a father wondering the same thing?

TK: Yeah, sure. Of course.

JFB: But we're less likely to sentimentalize that. It sounds like you want to leave your biological father alone. You're not driven to find him at this point. Is that right to say?

TK: No. It's more like she was easier to find. She was the first one I found, and you know, as I said, it's like having in-laws. I mean, I now have a whole other family. It's a lot. And I have complicated relationships with all those people, with both my birth mother and my two half sisters. You know, there's a lot going on there.

It would be like opening a second can of worms when the first can is still wriggling everywhere. Like, let's just leave it until we've gotten these worms all sorted out and in their special worm cases.

JFB: But those worms could wriggle—

TK: We'll never really have all the worms put away. It just seems like I've got a lot on my plate right now, with family number two, and then inviting family number three into my life would be more than I can handle at this time. I got a lot going on.

JFB: Who do you imagine he might be?

TK: His name is an unusual one, and it sounds like the name of a black man who would play piano. Although I do not appear to be black myself.

JFB: You do play piano, though.

TK: It seems possible that, by not knowing him, I just avoided years of being called a little pussy. I wound up being estranged from him without having to go through having known him in the first place. Who knows?

JFB: That's very efficient of you.

TK: Yeah. No, I don't know anything about the guy. I mean, it's— yeah, for some reason, it's easier to imagine your biological father just slumped over a beer in a dive bar somewhere saying, you know, after beer number eight, "Yeah, I've got a kid out there somewhere."

JFB: Would it cause trouble for your mom, too—your biological mom—if you got in touch with this man from her past?

TK: Well, maybe.

JFB: That, suddenly, old Dad is back in the picture.

TK: Well, I wouldn't necessarily have to put them in touch.

JFB: But you'd probably tell your biological mom.

TK: Yeah, I probably would.

JFB: So he asks if he could have her phone number. I mean, that would happen.

TK: Oh. Oh!

JFB: Can I just say, for the record, Tim is now grasping his forehead—

TK: In pain.

JFB: And holding his face in his hands.

TK: It just doesn't bear thinking about.

JFB: Yeah.

TK: Right. Yeah, see, this is the kind of thing I hadn't even considered yet.

JFB: So it's a good thing we're having this talk.

TK: That's another thing. It's not just you got two cans of worms open now. It's that those worms are now interacting. They're playing with each other. They're having little worm fights.

JFB: It seems to me if I were in the situation, I might think, Well, I opened up the door of mystery one time, and I was incredibly lucky that my mother and these two half sisters turned out to be wonderful and interesting people. Maybe I won that roll of the dice the first time. Why should I roll it again?

TK: Yeah. If you're on a game show, you wouldn't open the second door because you've already won the car and the trip to Japan.

JFB: And yet, I'm moved by this abstract idea of this man out there who has you for a son and doesn't know.

I mean, who wouldn't love you?

TK: You'd be surprised.

# III | MOMMY

▼

"I NEVER DOUBTED YOU'D RISE TO THE TOP.

YOU HAD SUCH A STRANGELY SHAPED HEAD."

© Heather Perry

*The Boylans, with Ranger and Indigo, on Long Pond,
in Belgrade Lakes, Maine, summer 2010.*

# THE JUMBLE

I opened my eyes in a dark room. Moonlight reflected off the snow. I went to the bathroom, brushed my hair, swallowed a tiny light green pill. Estrogen dissolved upon my tongue.

I walked down the stairs. The game was afoot. In the basement I split wood for the stove, carried it back up to the kitchen, and got the fire going. I woke up the boys and plugged in the waffle iron, put the bacon in an iron skillet. It was not quite six A.M.

I went into the laundry room. Zach's snow boots were still wet, and I turned on the dryer. The boots thunked and rang inside the drum.

Sean had gotten himself as far as the music room. The sun was just starting to break through the trees, and the early morning light shone off the piano's raised-up lid.

Zach's feet clumped up the stairs. A moment later came the rushing of water through the pipes as he turned on the shower.

I put a couple more logs on the woodstove. It was beginning to send out some heat. I removed a waffle from the iron, slung it on a plate. I put this on the table, along with the bacon and a pitcher of pure Maine maple syrup.

"Okay, Seannie," I said. "Let's get the day started."

Sean came into the kitchen and looked at his breakfast and smiled. "It's Waffle Tuesday," he said.

At six thirty, Deedie burst into the house with the dogs. "Oh my God is it cold!" she said, her cheeks red, tiny icicles clinging to the bottom of her blue wool hat. The dogs sat down in front of the roaring woodstove and raised their noses in anticipation. Deedie dug into the giant box of dog biscuits in the cupboard and then gave one to each of the creatures. Then she handed the newspaper—the *Morning Sentinel*—to Sean. "Here's the paper," she said. Sean opened the paper to the comics section, where once again Mark Trail was struggling with poachers in Lost Forest.

The dogs crunched their Milk-Bones on the floor. I got up and poured more waffle batter into the iron for Deedie. Zach came bounding into the room, fresh from the shower. "Hi, Mommy. Hi, Maddy. Hi, Sean." Deedie and I gave him a hug. Sean raised an eyebrow. "Hey, Baby Sean! It's Waffle Tuesday!"

"Mark Trail is chasing poachers," said Sean.

"Okay, Boylans," I said. "What do we got?"

"They have band this afternoon, and Sean's playing soccer. It's book group night for me," said Deedie.

"I've got a faculty meeting at four," I said, "and then I'm supposed to be playing rock 'n' roll."

"You have to take Sean to soccer. I told you about book group yesterday."

"Oh," said Zach. "I forgot to mention we're going on a field trip today to the Lobster Museum. I need you to sign some forms. Also, can I have ten dollars? Plus I said we'd bring snacks."

I pulled Deedie's waffle out of the iron and put it in front of her. Steam rose toward the ceiling. I poured one for Zach. Deedie looked at the clock. "The school bus is coming in ten minutes," she said. "I don't have any snacks for your class."

"I said you'd bring pumpkin muffins," said Zach.

"When was it you were going to tell me about this?" said Deedie.

"I just did tell you about this," said Zach.

"I can't make muffins now," she said. "Maybe I can buy some at the store and bring them by the school on my way into work. What time is your field trip?"

"I don't know," said Zach.

"Do you have the forms?" said Deedie.

"I think so," said Zach. He bounced toward the front hallway and opened his backpack. Juice boxes, crayons, notebooks, and rubber balls rolled onto the floor. "Here it is," said Zach, holding up a crumpled piece of paper. There was jelly on one corner.

"I can get the muffins," I said to Deedie, pulling Zach's waffle out of the iron.

"Will you remember?" said Deedie. It was fairly typical in our family for me to be given tasks that, since they were inherently annoying, I immediately forgot all about, thus saving me from the trouble of having to do them. It was a good system.

"Doubtful," I said.

"What is the Lobster Museum?" asked Sean. From beneath his chair came the sound of thick black tails slapping against the floor.

"Are you feeding the dogs your waffle?" said Deedie.

"Just the syrup," said Sean. Pink tongues lapped just out of the range of vision.

"It's time for everyone to start getting ready," I said. "I'll get the muffins and drop them by the school." Deedie signed Zach's forms.

"It's a museum about lobstering," said Zach. "You'll see when you're in fifth grade."

"So what do they have there? Famous lobsters?" said Sean.

"I said it's time to get ready," I said. "Zach, finish your breakfast. Sean, get your things together."

"It's about the environment," said Zach, climbing on his high pony. He took issues of ecology seriously and at that point was determined to devote his life to saving the manatee, a creature not known to have come within five hundred miles of central Maine. "It's about how to save the lobster's ecosystem. So the lobsters can have a future!"

Deedie finished her coffee and looked at the clock. "I have to be at work early today," she said.

"What kind of futures can lobsters have?" asked Sean. "They're still getting boiled. Aren't they?"

Zach stuffed an entire waffle into his mouth. "Oink," he suggested.

Launching children into a Maine winter is not totally unlike preparing them for life at the international space station. On a February day, for instance, the children had to be strapped into enormous snowsuits reminiscent of the various layers of sarcophagi encapsulating a boy-king of Egypt. Then they had to be equipped with both boots and shoes (they changed out of the boots and into the shoes once at school), high-tech mittens, thermal hats, scarves, earmuffs, backpacks containing all the right books and the completed homework and that day's permission forms. Sean had to bring his French horn. Both boys needed their music. (Zach, being a tuba player, did not carry his instrument on the bus; according to the school district, a tuba was a fire hazard.)

"I can't find my boots," Zach said.

"They're in the dryer," I said, and he went into the laundry room and pulled them out and popped them on his feet.

"Woo! Woo!" said Zach. He was hopping and jumping around the house. "Hot shoes!"

"Zach?" I said. "Are you all right?"

Sean looked at me with that ironic grin. "He's got hot shoes," he noted.

"Woo! Woo!" said Zach.

"Do you want me to try to find some other boots?" I asked.

"Are you kidding?" said Zach, still dancing. "This is the greatest thing ever! Woo! Woo! *Hot shoes!* Can I have hot shoes every day, Maddy? Please?"

Sean shook his head sadly. There were times when I feared Sean had fallen into the role of Marilyn on the old television show *The Munsters*. This was the one so-called normal child, brought up in a family of Frankensteins and vampires.

"Do you want hot shoes, Baby Sean?" said Zach.

Sean thought it over. "I'm good," he said.

He *was* good, now anyway. There'd been a season not too long ago, however, when Sean had lain in bed in the morning with tears in his eyes. We'd arranged for him to see a counselor at school, so that he could have someone to talk to about whatever was in his heart. I assumed that whatever was bothering him was a direct result of having me as a parent, but after a few weeks, the therapist said, *Actually, we think the issue is that he hates his math teacher.* In any event the weepy mornings had passed, which of course left his parents relieved. I wasn't certain we'd seen the last of the tears, though. I suspected that for the rest of their lives, I'd be waiting to see just how much damage I'd done to my children. I remembered holding Sean in my lap, the week he was born, as he struggled with supraventricular tachycardia. *Seannie, am I never going to stop worrying about you?*

The clock struck seven, and I opened the door and walked with the boys bearing their backpacks and French horns, wearing their astronaut clothes, down to the end of our driveway in the shocking Maine cold. Our breath came out in clouds.

We waited for the bus. The sun was now shining through the bare branches to our right; we could hear water moving beneath the frozen ice of the creek that bordered our property on its eastern side. Down the street about a quarter of a mile, we could see our neighbors, the Elliott brothers, waiting at the end of their driveway.

Zach hopped up and down. Sean looked at me knowingly. "That's my brother," he said dryly. "He's got hot shoes."

"Woo!" said Zach. "Woo!"

The bus came down the hill, and we saw its red lights flashing in front of the Elliotts' house. This was my cue to leave. Zach turned to me. "You won't forget the muffins, will you?"

"What muffins?" I said.

"Maddy," said Zach.

I walked rapidly up the driveway and stood on the porch. The yellow school bus came and the boys stepped on board.

As the school bus pulled away, I made eye contact with an older boy sitting toward the back. He laid eyes upon me, and his features curled into a malicious grin.

Deedie rushed past me.

"You won't forget the muffins?" she said.

"What muffins?" I said.

"Maddy," she said. She kissed me on the cheek and then headed toward her car. A moment later, I watched as the minivan turned right out of the driveway and climbed the snowy hill.

I stood there alone for a moment, listening to the silence. Then I went back inside.

I gathered up the dishes and loaded the dishwasher. I put the cap back on the syrup and put the eggs and milk and butter back in the refrigerator along with the bacon. I cleaned out the waffle iron and the skillet. I folded up the newspaper and put it with the recycling. I washed out the sink and dried it with a towel. I wiped down the table.

Then I poured another cup of coffee and sat down in a rocking chair and looked out at the snow. Tears flickered in my eyes.

Ranger came over and put his head in my lap, gave me that dog look. *What?*

A year or two before this, the boys and Deedie and I had been out at our place on Long Pond. A neighbor boy named Finn had befriended my sons, and on this morning, as on many others that summer, I found Zach and Sean and Finn curled up together on the couch, watching cartoons. They were eating Lucky Charms right out of the box.

"Green clovers," Sean noted. "Yellow moons."

Finn looked at me curiously. "Are you Zach's mom?" he asked.

"Well," I said. "Actually, Deedie is their mom. But I'm part of the family too." This vague answer was the best I could do at the moment, wanting neither to overtly lie (on the one hand), nor to embarrass my sons with an airing of the complex truth (on the other).

Finn seemed satisfied with my half-baked answer. But Zach looked at me aghast. "Maddy," he said sternly, shaking his forefinger at me. "You tell him the truth!"

I thought back to the morning on the beach at Sanibel, when Zach and I had found the dead seagull, and I'd tried to get him to believe that *its dreams were too wonderful to wake up from.* He hadn't bought that line from me then, and he didn't buy this one now.

"Okay," I said. "The truth is, Finn, that I used to be the boys' father. But I had a condition that made me feel like a woman on the inside. And so I took some drugs that helped my insides and my outsides match. They call me Maddy now. That's their combination of 'Mommy' and 'Daddy.'"

"Oh," said Finn. He ate another big handful of Lucky Charms.

"Pink hearts," said Sean.

"I don't know if that seems weird to you, that someone's insides and outsides wouldn't match."

"That's not weird," said Finn, fixing me with wide eyes. "I feel like that *all the time.*"

Finn's nonchalant response to the truth, to our surprise, had been the prevailing one, especially among children. We'd waited and waited for some terrible doom, but the days had passed and we all continued to thrive. It had seemed incomprehensible to us, that the world could be as forgiving as we had found it, especially since I'd heard stories first-hand from other trans people who, in nearly identical circumstances, had found only cruelty and rejection. Some had found violence. On the whole, it was hard to deny that our family had been very, very lucky.

But every once in a while something would happen to remind me of the strangeness of the journey I'd forced upon my family, and how close the danger was that still awaited us all. I thought of that kid on the bus, looking at me with those eyes of scorn.

In my heart I heard the words of Gandalf, considering the hopeless mission he had given to Frodo and Sam.

*I have sent them to their deaths. It's only a matter of time.*


AT THE END of the day, the school bus pulled up in front of the house again. I opened the front door. The dogs galloped down the driveway. Usually the boys threw their backpacks down in the snow and spent a few minutes cavorting with Ranger and Indigo. On this day, however, Zach walked toward the house with his head down.

*Uh-oh,* I thought.

They came through the door with the dogs. Zach headed for his room.

"Hey, Seannie," I said. "Is Zach okay?"

"I don't know," said Sean, as if it were impossible to know anything about his brother's state of mind. As Sean settled down at the kitchen table to start in on his homework, I went down the hall to check in on Zach.

"Are you okay?" I said through the door.

"I'm fine," he said, in that voice that means, I'm not.

This much was clear: His shoes were no longer hot.

A few hours later, he came out of his room. Deedie was home by now. The two of us were sitting by the fireplace in the living room.

"Mommy, Maddy," he said. "There's something I need to talk to you about."


EARLIER THAT DAY, the phone had rung. I had a pretty good idea who it was and what she wanted.

"Jenny. Can you help me? I'm stuck."

We had this same conversation every day, my mother and me. It's worth mentioning that my mother's name, incredibly, is Hildegarde. I remember lying on the couch in my parents' house in high school, thinking with a kind of adolescent terror, *My parents' names are Dick and Hildegarde!* I had the sense that no one whose parents were thusly named could ever hope for a normal life. *Forget the transsexual thing; my parents are named Dick and Hildegarde!*

There were times when I figured the odds against me were just too long.

"How many have you got, Mom?"

"I have the first two and the fourth one. The number three has me stumped."

"Okay, let me get the—" I paused to snuff back some tears. Mom had a way of calling at exactly the moment when I found myself *verklempt*. Would I have this same ability, decades from now, to know when Zach or Sean was in trouble? Would something in me reach for the phone and dial my sons, wherever on the planet they'd be by then?

"Are you all right, Jenny?" I was in the recycling pile now, hauling out the comics. There was Mark Trail, right where I'd left him, hunting poachers.

"I'm okay, Mom," I said.

"Oh, Jenny," said Hildegarde. "What is it?"

"Nothing," I said. "It's just the boys. I worry about them." *I have sent them to their deaths. It's only a matter of time.*

"Well, of course you do," she said. "That's what parents do. You worry about your children! If you weren't worried about them, you wouldn't be doing your job."

My mother had an unsettling talent for looking on the bright side of things. She'd always been this way. When I was a teenage boy, and my friends and I came up with cruel nicknames for all our parents, the name we'd devised for Mom was Glinda the Good Witch.

There really was a fair amount of Billie Burke in Hildegarde. *Only bad witches are ugly.*

I looked at the Jumble. It was a crazy mixed-up word game. "What can't you get, the third one?"

"Yes. TETREL. I tried *title* and *titter,* but those don't work. What do you think? Is it *litter?*"

I thought for a moment. "I think it's *letter,* Mom."

"*Letter!* Of course."

"What did you get for the first two, Mom?"

"Well, RTCIK is *trick,* of course, and OFPOR is *proof.*"

"And number four, EKDDEC, is *decked,* isn't it?"

"Decked?" she said. "I didn't have *decked,* I had *docket.*"

"Mom?" I said, wiping my face. "There's no *T.* And there's no *O.*"

"I know," said Mom. "But it's so close. I didn't think anyone would mind."

My mother's cheerful, buoyant optimism had carried her through two world wars; the Depression; an abusive, abandoning father; poverty; the death of her husband; and her son's sex change. Still, there were times when she placed too much faith in the idea of things just working out. When she drove her car onto the interstate, for instance, she rarely checked her mirrors as she merged into traffic. Hildegarde just assumed things would "work out for the best," and that "nice people would make room."

"It's *decked,*" I snapped. "You can't just put in any letters you like, Mom. You have to use the ones they give you!"

Mom paused before replying. "Are you sure you're all right, Jenny?"

"I'm fine," I said. I looked at the cartoon. There was a drawing of a man hanging a portrait on the wall. The clue was: *The Farmer's Photo of His Cornfield Wasn't Perfect Until He Did This.*

"Sowed his oats?" said Mom.

"There is no *S*." I sighed. "There's two *P*'s. It can't be 'sowed his oats,' Mom. Okay?"

"Of course. You know best."

"Cropped it." I said. "He cropped it."

"Davy Crockett?" said Mom. She was totally deaf in one ear. I hoped that wasn't the one she had toward the phone at this moment.

"Cropped it!"

"Oh, 'cropped it.'" She wrote it in the little squares. "There!" she said. "Another success!"

I nodded. I loved my mother, but there were times when all of her optimism and cheer made me feel as if I had strayed into some fantasy world where people lived wholly on marshmallows. I wondered if people felt the same way after hanging out with me for more than three minutes.

"I'm so glad my daughter is an English professor," said Mom. "If it wasn't for all those years at Johns Hopkins I'd never be able do the Jumble."

"I know," I said. "Thank God it's good for something."

I heard the sound of her putting the *Philadelphia Inquirer* down on her table.

"You know they're very good boys," said Mom. "I just believe they're going to be fine."

"I know," I said. "I just worry. I don't know how to help them sometimes."

"Well, you love them all the time," said Mom. "What more can you do? Let them alone, and give them time to become themselves."

My parents had had a strangely hands-off approach to raising my sister and me. Maybe it was because we lived in such a giant, drafty old house; in our falling-down haunted mansion, if you played your cards right you could go for days without running into another member of the family.

"Mom," I asked, "when I was a boy, did you ever worry that I wasn't going to make it?"

I heard Mom sip her coffee. "Oh, sometimes," she said breezily. "But I never doubted you'd rise to the top. You had such a strangely shaped head."

IN EARLY 2001, I had taken my strangely shaped head down to Pennsylvania to tell my conservative, religious mother the news. I spent the night in my old high school bedroom, in the very bed where for the first eighteen years of my life I lay on my back and dreamed that I was someone else. That night, I opened my eyes in the middle of the night to see my father standing next to my bed smoking a cigarette. There were at least two things wrong with this. For one, he had been dead for fourteen years. For another, why was he smoking? Surely in the world beyond this one there are pleasures more satisfying than tobacco? It didn't make any sense. All I could think was, *Once you start a habit like that, it can be tough to break.*

*I've been watching you,* said my father, without his lips moving. *There are a lot of things I understand now, Jim, that I didn't understand when I was alive.* He inhaled his L&M King and blew out the smoke. *If you have to become a woman, you should know that I will always love you, and that your mother will always love you. But if you do go through with this, there is something you have to know.* He gave me a cold look.

*I'm not going to be watching out for you anymore.*

He stared at me with that harsh, judgmental expression. And then he disappeared.

I sat up from the dream into the darkness of my high school bedroom. I turned on the lamp, my heart pounding away.

The room was full of the smell of his hair tonic. I'd have recognized it anywhere.

IN THE MORNING, I went for a long walk around the old neighborhood. I stood by my friend Mark's old house, a house not unlike the one my mother lived in. After Mark's family moved out, Lenny Dykstra had moved in. He had been the center fielder for the Phillies, but he was gone now too. I didn't know the people who lived there now, or what was inside their barn, the place where we'd had the cast party for *Our Town* back in 1975. I thought of a poem by Edwin Arlington Robinson, and the man who looks down at the town "where strangers would have shut the door that friends had opened long ago." I walked down the street and stood by the meadow with the stream, where once Mark and I had spent a whole evening watching fireflies electrify the night.

Then I walked back to the house, and I sat down with my mother, and I said, "Mom. There's something I need to tell you."

She put down her knitting. Day after day she made baby booties for her church's charity. I can't even imagine how many pairs she'd made, all those booties for babies she did not know.

"Is it something good?" she said, although she knew better.

"I don't know what you're going to think," I said. "But I'm afraid it's something that's going to hurt you, no matter how much I want not to hurt you."

My mother drew into herself a little bit. I could feel her raising her shields, as if to prepare for whatever blow was surely coming next.

"You need to know I'm not sick," I said. "I'm not gay, and Deedie and I aren't getting divorced." And for a moment my mother relaxed a little bit, since the three of these were the obvious first choices. That there was something other than these, that it was something she had hardly heard of, was what she did not yet know.

"You have always been the best mom," I said. "You have always had that optimism and faith in everything, and I think I've inherited that, too; it's given me a sense that things are always going to get better, no matter what happens."

I was reaching the hard part. I couldn't believe the words that were falling from my lips, couldn't believe the pain I was about to cause her, wondered even now if there was any way to protect her from what I had to say. Hadn't that been my job as a man, protecting my mother and my sister and Deedie and the boys from all the battering evils of the world?

"I have had a happy life," I told her. "There's been pain and sadness but mostly it's been a happy life. In part because you and Dad always loved me, but in part because I have that optimism of yours, that same faith in the goodness of people."

My mother sat there in silence. I could hear her thinking, Yes, honey. And what's the catch?

"But I have had a secret from you, all these years. Ever since I was a child. And now I'm afraid to tell you, because I'm afraid that if I tell you the truth about my own heart that you won't love me anymore."

The tears were coming down now, and my mother still looked at me, waiting. It was lucky I had rehearsed this speech, oh, about a hundred thousand times. I'd given it to her in my head so many times that it was hard to believe it was actually happening now for real.

"But the reason you haven't known this secret is because I wouldn't share it with you. I have barely been able to share it with myself, because of the shame I've always feared it would bring on us. But I've reached a point where I have to tell the truth, where I have to accept myself, or I can't go a step farther."

My mother spoke softly. "What is it, honey?"

"The fact is, Mom," I said, pulling back the string of my bow, "that I'm transgender. I'm a transsexual. Someone who's always believed herself to be female, even though I was born male. I've fought against it my whole life, because I didn't want anyone to be ashamed of me, because I wanted you to be proud of me. I wanted you to—"

But at this point I was unable to speak further, because I was weeping too hard. My mother looked at me hard. Tears began to stream from her eyes as well.

Then she stood up, and she sat down on the couch next to me and put her arms around me.

"Oh, Jimmy," she said, her voice shaking with tears. "I love you, and I'll always love you. I would never desert my child. I would never abandon you or turn my back on you. And even if you're my daughter, instead of my son, I'll always be your mother. And we'll always have each other."

And then she held me, and the two of us cried until each other's shoulders were wet.

"But, Mom," I said. "Don't you understand? If I become your daughter, won't that be an embarrassment? Won't you be ashamed? Won't it be a scandal?"

"Well, yes," she said thoughtfully. "Probably it will be a scandal, for a while at least." Then she shrugged. "But—I will adjust."

We talked about the logistics of the situation, which, given the particulars of transition, were complicated and took a lot of explaining. But in the end, when she got her mind around the most important facts—that Deedie and I were trying to stay together, that the children were generally okay about things so far, that I was under the care of a doctor and a specialist and a social worker—she seemed content to trust that I knew what I was doing. Looking back now, I also know that she hadn't given up all hope of talking me out of it, or abandoned the hope that somehow she could "fix things" all by herself, through the force of her own kind, generous, carbonated personality.

But for the moment she just held me in her arms. She said, "Love will prevail."

That evening, she sat me in front of a fire in a room filled with books and showed me how to knit. She didn't feel there was a lot she could teach me about being a woman, at this point, but she thought that knitting might help.

"Now you have to remember," she said, as she parsed the differences between knitting and purling, "that I learned this in East Prussia, a long time ago, from my own mother. Which is why I do it backward."

"You knit backward?" I said, a little confused.

"Well, that's what everyone tells me. I just knit the way I was taught. So if you knit the way I teach you, you need to know one thing. You're going to knit backward too."

"That's okay, Mom," I said. "I'll do it the way you teach me."

And so we sat there by the fire together, knitting booties for babies we did not know.

✦

ZACH LOOKED AT US in anguish. "Mommy? Maddy? There's something I have to talk to you about."

In my heart I again heard myself speaking to my mother. I remembered her looking at me and saying, *Is it something good?*

"I've reached two important decisions in my life," he said.

Deedie and I exchanged a glance.

"Okay," said Zach. "First off, I've decided—" He looked down. "Man, this is hard to say."

Deedie and I looked at each other, in agony. What was it our son was about to let loose upon the world?

"I've decided that I want to become—"

I closed my eyes. Please, no.

"A pacifist."

Deedie and I exchanged glances again. "A pacifist?" I said.

"Yes," said Zach. "I want to work for peace."

There was a moment of silence as we thought this over. Then Deedie spoke for us both. "Good for you, Zach," said Deedie. "We're proud of you. We'll go online, see if we can find, like, some peace marches we can all go to. If you want."

"Yeah," I said cautiously. "But you said you'd made—two decisions? What was the other one? Do you want to share that with us as well?"

"Yeah, okay." He blushed. "This is the hard one." He looked at me and said, "Maddy, I really don't want to disappoint you. . . ."

"You could never disappoint me," I said, and shot him a look. I wondered, briefly, if the look I was giving him was similar to the look my father had given me, years earlier, when we'd shared a fleeting glimpse of Frank-N-Furter together, dancing in his fishnets.

"All right," he said. "I think I want—to stop playing tuba? And instead to start playing—the Irish fiddle."

He let this sink in.

"That's it?" said Deedie.

"Yeah," he said, looking at the two of us, still biting our nails. "What did you think I was going to say?"

"Nothing," I said. I went over and hugged him. *Love will prevail.* "It's okay, Zach," I said. "You were great on tuba. I know you'll be great on fiddle."

He heaved a sigh. "Whew," he said. "That was really hard." He looked at me. "Did you ever have to tell Grandmama anything like that?"

"Once or twice," I said. "Why? Were you scared? You should never be scared to tell the truth."

"I wasn't scared," said Zach, and he looked out the window at the snow. "I just hate to let anybody down."

# THE MUFFLE VOICE

Dick Clark had had a stroke. We couldn't quite make out what he was saying, although we knew he wished us well. The Waterford crystal ball in Times Square was slowly descending toward the earth. Our guests counted down the seconds remaining in the year of 2009. Five . . . four . . . three . . . two . . . And then the lights were flashing and strangers were embracing and bands began to play "Auld Lang Syne."

I turned toward Deedie. She did not kiss me.

That look of loss crept over my face. It'd been ten years now since I'd stood by the banks of Great Pond in Belgrade, Maine, my six-year-old son in my arms, watching the fireworks over the frozen lake inaugurate the new millennium. It had only been days later—January 6, 2000, to be exact—that I had looked up into the night sky and seen Orion the Hunter shining down at me, asking me, *How much longer do you intend to avoid the truth of your own life?*

Later, I'd learned that January 6 that year was the date of the Feast of the Epiphany. Now here we were in our home, a decade later, surrounded by many of the same friends with whom we had crossed over from the twentieth to the twenty-first century. Our family had endured. Here was Deedie Finney, a straight woman, still married to me.

I'd hoped that as the years passed, she'd find herself more attracted to me, in spite of the bosoms. But this wish—alone of so many of the insane, ridiculous wishes I'd carried in my heart all those years—had not been granted. Deedie could spend her life with me and love me as her soul mate. But she could not kiss me.

"Don't be sad, Jenny," she whispered to me. "You know I love you."

"I love you too," I said as she rubbed my back.

On the television, Dick Clark was trying to make his impressions clear. *Hppy Nnnh Yr!,* he said. *Hppy Nnnh Yr!*

I thought that he was very brave.

WE WERE SITTING in the auditorium of an ancient building on the campus of the University of Maine at Farmington. I suspected that this large, ornate chamber had once been a chapel. There were stained glass windows and a dusty chandelier.

The conductor raised his baton. The violinists placed their bows upon their strings. The trumpeters pressed their lips against their mouthpieces. A young, terrified xylophone player raised his mallets in the air.

The "Jupiter" movement of Holst's symphonic piece *The Planets* begins with a trembling upon the strings. Then the horns come in. The full title of this movement is "Jupiter, the Bringer of Jollity." I'd had a long history with this piece of music. When I was a teenager—although I did not know this at the time—I'd heard it quoted by Frank Zappa and the Mothers of Invention in their composition "Call Any Vegetable." Later, at college, my friend Beck had used the "Uranus" section as backdrop for the conclusion of his production of Ibsen's drama *Ghosts.* When I was in graduate school I started sketching out a novel based on the symphony, using the titles of the movements as titles for chapters. In 1991, three years after I got married, *The Planets* was the title of my first novel.

"Jupiter" was one of my favorite pieces of music in the world, a composition so abundant with hope and celebration that there was nothing to do in its presence except smile broadly and let the tears roll down my cheeks.

Sean's eyes were fixed upon the conductor, waiting for the downbeat. He was in ninth grade now. My younger son had continued to thrive as our family's wry, loving savant. Unlike his older brother, it was harder to know what Sean was thinking sometimes; he kept his emotions closer to his vest. Now and again evidence of his wild brain and sweet heart would surface, however.

One day I came home to find him cutting and gluing paper. At dinner, he came to the table holding a sphere with ninety-two sides. "What's that?" I asked.

"Snub dodecahedron," Sean said.

Deedie put a bowl of green beans on the table, next to a platter of chicken.

"Look at Ranger," said Zach. The dog was underneath the table, praying for beans.

"A snub dodo—" Sean could apparently build what I could not even pronounce.

"Dodecahedron," said Sean. He looked at the green beans as if he were observing a distant star.

"You made that?" said Deedie.

"Sure," said Sean.

"Is this a project for school?" I said.

Sean smiled, as if I had said something very, very funny.

"No," said Sean. "It's just something I made."

"Ranger is cute," said Zach.

"Are you going to eat your green beans?" asked Deedie.

Sean thought it over. "I don't *think* so," he said.

SEAN'S HAIR turned curly. Like his brother, he decided that he liked growing it long. It was thus impossible not to know where my son sat in the orchestra, even though his face was partially obscured by a line of clarinetists and oboists. His huge head of abundant blond curls shook and shimmered with the music. Earlier, as the musicians had taken their seats, a man in front of me had turned to his wife and said, "Boy, look at the hair on that kid."

I wanted to shake the man's shoulders and say, *Yes. Look at it! Isn't it insane? Have you ever seen such hair! That's my son. He builds snub dodecahedrons in his spare time.*

I could not wait for the music to begin. I looked at the glowing cloud of Sean's hair. I thought at that moment that I may have never loved anything as much as I loved our lives together.

I turned to my right. There was Shannon,* Sean's girlfriend. She was looking at him too.

ZACH AND I went out to dinner one night while Deedie drove Sean to a soccer tournament. (In addition to being a hornist and a dodecahedron builder, he was also a remarkable athlete, nicknamed Bee Sting on the field because of his intensity and speed.) Zach wore a tie.

The waitress fawned over him. At first I thought she was putting on a show, but as the evening went on it was clear enough that this young woman thought my son was cute. It was hard for me to remember that, at sixteen years of age, other people saw Zach for what he was—a young man—rather then what I saw, which was the person he had been: a four-year-old weeping when the lemurs in the Cork city zoo had stolen his ice cream.

He had a steak. I drank a glass of red wine.

"Maddy," Zach said, "can I ask you about something?"

"Sure," I said. My heartbeat quickened slightly.

"What do you do—" he asked. "If the person that you love . . . doesn't love you?"

I opened my mouth, then shut it. I wanted to tell him, *Well, you just love them anyway. No one can take that away from you.* But I wasn't at all sure it was the right advice.

"Are you in love with someone, Zach?" I asked.

He shrugged. "I don't know," he said.

*Hppy Nnnh Yr!*

"Have you told her?" I paused. "It is a girl, isn't it?"

Zach nodded.

"Because if you're ever attracted to a boy, you know that would be just fine. Your mother and I will love you and support you no matter—"

"Maddy," said Zach, with just a hint of exhaustion. "I know."

---

*   This name has been changed. Later in this chapter, the name of the character "Spike" has been changed as well.

"And it's okay if you're trans, too," I said, although to be honest, this was more of a statement of general principle rather than an actual commitment. The last thing I wanted either of my sons to be was transgender. And this was not because I wouldn't stand with them, and love and support them throughout whatever journey fate demanded of them. But I knew better than anybody what a hard life it was. Even in the best-case scenario—which by many people's measure, mine was—it was a condition replete with miseries. I hoped my children would not be trans in the same way that my own parents had hoped I would not become a writer.

"She doesn't know," said Zach. "She's in love with someone else."

"Is this a girl I know?"

He shook his head. "No," he said. "I'm not sure she even knows who I am."

"Who is this other person she's in love with?" I asked.

"Some random guy," said Zach with contempt.

I felt a strange anger for this girl, this creature who could look over all of the men in the world and somehow give her love to someone other than my son.

The waitress came over. "How's your steak, sir?"

"It's really good, thank you," said the young man. He turned to look me in the eyes again. "So what do I do? Do I just keep waiting for her, forever? Or do I try to forget what I feel?"

My throat closed up again. I thought back to my early twenties, when I had lived in New York City and shared an apartment with another young writer named Charlie Kaufman. Years later he became a revered filmmaker, the writer of, among other things, a movie called *Adaptation*. In that film, Nicolas Cage turns to his twin and says, "You are what you love, not what loves you."

I remembered Charlie and his girlfriend back in the day, the three of us going out to close down bars in Morningside Heights after long evenings pounding our respective typewriters. Eventually Charlie had moved out of the apartment we shared and moved in with his girlfriend in an apartment way uptown. That had left me living in our apartment on 108th Street by myself, occasionally sitting on the radiator by the window, wearing a pair of pearl earrings.

"You are what you love, Zach," I said to my son. "Not what loves you."

Zachary thought this over. He looked at the waitress, who was now pouring the wine for another couple at a table across the room.

"What does that even mean?" he said.

"It means you love the people that you love, Zach," I said. "Sometimes it means you hurt."

A FEW YEARS before I took my son to dinner, I was a long way from home, doing a story for a magazine. I pulled my rental car into the lot of a hotel in Kentucky. I was ready for bed. As the clerk handed me my room key, I noticed a sign: WELCOME NATIONAL VENTRILOQUISTS' ASSOCIATION CONVENTION.

*Oh for God's sake,* I thought.

"Lady," said a high-pitched voice.

I turned to my right. There in the lobby was a good-looking young man with short hair, twinkling eyes. "Hey, lady, hey, laaady!" said his dummy.

I turned back to the man at the front desk. "Ventriloquists' convention?" I said.

He nodded back at me, with a subtle roll of his eyes, like, Sweet weeping Jesus, don't get me started.

"Laaady!"

The dummy stuck his tongue out at me. I didn't even know they had tongues, dummies.

I was exhausted from the road. I'd spent the day looking at covered bridges. One of them had been built by my great-great-uncle. His name was Elmer.

"You want to get out of here?" said the dummy, and it wasn't bad advice, considering what followed. The figure cast a glance at the guy whose hand was up his neck. "This guy's a real drag."

There's a scene in Cormac McCarthy's *All the Pretty Horses* where one cowboy says to another, *I'm goin to tell you somethin, cousin. Ever dumb thing I ever done in my life there was a decision I made before that got me into it. It was never the dumb thing. It was always some choice I'd made before it.*

I could have kept my mouth shut at this moment, taken my bag and headed up to my room.

Instead, I said, "What's your dummy's name?"

"Spike," said the dummy.

"No, I mean—the other dummy." Spike smiled, and as he smiled I realized: The ventriloquist is cute. "This here," he said, "is Mikey Splinters."

Mikey spun his head all the way around, like Linda Blair in *The Exorcist*. He wiggled his ears.

"So," Spike asked, "where's *your* dummy?"

I stood there for a moment, unexpectedly tongue-tied. All at once, it struck me as a damned good question.

AT THE TIME I stumbled into the ventriloquists' convention, I was a forty-four-year-old woman who'd never had sex with a man. I'd had sex *as* a man, of course, but as it turns out, that's hardly the same thing. I was curious about men, though. Wouldn't you be? I had lots of friends who'd say things to me like, *Jenny, you just spent twenty thousand dollars on a new sports car. Now you're going to just leave it in the garage?*

The Drawbridge Inn—site of the ventriloquists' convention—had a nice bar down in the basement. There, at eleven that night, I could have been found drinking a pint of Guinness. It was a big place, with a disco dance floor and a wide-screen TV in the corner. I was about halfway through my second pint when the voice spoke to me again.

"Lady. Hey, lady."

I looked over. There they were.

"Hey," said I.

"Hey, lady," said the dummy. "What's your name?"

"Jenny?"

*I love you, Jen-nay,* said a voice that appeared to be coming out of a trunk on the floor. For a moment I was confused.

"We call that the *muffle voice,*" said Spike. His dummy got the bartender's attention.

"Get her another round," the dummy said magnanimously. "Get everyone another round!"

"Who's in the trunk?" I asked. From the box on the floor the voice came again. *Let me outta here. Hey! Let me outta here!*

"Yeah," said Mikey Splinters, giving Spike a hard look. "Who *is* in the trunk?"

There were a lot of guys sitting at the bar with dummies in their laps. Some of the dummies were talking to each other. On the dance floor were a half a dozen people dancing with their figures. It was a strange sight, both touching and pathetic.

As I watched the ventriloquists dancing, though, it was hard for me not to view them as distant relations. Back when I was a guy, there'd been plenty of times when I'd felt a little like a ventriloquist's dummy myself. For forty years I'd been at the controls of an unwieldy figure, rolling my eyes and sticking out my tongue and raising my eyebrows. Sometimes I spoke in a funny voice. You had to admit there were times when I had been very entertaining.

Spike took the puppet off his hand. He gave me a look that Mikey Splinters could not duplicate. "So, Jenny," he said. "You want to dance?"

I said, "Sure."

And so Spike the ventriloquist and I found ourselves on the dance floor, swaying to a slow song. I felt something that I'd never felt until I was forty—the scratch of a man's stubbly face against my smooth cheek. The weird thing is how natural it all seemed to me, as if I'd been dancing backward all my life.

"I don't think I've ever danced with a girl so tall before," said Spike, and it was true. I towered over him.

"I know, I'm sorry."

"Nothing wrong with being tall," he said. "There's more of you to enjoy."

While all of this was going on, I had not forgotten my sons or my wife, back in Maine. I didn't particularly want to have an affair, or a one-night stand, in a motel full of ventriloquists. But did I really want to live my entire life without ever having sex with a guy—not even once? A stupid thought went through my head, a thought that I knew was wrong, but I thought it anyway: *Maybe I'd never be wholly female until I'd experienced what it was like to have sex with a man. I'd come this far on the journey,* I thought—*shouldn't I go the final six inches?*\*

It took no time at all to counter these ridiculous thoughts with common sense—that womanhood comes from within, not from your relations with others. If Betty Friedan had taught me anything, it's that who I am in the world is for me to define, not the men I'm with.

Still, Spike was cute. There was no getting around that.

"What do you say, Jenny?" he asked at last. "You want to get out of here, head up to my room for a while?"

As I considered the question, I looked again at all the other couples around us—men and women, some of them clutching puppets, some of them dancing alone.

I don't know. What would you have done, if you were me? If you were a forty-four-year-old virgin, would you have slept with him, just the one time?

On the wide-screen TV in the corner I noticed that they were playing the old Beatles movie *A Hard Day's Night,* the scene where John Lennon encounters the showgirl, backstage, who says, *You don't look like John Lennon at all.*

Lennon sighed and walked away. As he walked, he muttered. *She looks more like him than I do.*

When I was a man, there were times, with my long hair and round wire-rimmed glasses, that I looked a little like John Lennon.

"Well?" said Spike. "What do you say, Jenny? Do you want to do it?"

I'D BEEN DRIVING home with Sean. He was just about to turn fifteen. He had a funny expression on his face.

---

\*  Or, in the case of a ventriloquist, three?

"What?" I said.

"I had a conversation after morning meeting today," he said.

"With whom?"

"Shannon," he said.

Shannon was a friend of his who lived not far from the school. She and Sean had the top two GPAs in the freshman class. They had spent much of the fall Skyping together, reviewing their notes for biology, preparing for their tests in Western Civilization.

"What was this conversation about?"

"Well," said Sean, "Robbie came up to me after morning meeting and told me, 'Dude. It's time to step up your game.'"

"It's time to what?"

Sean didn't go into details. "Step up my game," he said. "So I went up to Shannon, and I asked her if she wanted to go out with me."

We drove toward home in silence for a moment.

"And?" I said.

"And what?" said Sean, and he gave me that mysterious smile of his again.

"And what did she say?"

At this moment, a huge grin broke out all over my son's face. "She said yes."

I nodded. "Sean Boylan," I said. "I am so proud of you. You—" I wasn't quite sure how to put it.

Sean nodded. "I stepped up my game."

SEAN'S STEPPING UP his game was a delight, of course, and not least because Deedie and I were already crazy about Shannon. She was thoughtful, smart, and elfin.

Zach, however, was perhaps just slightly unsettled by it. For one thing, it irked him that his younger brother had landed a girlfriend before he had. For another, it wasn't clear to Zach what the nature of Sean's relationship was. "When they're together, Maddy?" he said, with disbelief. "I think they study."

Studying probably wasn't all they were doing. At various moments

Deedie and I tried to have the Big Talk with Sean. The irony of having teenagers, of course, is that at the exact moment they need to know the things that you alone can tell them, they have reached a moment in their lives when you, as their parent, are the only person they cannot get this information from. There were plenty of dinners when Deedie or I would turn to Sean and say, "You know, speaking of bodies—"

Sean would raise his hands to his ears until we stopped talking. Then he'd lower them and say, in a tone of voice that was less reassuring than he intended, "Mommy. Maddy. I got this."

"But you need to know how to—"

"Mommy," Sean said firmly. "I said I got this."

The advent of Shannon in our lives, I admit, helped put my mind at ease regarding at least one important question. I had wondered what effect having a transgender parent—not to mention having two loving parents who weren't particularly physically intimate with each other—would have on my sons. Would they, obliquely following our example, be afraid of falling in love?

A few days later, Zach told me some news of his own. "I joined the GSA," he said.

"What's the GSA?"

He couldn't believe I didn't know this. "The Gay-Straight Alliance?"

"Wow," I said. "That's great." I was driving him home. Sean wasn't there. He was over at Shannon's. "I guess I should ask you—does that mean you're interested in guys?"

Zach looked at me as if I were crazy. "No, Maddy," he said. "I'm an ally. I'm trying to work for justice."

He was given to saying things like this now and again, particularly since he'd become part of the school's Amnesty International chapter. He'd even gone on a trip to New York earlier in the fall in order to march around in front of the Chinese embassy, holding a sign that said, SHAME ON CHINA! HUMAN RIGHTS NOW!

"Well, I'm very proud of you," I said. "And you know, Zach, if you ever feel like—"

"Maddy," he said, and patted me on the shoulder. "I know."

✦

I LOOKED AT SPIKE. "Yeah, okay," I said. "Let's do it."

The ventriloquist smiled. "I love you Jen-nay," he said, in Mikey Splinters's voice. He gave me a kiss, and all the hairs on my arm stood on end. Then he said, "Give me one second, okay?" He headed to the men's room.

I waited for him at the bar. Mikey Splinters sat on the stool next to me, looking at me with his hungry, lascivious expression. *What do you think, Mikey?* I asked the dummy. *Is Spike going to be able to tell?*

This was more than a minor concern. A lot of men would find it disconcerting if they learned that the woman they'd had sex with had once been male. You want to know how I know this? Because back when *I* was a man, if a woman I'd had sex with told me *she* used to be a man? I'd have found it disconcerting.

*Maddy*, said the figure next to me at the bar. *You tell him the truth. I don't think so,* I replied. *Not this time.*

It wasn't as if Spike was going to be able to conclude anything from my anatomy, thanks for asking. Everything looked just like it was supposed to. I'd even seen several doctors for checkups since the exciting days of the big switcheroo, who did not know my history and could not tell. One of them wanted to know if I was pregnant.

Anyhow, between the surgery and the hormones, it was unlikely that Spike would be any the wiser simply on the basis of my appearance. But then, it wasn't my appearance I was worried about. It was that I was a virgin, at age forty-four, an innocent, a wide-eyed thing who, since the transition, had somehow stumbled through the world protected from danger by little more than her own naïveté and a healthy portion of luck. What could I say if he asked me, as he inevitably would, if he was the best I'd ever had?

*Hey. Let me outta here! Let me outta here!*

Mikey Splinters gave me the eye. I thought about my family, about Deedie and the boys and the two black Labs. Our house in Maine. The tears my wife had cried when she realized that she was going to lose her husband, even if she got to keep me. For a while it seemed as if we'd spent the better part of three years lying in our bed in Maine, one of us holding the other, as we wept and wept.

Mikey Splinters, sitting there with his gin and tonic, stared at me with his sad, blank face.

*Please?* I asked him. *Just once?*

But the dummy had nothing to say.

I grabbed my purse. Halfway back to my room I kicked the wall. *Goddamn it.* My shoe made a small dent in the wall, and I realized, as I looked at the hole, that there was another one just like it, only a few inches away from mine. Apparently I'd entered a world where people kicked the walls all the time.

I opened the door to my room and lay down on the bed alone and stared at the ceiling. This went on for a while until at last I went into the bathroom and looked in the mirror.

I stared at the person reflected before me. *Laady,* I said.

WE SAT THERE in the former church, Deedie and me, Zach and Shannon. The conductor held his baton aloft. I looked at Sean and his halo of curls with a sense of wonder. I thought of my father, who had wanted to be a professional pianist in his youth. The week before Dad died he claimed he'd seen a specter dressed in tails come into his room and stand next to his bed. *Come away with me,* said the maestro. He reached toward my father with one skeletal hand. *And conduct my orchestra.*

*I was afraid,* my father later told me, through his morphine haze. It was one of the last things he ever said. *Because I did not know the tune.*

Tears flickered in my eyes, and Deedie took my hand. *I love you, Jenny,* she whispered.

The conductor's hand swept through the air, and the chamber filled with music.

# I'LL GIVE YOU SOMETHING TO CRY ABOUT

I was in a hotel in New York when I found it first. This was winter of 2010—the boys now in eleventh and ninth grades, respectively, Deedie and I in our fifties. I was in the fancy hotel bathroom, in a shower with seven different showerheads and mood lighting and a cluster of votive candles. I had twinkly New Age music playing on the stereo, the kind Thomas Pynchon once described as *mindbarf.* If you're going to find a tumor in your breast, this was a pretty good space for it.

I'd felt it before, during one of those monthly self-exams you're supposed to do. Given the fact that I hadn't had any breasts in the first place until I was forty, and given the fact that, compared to most women, anyhow, my estrogen level had been well below average until I reached the same age, the chances of my contracting breast cancer were less than that of other women I knew. So the first time I felt the lump I thought, *This? Oh, this must be nothing.*

Then I found it again. Every now and again I'd check it out and think, *This thing isn't still here, is it?* Sometimes it seemed to disappear.

But there in the hotel, the hot steaming water surrounding me, I put my fingers right on it. It seemed larger.

I got out of the shower and turned off the twinkly music. Somehow it wasn't relaxing me anymore.


I STARTED PLAYING rock 'n' roll with a new band called Nasty Habits in January of 2011. I'd known the guitar player, Steve, from another band, the Deadbeats. We started playing in a bar near my house, where they were the house band on Friday nights. We sounded good, and they even gave me a chance to play a Farfisa effect in a couple of Doors tunes, "Riders on the Storm" and "Light My Fire." Fun. Over the years, I'd played with a half dozen other bands, and been thrown out of every one. *Sorry, Jenny,* they'd tell me, although they never sounded sorry. *It's just not working out.*

As I played with Nasty Habits, popcorn popping in the popcorn machine, Boston Bruins slapping the puck around on the big bar television, I felt that thing still throbbing in my left breast. I'd called up my doctor when I got back from New York a month earlier, tried to get an appointment. I have a lump in my breast, I said. The receptionist at my doctor's office said she couldn't get me in to see her for a month. They finally slotted me in for an appointment at nine o'clock on a Friday morning, but they warned me I had to call in at eight that morning to confirm. They said that if I didn't call them they'd give the appointment away. It was only fair to the doctor's other patients, they said.

I said, "Did I mention that I have a lump in my breast?"

And so I waited for the appointment, week after week. It was a cold, snowy January in Maine. I kept the fires roaring in our woodstoves, and I shoveled the ice and snow off our front walk.

On the day of the appointment, a classic nor'easter screamed up the East Coast, taking down power lines, closing schools, blocking off roads. I got a call from the doctor's office. "Sorry," she said. "We'll have to reschedule."

I said, "When can we reschedule?"

The receptionist made a sad sound. "I'm sorry, Jennifer. We're really booked. I think I could get to you in the last week of March."

"Okay, that's fine," I said. *Last week of March.* My breast throbbed.

I hung up the phone and looked outside. Snow blew horizontally past the window, past the four-foot-long icicles hanging off our gutters.

I built up the fire and sat down to read Jennifer Egan's *A Visit from the Goon Squad* in my rocking chair. I heard the ding from my computer that indicated there was fresh e-mail. So I put down the book and checked it out. It was a letter from the rhythm guitarist in Nasty Habits.

*Sorry, Jenny*, he wrote. *It's just not working out.*

THEN THE HEADMASTER called. "It's about your son," he said.

"What about him?"

"We're asking that you remove Zach from the campus community. We'd like you to have him see a psychiatrist. If he gets a clean bill of health, we can talk about him returning to the school."

"What's this all about?" I asked. "Did he do something?"

"You'll have to discuss that with him," said the headmaster. "He's posted something on his Facebook page. It gave me chills."

"Wait," I said, still trying to catch up with this conversation. "He's being suspended? For something he put on Facebook?"

"It gave me chills," said the headmaster.

ZACH HAD A FRIEND we'll call Pete. Pete was a sweet, ironic young man who wore his hair short and, like a lot of Maine kids, liked going hunting. He had put a photograph of himself on Facebook wearing camouflage and holding a toy gun. Zach thought it would be hilarious to put a caption below this photo. The caption was "Guns don't kill people; I kill people."

This was just about a month after the shooting of Congresswoman Gabrielle Giffords in Arizona.

I drove to the school and picked Zach up and took him home. As we drove, he stared out at the snowy mountains of central Maine, the frozen lakes, the pine trees burdened with icicles.

"They're acting like I'm a stranger," he said. "I've been part of that school for three years now. I'm the head of Amnesty International. I'm part of the GSA. Everyone knows I'm a pacifist. And now I'm being thrown out of school for making one joke? On Facebook?"

Deedie and I started calling psychiatrists. Thanks to her deep connections among the social work community in Maine, we were able to find a therapist qualified in counseling "student threats" within a day or so.

Unfortunately, Deedie was, at that same hour, heading down to Pennsylvania to escort my mother to her annual retreat in Florida. And so it fell to me to drag Zach to two consecutive days of therapy, each session lasting over four hours.

As Deedie headed for the airport, she hugged us all in turn. She was feeling the same ambivalence that I was, although it's fair to say her exasperation with Zach was winning out over her anger at the school. Her last words as she left were, "What were you *thinking?*" a phrase so handy among parents of teenagers I sometimes thought we should get T-shirts made up bearing exactly these words.

That night, I turned off the lights and lay in bed. Ranger jumped up and lay down in Deedie's spot, and moaned sympathetically. But I would not be consoled. I could only imagine Zach interviewing at colleges next summer and having to explain his suspension. *Yeah, like I posted on Facebook about this friend of mine who I said was going to shoot people. It was supposed to be funny.*

I woke up in the middle of the night and sat bolt upright in bed. Something had happened to my family that I could not fix. But then, this was hardly the first time this was true.


IN THEORY, DEEDIE was supposed to get my mother as far as Delray Beach in Florida, stay with her for a couple days, and then hand responsibility for her care over to a series of friends and cousins. My mother was ninety-four years old at this point, not that you would have thought she was a day over thirty-nine to judge from her buoyant nature. Plus, she had amazing skin; even now it was as soft and elastic as a pair of underpants.

But Deedie called me from my mother's house the next day to tell me that Mom was out of sorts—the lifelong pain she had suffered from a back injury in 1966 had flared up again, and she didn't seem to be able to get out of bed.

"I'm calling her doctors," Deedie said. "Something's not right."

In the days that followed, my wife shepherded Mom to the hospital and back. Nothing seemed to help Hildegarde except painkillers, and these made her deranged and depressed.

She never did get to Florida that year. As it turned out, Hildegarde never went south again.

SEAN GOT LICE.

Now, when you're in this situation, the only thing you can do is give them (the children) special shampoos and then coat their heads with olive oil or mayonnaise, and wrap their juicy craniums with cellophane. The idea is to drown them (the lice). This also has the effect of permanently spoiling one's appetite for mayonnaise.

And so: It came to this. I was out of the band. My older son had been suspended from school. I had a lump in my breast. We all had lice. My mother was dying.

Sean and Zach and I sat around the dining room table eating Kentucky Fried Chicken with Saran wrap wrapped around our heads. Liquefied mayonnaise dripped down our temples.

"So," I asked. "How's everybody doing?"

MY FRIEND RICK RUSSO sent me a letter concerning the situation with Zach. He wrote, "Now that I've had a chance to digest what you told me, I hope you won't mind my sharing a couple thoughts. While I understand that this is serious business and that the school, for liability reasons, has to take it seriously, what we're really talking about here is a bad joke and poor historical timing. Also, there's context. If inappropriate jokes were a criminal offense, you'd be serving a life sentence, and I'd be in the adjacent cell. Zach has grown up in what might be called the Boylan/Russo school of comedy, which requires all goofs, amateur and professional, to joke tonight and regret the joke in the morning.

"The only reason this seems important to say is that Zach's now living in a world where it seems to him that people who thought they knew him—friends, teachers—suddenly aren't so sure, and it's important for him to know that those who love him most harbor no doubts. That's another reason you might consider consulting a lawyer. Zach needs to know that while you're seriously pissed at him for making such a boneheaded mistake, you're going to defend him because you know better than anyone who he is. Don't let him wonder if Deedie's profession or your personal politics (gun-wise) have you feeling in any way conflicted about what you should do.

"I don't worry about Zach learning the lesson he's supposed to learn, but I worry about other more insidious lessons that might trail in its wake. Don't get me wrong. I know you're on his side. Just don't treat what he's done as seriously as everybody else is going to.

"I'll end this the way I should end every letter: But what do I know?"


SEAN AND SHANNON had a fight. I didn't know what it was about. The only way I knew they were having trouble was that I overheard Sean Skyping with her, using a tone of voice entirely new to me. Later I saw him looking out the window with a melancholy expression.

"Anything I can help you with, Seannie?"

He just shook his head, but I thought I saw his eyes shimmer. For a moment I thought of the days back in fourth grade when he'd had such a hard time getting out of bed in the morning. One of the strategies I'd used back then to raise his spirits was to purchase a life-sized stuffed black Labrador retriever toy and leave it in his room smiling at him.

It occurred to me that my sons had reached an age at which their problems could no longer be solved with stuffed animals.

"Seannie," I said. "I know it's not my business. But if I know anything it's that if you love someone, you should always forgive them. There's nothing more powerful than forgiveness."

He looked at me as if I were speaking a language he'd never heard before. He thought this over. "Seriously?" he said.

✦

WE SPENT TWO full days with the psychiatrist. When all was said and done, the doctor produced the following report: "Zachary's teachers, coach, and administrative personnel at Kents Hill consistently describe him in very positive terms. Overall, Zachary is seen as a very well adjusted young man who is at extremely low risk for violent behavior. He is much more likely, and better equipped, to be involved in efforts to reduce violence in the lives of others."

He headed back to school the following week. The school decided not to enter the incident on his permanent record, and we all chalked the experience up as a Lesson Learned. He and Sean jumped out of the car that morning, and halfway to class, he turned back to me and grinned sheepishly. As I watched him, I thought of my favorite line from the report.

"He is well aware that his posting of an image of another student with a gun and a caption referring to killing people was a serious mistake."

*Yeah,* I thought. *You think?*

DEEDIE RETURNED FROM Pennsylvania after two weeks, having helped set up ongoing home health care for my mother. Hildegarde had plateaued after her terrible first week or two and now had aides on hand to help her get through her day. Still, it was clear that the long years of good health that my mother had enjoyed seemed to be ending at last. Her doctor had told Deedie that we all needed to start being philosophical about her, and what the future might hold.

I WENT TO DINNER with some of my friends from the best band I was ever in, Strangebrew. (I had ingeniously called the band "Blue Stranger" in earlier published works, thinking that this camouflage would make us all undetectable.) Another friend of ours, Dave, was there. "Jenny," he said. "We were just talking about you."

"Who's 'we'?" I asked.

"Me and Tom. Remember Tom Ferris?"

I did remember Tom. Once he'd tried to pick me up at a bonfire, which is a good place for it.

"We got a new band. It's Tom and me, Randy on the bass, and this guy Luke playing fiddle. We're called the Stragglers. You want to play with us? It'd be wicked awesome."

I thought about it. "Okay," I said. "I'm in. Only you have to promise me that you'll never throw me out of the band."

Dave thought about it. "Jenny," he said. "How can I promise that?"

ONE DAY I SAW Sean looking out the window with that look again. "Well?" I said.

"I was thinking about what you said," he said. "About forgiving people for things."

"What were you thinking about it?"

"I was thinking I might give it a try."

I nodded. He walked into his room and closed the door. Later, I heard him speaking quietly, and I knew that he and Shannon were Skyping. I couldn't hear the words. But the low murmur of my son's voice made me think about the concert, when Sean had played Gustav Holst and Shannon had sat by my side gazing at the French horn section with love.

A little later, my son came out of his room.

"How'd it go?" I said.

He gave me that wry grin of his. Then he gave me the thumbs-up sign.

I GAVE UP on my family doctor and went to a local health clinic, where a physician's assistant felt my breasts. It didn't take her long to find the lump. "Okay," she said. "I'm setting up an appointment for you at the hospital for tomorrow. I want you to have a mammogram and a sonogram."

"What do you think it is?" I asked.

She looked at me sadly. "Nothing good," she said.

Another nor'easter blew in the day of the procedure. As I headed toward the hospital, howling winds and swirling snow whipped around my car. I drove toward Waterville—the nearest big city—at fifteen miles an hour. It took me over an hour to make a journey that usually took twenty minutes.

I was wearing a pair of boots I had just mail-ordered from the Internet, made by a company called Sorel. It was a good thing I was wearing those boots, too, because just getting from the parking lot and into X-ray was like hiking the Appalachian Trail.

I was ushered into the mammography chamber, removed my shirt, wiped off my antiperspirant using a special pad, and then, with the technician's help, lowered my breasts one at a time onto the glass platters, where they were, in turn, squashed like a panini.

"Hm," the technician said, examining the image on her computer screen. "Can you point to exactly where you feel the lump?"

I did so.

"Hm," she said again. Then she turned to me. "Okay, I'm going to do a sonogram now. I'm not entirely certain what it is I'm looking at."

"Okay," I said.

I sat in the room by myself waiting for her to return with the equipment. There was a clock in the room that ticked loudly. I sat there listening to it, trying to imagine the future.

I thought about my boys, and Deedie, and the journey we had all been on together. What could I do but give thanks for the gifts I had been given? I tried to imagine my sons growing old without me, thought for a moment about all of the adventures and sorrows yet to come.

The technician returned. She had me lie down, then started sliding the sonogram wand around my chest. The last time I'd seen one of these was when we had gone to the obstetrician together, Deedie and I, when she was pregnant with Sean. Out of the mysterious murk we had seen a tiny face emerge.

"Okay, so is this it?" the technician asked.

I nodded, unable to speak. That was it.

"Okay," she said. "That's not a tumor. That's what we call a pseudo-lump."

"A pseudolump?"

"Yes," she said. "You see?" She pointed at the image on the computer screen. "Right there? Is that it?"

"Yes," I said. "That's it."

She snapped off the machine. "It's nothing," she said. "Get yourself dressed. You're going to be fine."

She left the room for a moment and I lay there in a strange mixture of embarrassment and gratitude. *So you're saying—I don't have cancer? You're saying—I get to stick around just a little bit longer? I'll hear my Seannie blow his horn?*

When the tech came back in the room, she found me in tears. "Well, this is a surprise," she said. "Usually, people cry at bad news."

"I'm just so grateful," I said. "I was expecting the worst."

"You're very good to find that. That means you're doing your self-exams. You should keep doing them."

"I will," I said. "I promise I will!"

I sat up and put on my bra, and then began to button my shirt.

"I hope you don't mind my saying this," said the tech. "But you have really nice boobs."

This caught me by surprise. It didn't seem exactly like the professional thing to say. Still, it was nice enough.

"Thank you," I said.

"No, seriously," the woman said. She smiled enthusiastically. "They are really beautiful."

Now I was getting a little bit weirded out. Wasn't she supposed to buy me a margarita or something first?

"Thank you," I said again, a little more tersely.

"Do you mind if I ask you where you got them?"

I was just about to say, *Well, Wisconsin, actually,* when I suddenly realized that she hadn't been saying *boobs*. She had been saying *boots*. She thought I had nice boots. My mouth opened wide in surprise.

"What?" she said.

"I'm sorry," I said. "But I didn't think you were saying *boots*."

"Really?" she said. "What did you think I was—?"

Her mouth opened wide, and her cheeks flushed red.

"Oh," she said. "I'm so sorry."

"No, please," I said. "My mistake."

She started laughing. "Oh my God," she said. "You must've thought—"

"I didn't think anything," I said.

I left her office, amazed by the unexpected prospect of being alive. The snow howled all around.

I CALLED MY MOTHER on the phone the next morning, after I had fed everyone their bacon.

One of her home health care aides answered the phone and then got her on the line. "Hi, Mom," I said. "Do you want to do the Jumble?"

"The what?" she said. "Who is this?"

"It's Jenny," I said, and I felt my throat close up. There was a long pause. I wondered if I needed to remind her that this wasn't the name she'd given me, fifty-three years earlier.

Then she snapped back. "Oh, Jenny," she said. "I've been waiting and waiting for you to call. What ever happened with your breasts?"

"It's fine, Mom. It turned out to be nothing."

"Oh, I'm so glad." She laughed to herself.

"What's so funny?"

"I was thinking if you ever wrote another book, you could call it *Thanks for the Mammaries*." She laughed again. "Wouldn't that be terrible?"

At my end of the line, I nodded. *Yes, Mom,* I thought. *That would be terrible.*

"So, Mom," I said. "Do you want to do the Jumble?"

She thought this over. "Do the what? What do you mean?"

"The Jumble," I said. "You know. The puzzle. In the newspaper."

"The—?" Mom thought about it for a long while. She'd never heard of any Jumble.

"You know," I said. "It's a word game."

"Oh, that." She thought things over for a while, as if she were searching for just the right words. "Jenny," she said, her voice falling to a whisper. "I'm beginning to think—" She paused again. "I think my Jumble days are through."

# IN THE HALL OF THE MOUNTAIN KING

My father and I set sail. First stop was Trinity College, up in Hartford. After that we went to Williams, Wesleyan, Middlebury. He let me do the driving. I shifted the VW Bug as Dad sat placidly in the passenger seat chain-smoking L&M Kings. The car, which he had bought new in 1963, had no seat belts. I would total it just a few months later in a spectacular wreck on the first day of my senior year. I'd nearly lose my right ear in the crash. But they'd put it back on all right.

It was the summer of 1975. Gerald Ford was president. Saigon had fallen to the Vietcong back in April, the same week this girl Dell had broken my heart. First rejection, then communism. I watched the last chopper take off from a roof in Saigon and thought: Figures.

At Trinity, the dean of admissions got up in the middle of our interview and went over to the window. "Hey!" he said. "I see a rat!"

I didn't apply there.

At Wesleyan, I heard the Grateful Dead playing from a dormitory window. *Well the first days are the hardest days, don't you worry any more.* People were sitting on Foss Hill, reading books. Someone threw a Frisbee to a dog. On the sidewalk I saw a crushed-flat can of Maximus Super beer. I'd never seen an actual can of it, but a friend of mine had a poster with this beautiful girl on it, holding a can. I wanted to look like her, although I did not share this longing with my father.

I figured Wesleyan would be a pretty good place to go to school, if they had cans of stuff like that lying around.

◆

THIRTY-SIX YEARS LATER, Zach and I set sail on the very same ocean. We drove all the way to Ohio to visit Kenyon and Oberlin. On the way home we stopped off at Gettysburg, took the college tour, and then crouched behind the wall on Little Round Top, imagining Joshua Lawrence Chamberlain and the Twentieth Maine staring down the Alabamians. My gentle, pacifist son picked up a long stick, turned in my direction. "Affix bayonets!" said he.

Before that, he'd been behind the wheel of the Hyundai as we drove from Oberlin, Ohio, to Gambier. He didn't have his license yet. As we hurtled along the highway, we listened to the radio. The Youngbloods came on: *Some will come and some will go, but we will surely pass. We are but a moment's sunlight, fading on the grass.*

As my son weaved from one side of the road to another, I clutched the oh-my-God strap on the passenger's-side ceiling, quietly reviewing the Lord's Prayer. At one point we had to merge onto a six-lane highway as giant tractor-trailers barreled toward us, air horns blasting. "What am I going to do?" Zach cried as we accelerated toward our certain deaths. "Where am I going to go?"

"You can do this," I said, hoping that saying this would make it so. "I know you can do this."

We failed to die. That night we sat at the edge of the Kenyon campus at an inn named after the college. I drank a cocktail that was Kenyon purple. I had stayed at this same place with my father back in the summer of 1975. He'd tried out the bourbon.

Over dinner, Zach and I talked about some of the things he might study. He was getting more and more enthused about theater, although he said he would also major in bio because "you have to exist in the world."

"You know what I want to do, Maddy?" said my son. "Next year, for my senior project? I want to direct a full-length play."

"Which play?"

"I don't know. What plays do you think would be good?"

It didn't take me long to come up with a suggestion. "*Our Town*'s good."

"*Our Town?*"

"By Thornton Wilder."

It had been my class's senior play, back in high school. I still remember looking out at all the adults in the audience, tears streaming down their faces. I couldn't figure it out. What were they all so upset about?

EMILY: I didn't realize. So all that was going on and we never noticed. Take me back—up the hill—to my grave. But first: Wait! One more look. Good-by, good-by world. Good-by, Grover's Corners. Mama and Papa. Good-by to clocks ticking . . . and Mama's sunflowers. And food and coffee. And new ironed dresses and hot baths . . . and sleeping and waking up.

I described it to him. It was the story of a small town, not unlike the one we lived in up in Maine. It was about the preciousness of life and how hard it is to be aware of the gifts we have been given.

"Plus," I said to my son, "it will make all the adults cry their brains out."

Zach looked thoughtful. It was the same look I'd seen when he'd crouched behind the wall at the end of the Union line. "Hm," he said. "I have to admit that's appealing."

"It'd be an incredible amount of work, though," I said. "You, directing a whole play."

"You don't think I can do it," he said. From the Kenyon campus, a young couple approached. They had books and sunglasses and a Labrador retriever.

"Of course you can do it," I said. "Have I ever doubted you?"

I sat there in the twilight with my purple Kenyon cocktail. My father and I had had a conversation like this, thirty-six years earlier, perhaps at this same table. I told him I wanted to be a writer. Dad looked at me with concern. *You don't think I can do it.*

"It's not that," Dad had said. "It's just—I don't want you to go hungry."

The young people on the quad threw a Frisbee, and their dog caught it in his mouth. I sipped the Kenyon cocktail. Zach was watching the couple and their dog.

"I am going to direct that play," said Zach. "You'll see."

*Oh earth, you're too wonderful for anybody to realize you. Do any human beings ever realize life while they live it?*

I THOUGHT A LOT about my father on that trip. It was hard not to wonder about the many ways Zach resembled my own seventeen-year-old self, not only with his long hair and glasses, but in his humor and imagination and ridiculous, buoyant hope. And if Zach was walking in my shoes, was I not walking in those of my father, vagina notwithstanding? Was I not, after all this time, still more of a father than a second mother to him? What was the difference?

*If you're a father,* Edward Albee had said to me, *it means you've had sex with a woman, your wife or someone else, and impregnated her.*

I hadn't known how to respond to this. I'd sat in Edward's incredible loft, surrounded by primitive sculptures and modern paintings, flabbergasted. *You think that's what it means?* I'd said. *Seriously?*

*You never birthed those two,* Edward replied. *Isn't that a different quality of parenthood?*

It *was* a different quality of parenthood.

But there is a lot more to parenting than birthing, just as there is a lot more to a novel than its opening sentence. James Joyce, for whatever it's worth, had once managed to write a novel that didn't even have an opening sentence. *riverrun past Eve and Adam's from swerve of shore to bend of bay, brings us by a commodius vicus of recirculation back to*

*Does it mean making,* Edward had asked, *or is it the being?*

I think it's the being.

There was a time once when motherhood and fatherhood were states as simple to define as *woman* and *man*. But as the meanings of *male* and *female* have shifted from something firm and unwavering into something more versatile and inconstant, so too have the terms *mother* and *father* become more permeable and open-ended. I understand the reluctance many people have to embrace this thought; a world in which male and female are not fixed and unmoving poles but points in a wide spectrum is a world that feels unstable, unsafe, unreal. And yet to accept the wondrous scope of gender is to affirm the vast potential of life, in all its messy, unfathomable beauty. Surely, if we make room for the mutability of gender, we have to accept that motherhood and fatherhood themselves are no longer unalterable binaries either.

How many different kinds of fathers and mothers are there? My friend Richard Russo had loved his father even though he'd essentially been abandoned by him. *You can either take what he's offering—maybe he should be offering more—but you can either enjoy it and let the rest go, or you can be bitter and resentful. . . . For me, it was . . . just an easy choice. He was endlessly, endlessly entertaining.* Augusten Burroughs, on the other hand, was still trying to come to terms with his father, a man whom he'd long thought of as a monster, although Augusten's dad surely had never chosen monstrousness for its own sake. *But what's a father? What did you really take away from [your sons]? You took the ability for them to call you Dad, or Deedie to call you her husband.*

Dr. Christine McGinn had told me that gender is a mystery and said, *I think it always will be a mystery.* She had been born male, but she'd changed genders, and using the sperm she'd saved, she and her wife had had twins. There she was: Christine McGinn, her babies in her arms, breast-feeding. *And every one of us is in heaven.*

Timothy Kreider was adopted and raised by a loving family. When he made contact with his biological mother and his half sisters at age forty, he felt the world move beneath him. *I felt totally blindsided by this affection for them. I mean, I adore them horribly. I can't help it.*

Veronica Gerhardf, our former nanny, had become pregnant herself in her late twenties, then learned that her child would be stillborn. After the birth, she held her lost child in her arms and wept. She named her Penelope, after Odysseus's wife. *She spent all day making this quilt and then at night she spent her time unraveling it so that she's never done. For us it meant the task that is not completed, the end that is never met. It meant the promise unfulfilled.*

Only 7 percent of American households, according to the Population Reference Bureau, now consist of married couples with children in which only the father works. As it turns out, the biggest outlier in our culture is not same-sex couples, or transgender people, or adoptive parents, or single fathers, but the so-called traditional American family itself.

What does it even mean, at this hour, to call anybody traditional? Surely it is not the ways in which we all conform that define us, but the manner in which we each seek our own perilous truth.

DJ Savarese, considered retarded at birth, wound up going to Oberlin. *You are the dad I awesomely try to be loved by. Please don't hear my years of hurt. Until you yearned to be my dad, playing was treated as too hard. Until you loved me, I loved only myself. You taught me how to play. You taught me how to love. I love you.*

Every single family in the world is a nontraditional family.

I used to worry about my sons, about the ways in which our family's difference would be a hardship for them. One day, when he was about eight, I'd dropped Zach off at a bowling alley for a friend's birthday. I looked at the other kids there, putting on their rent-a-shoes, trying out different bowling balls. There were white kids and African-American kids. One boy was on Ritalin because of his attention deficit disorder. One girl's mother was in the hospital after suffering a nervous breakdown. One kid was being raised by two dads. Another one had six fingers on one hand, four on the other.

As my son entered the bowling alley, all the kids cheered. They loved him. "Hi, Zach!" they shouted.

Then they looked at me. What could they say to a father who had become a woman? What possible words were there for these children to describe the world we lived in now?

"Hi, Maddy!" they said.


ON THE WAY back from Gettysburg we pulled into my mother's house. They had her in a hospital bed on the first floor now. She didn't recognize Zach and me at first, but after a moment her face lit up and she spread her arms wide and gathered us all to her.

"I'm so glad you're here," said Mom. "Now you can take me home."

"But, Mom," I said. "You are home."

I could see disappointment and betrayal play across her face. "Oh, Jenny," she said. "Not you too."

Zach gave me a hard look. "I'll carry our stuff upstairs."

The aide pulled on my elbow. "Just play along," she said.

"How are you feeling, Mom?"

"Well, I have a lot of pain in my back still. But the main thing is, I just want to get out of here. If I were back in my own house, I know I'd feel better."

The aide gave me an urgent look. "Have you seen the doctor recently?"

"Well, your uncle Dave was here," she said. "He made me a strawberry pie." This made a little bit of sense, since my uncle Dave was known for making pies. On the other hand, he had died seven years ago, so if he'd come by to visit my mother he'd brought that pie from a long way off.

"It's not that I don't appreciate what you've done for me," said Mom. She looked around the room, which was filled with her favorite paintings, a green sofa, a big green chair.

"What have I done for you?" I asked Mom.

"Bringing all these things from my house. Setting everything up to look just like my room. Did you have this place built right on the side of the hospital? It must've been so much work."

I looked at the aide, who was now sitting down on the sofa with the *Philadelphia Inquirer*. "Mom, we didn't build a room on the side of the hospital and fill it with your things and make it look like your house. This really is your house. You're at home, just like you wanted to be."

My mother gave me the same look she used to give me back in high school. "I can always tell when you're lying," she said.

"Mom," I said. "I'm not lying. This really is your house. You're right here. I'm with you."

She shook her head in disappointment. "Jenny, she said. "I was counting on you to be the one person who would tell me the truth."

"But, Mom—"

The aide, who had clearly been through this conversation before, cleared her throat. "Mrs. Boylan," she said, "the doctor is coming to-morrow. We'll talk about all this with him then."

"Tomorrow," my mother said. "All right then. Jenny, you make sure you're here when the doctor comes. And tell your father I need to speak with him."

I felt my throat close up. "Okay, Mom," I said. "I'll tell him."


I WOKE THAT NIGHT from a strange dream. I turned on the light and found myself in my high school bedroom. I had often dreamed as a child that I would wake from a mysterious slumber and find myself magically transformed to female. Back then, though, I'd always imagined myself waking up as a young woman, some sort of beautiful teenage thing. It hadn't occurred to me that someday I would sit up in the middle of the night as a mother of two. I lay back on my pillow thinking how strange it was that most of the wishes I had ever had in this life had come true—although almost never in the manner that I had expected.

A phrase came to me from the dream world I had just left. "My mother is a fish," I said out loud. Then I turned off the light and went back to sleep.

In the morning I remembered this whole incident and thought, *My mother is a fish? What?*

It didn't take too long to recall the line from Faulkner. The little boy Vardaman thinks it. In *As I Lay Dying*.


I DESCENDED THE STAIRS to the kitchen, got a cup of coffee, waiting to see what my mother was up to. "*Guten Morgen,*" she said to me. I looked at the aide, whose name was Monica.

"Don't look at me," said Monica. "She was like this when I got here."

"*Meine Schwester,*" she said, taking me by the arm. "*Du bist so schön.*" My sister, you are so beautiful.

German had been my mother's language until the age of seven, when she and her family had come to America through Ellis Island, fleeing the chaos of the Weimar Republic in East Prussia. It had been important to her, at one point, that I understand the difference between Germans and Prussians. The Prussians were scholars, she said. The Germans? Were not. Other times, she felt bad that Prussia was a country that they didn't have anymore. "They carved us up between Russia and Poland," she said sadly. "I come from a country that no longer exists."

The country might not have existed anymore, but she seemed to have settled happily back into its language after eighty-seven years. Using what was left of my high school German, we had a nice little talk together, although in order to sustain it I had to pretend that I was my aunt Gertrude.*

My mother looked tired and sad. "*Es tut mir Leid,*" she said. "*Aber müssen wir nach New York zuruck gegangen. Wir müssen ihn finden.*" I'm sorry, but we have to go back to New York. We have to find him.

I knew where she was headed with this, and it was not a particularly good place for her to be traveling. After my mother's family had landed in America, my grandfather had abandoned his family. He would be gone for years at a time, only to turn up unexpectedly, drunk as a gas station. *I used to have to pull him out of the pigpen,* my mother used to explain. *I was afraid the pigs would eat him.* One time he showed up with part of his third finger missing.

Then he disappeared for good. Years passed. The suspicion was he'd finally fallen into a pigpen someplace where there was no one to pull him out.

The phone rang at my aunt Gertrude's house in 1965. The New York City morgue was on the line. "We've got your father," they said.

My mother and her sister took the train to Manhattan, got off at Penn Station, walked over to the medical examiner's office on Thirty-third and First. On the wall was an inscription in Latin: TACEANT

---

* In previous works, I gave her the pseudonym "Nora." There's a chapter about her in *She's Not There* in which I describe the morning my aunt became convinced she'd died. My mother had recommended that the best response to this situation was for my aunt to drink a nice glass of milk.

COLLOQUIA EFFUGIAT RISUS HIC LOCUS EST UBI MORS GAUDET SUCCUR-
RERE VITAE.

Let conversations cease. Let smiles fade away. For here is the place
where death is glad to help the living.

The two sisters were brought into a room where a body lay upon
a table. A man in a white coat pulled back the sheet. They didn't recognize him at first. Then they saw that the body was missing a finger.

"That's him," said aunt Gertrude. My mother nodded.

"He had your address in his pocket," said the man in white. This
unsettled my aunt. Considering that they hadn't heard from him in
thirty years, it seemed odd that he'd know exactly where she lived.

Later, in hearing this story, I thought of the line from Father Brown
(and quoted in *Brideshead Revisited*). "I caught the thief," said Father Brown, "with an unseen hook and an invisible line which is long
enough to let him wander to the ends of the world and still to bring
him back with a twitch upon the thread."

"What do you want done with the body?" asked the man in white.
"Shall we release him to you?"

My mother and my aunt looked at each other. It didn't take them
long to decide. "We don't want him," said my mother. "He abandoned
us; now we'll abandon him. See how he likes it."

They left the morgue and got back on the train and went back to
Philadelphia without him.

My grandfather was buried in the potter's field of New York City,
a small island off the Bronx called Hart Island. Prisoners from Rikers
Island bury the dead there in pine boxes, one stacked up on top of
the other.

In my twenties, I had gone to Hart Island to do a story for a magazine. It was a spectacularly haunted place, accessible only by a ferry run
by the Department of Corrections. In addition to the potter's field,
the island featured an abandoned mental hospital and the remains of
a nineteenth-century village. The prisoners from Rikers, dressed in or-
ange, shoveled the graves as guards stood there with guns trained upon
them and the sun shone down.

I had no idea at the time that I was standing upon the grave of my grandfather.

"*Wir müssen nach New York zuruck gehen,* Gertrude," whispered my mother. She clutched my arm fiercely. "*Wir einen Fehler gemacht. Wir müssen ihn retten.*"

We have to go back to New York, Gertrude. We made a mistake. We have to rescue him.

It appeared as if my mother was having second thoughts—fifty years later—about having abandoned my grandfather. This wasn't completely out of character, either. Of all the people I have ever known, my mother is the one least likely to bear a grudge. At age ninety-four, just as when she was a child, my mother was still trying to pull her father out of the pigpen.

I imagined going up to New York, retrieving my grandfather's body from Hart Island. When I'd written that story, back in 1984, I'd learned that people did that all the time.

The world is full of second thoughts.

Zachary entered the room. He was sleepy. "Good morning, Grandmama," he said. My son wrapped his arms around my mother.

"Hello, Zach," she said, in English. "I understand you've been looking at colleges."

"Yes I have," he said. "I'm thinking of majoring in biology and theater. And I want to start an Amnesty International chapter."

My mother looked at him proudly.

"I wish you'd known your grandfather," she said. "He'd have been so proud of you, Zachary. So proud."

Then her eyes fell to me. "Oh, Jenny," she said. "When did you get here?"

"I just flew in from Maine," I said. "And boy are my arms tired."

She gave me a familiar, exhausted smile. "Always with the jokes," she said, and looked at Zach. "The two of you. I don't know which one's worse."

"She's worse," said Zach.

"Well, you'll be glad to know I've been talking to real estate agents," said Mom. "I've decided I don't want you to take me back to my house. I'm buying a new house. I'm moving to a place I've never been before."

Zach cast a worried glance at me. "That's good, Mom. We really didn't want you going back to the old house. We don't think you'd be happy there."

"So you admit it," Mom said. "This is a room you had built onto the hospital. And filled it with all of this duplication furniture."

Monica looked at me. She nodded and mouthed the words, *Say yes.*

"Okay," I said. "I admit it."

"It was a very, very sweet thing to do," Mom said, squeezing my hand. "I just don't understand why you couldn't tell me the truth."

"We thought it might upset you," said Zach.

Mom thought this over. "Yes," she said. "I see. But it's going to be all right now. I'm moving on. Don't you think that's exciting? I'm making a new beginning."

"I'm glad you're moving, Mom," I said. I felt my heart in my throat. "It will be nice to have a new house."

She reached up and squeezed my arm. She sang, "*Du, du liegst mir im Herzen! Du, du liegst mir im Sinn. Du, du machst mir viel Schmerzen, weißt nicht wie gut ich dir bin!*"

Which of course means, You're in my heart, you're in my mind. You cause me such pain! You don't know how good I am for you.

"Is that German?" Zach asked me.

"Prussian," I said.

Mom looked at Zach proudly and turned to me. In German she said, "I'm so proud of my son." Meaning Zach. Then she looked at me. "*Es tut mir Leid für dich, Gertrude,*" she said. I'm sorry for you, Gertrude.

She didn't say why she was sorry for her sister, but I had a guess. My aunt Gertrude had never had any children of her own.

❖

LATER, I SAT by myself in the living room in what had once been my father's chair. The piano sat silently in the corner. It was as if the whole house was waiting now, preparing itself for what was about to happen.

I looked up at the mantelpiece. Just before Christmas in 1985, some carolers had come to the front door and sung for my mother and me. *Said the north wind to the little lamb, do you hear what I hear?* There were footsteps on the stairs behind us, and down the steps came my father, bald from the chemo, wearing his bathrobe. "Oh, Dick," my mother had said. "You shouldn't be out of bed."

"I wanted to hear the music," he said.

My mother and my father and I stood there in the front hallway, listening to the carolers. Some of the people singing were in their twenties. When we'd first moved into the neighborhood, they were little kids.

*Said the king to the people everywhere, listen to what I say. A child, a child, slumbers in the night, he will bring us goodness and light.*

My mother guided my dad back up the stairs when the singing was done. I heard their footsteps go down the hallway, the springs in my father's bed groaning as he lay back down.

I stood and leaned against the mantelpiece, and the tears poured out of me. It was a few months later that the maestro came for my father, in his tie and tails, and asked him to come away and conduct his orchestra.

Now I sat in his chair as my mother drifted through time and space. There were footsteps as someone came down the stairs. For a moment I half expected to see my father in his bathrobe. *How are you, old man?*

Instead, there was my son. "Are you all right?" he asked.

"Oh, I'm sad, Zachy," I said. "I'm just so sad."

He gave me a good, long hug. "I know," he said.

I blew some air through my cheeks. "I am glad that you are with me, Sam," I said. "Here at the end of all things."

"Mr. Gandalf told me not to let you out of my sight," my son replied, right on cue. "And I don't mean to. I don't mean to."

❖

I TALKED TO Deedie on the phone. She and Sean arranged to fly down to Philadelphia in order to say good-bye. Then the two of them and Zach would get in our car and drive back to Maine. I would wait with Mom. My sister was on her way from the UK. Time was running swiftly now.

As we waited for Deedie and Sean to arrive, Zach began to sketch out his college admissions essay, sitting in the library of the old house.

This is what he wrote:

Oprah Winfrey asked me what my family was like.

It's 2001, and I was seven years old. We were sitting around the dining room table. I looked over at my father and said, "We can't really call you 'Daddy' any more now, can we?" She said, "No. I don't suppose you can." She was a year into her transition. "But you could call me Jenny. That's the name I'm using now that I'm female." I laughed. "Jenny?" I said. "That sounds like the name of a girl donkey." "Well," she said. "What would you like to call me?" I thought about this for a moment. "What about—Maddy?" I said. "That's half mommy and half daddy—Maddy." I sat back in my chair, satisfied with my work. My younger brother, five at that point, sat up in his chair and said, "Or Dommy." We all laughed at this.

It's 2008, and I was fourteen years old. It was the day before I started my first year of high school. I was nervous, not just because this was high school, but because I'd finally left the public school I'd been attending for nine years. Would I be able to handle all the work? Would I have friends? Maddy sensed that I was worried, and told me to come down to the dock. We live on a lake in Maine, in a small town called Belgrade. We walked down to the dock in silence, and sat in the Adirondack chairs by the water. Together we gazed upward at the vast mystery of space. Stars twinkled in the sky; the Milky Way was just barely visible. A few clouds drifted across the almost-full moon. There were no human noises; we heard the chirping of crickets, the hooting of great horned owls, the long mournful call of loons. We sat there looking at the sky and at the water for what seemed like a long time. Although not a word had been exchanged, I felt like things were going to be fine. We walked back to the house together.

It's 2011, and I'm seventeen. It was a beautiful summer day. The family had decided to go to our favorite local tavern, The Village Inn, across the lake. It was the first time that our family had been together for what seemed like a long time—my brother had been at music camp for the last three weeks, and I a camp counselor for eight. My mother was sitting next to my brother, and Maddy was in the stern with a smile on her face. As my brother took the wheel and guided our slow aluminum boat across the lake, the sun reflected off the water of Long Pond and illuminated the four of us, each one contented by the presence of the others.

It's 2010, and Oprah was having a "Most Memorable Guests" Special. "So Zach," Oprah asked, "what's your family like?"

I smiled. "My family is good," I said.

SEAN SAT BY his grandmother's side. She was very sensible with him. Mom wanted to know all about the pieces he was playing at summer music camp.

"It's Handel, and Vivaldi," said Sean. "And Grieg."

"Grieg, what pieces by Grieg?"

"*In the Hall of the Mountain King,*" said Sean.

My mother started singing it, softly and slowly at first, then more loudly and swiftly. It was alarming to watch her singing it. "Dee-dee, dee-dee, dee-dee-dee, dee-dee-dee, dee-dee-dee."

"Mrs. Boylan," said Monica, "we don't want you to get riled up now."

Mom relented. "Oh," she said. "I used to think that was the scariest music in the world."

Sean took this in. "It's fun to play, though," he said.

Hildegarde thought this over. "Is it?" she asked.

THE NEXT MORNING, just before dawn, the boys and Deedie prepared to head back to Maine. Mom was still asleep.

"We love you, Hildegarde," Deedie whispered. She had known my mother for twenty-four years; her own mother had died when Deedie was twenty-four. Sean looked at her, his lips tight. Zach's eyes shone.

"I appreciate you understanding about my staying here," I said to the boys. "I'm glad you're okay about my having to spend time with her now."

"It's all right, Maddy," said Zach. "Someday, you'll be the one who's all old and feeble. And then it'll be my turn, to stay with you."

It was a nice thing to say.

I stood in the doorway and watched as the three of them piled into the van and headed down the driveway. There was a flash of headlights against the neighbor's house, the sound of tires shushing against the wet street, and then they were gone.

For a moment I stood there, listening to the silence. I thought about how many times I had passed out of these doors, on my way to some adventure. I remembered climbing into the Oldsmobile Omega at dawn on the first of September 1976, the car packed full with my steamer trunk, a pair of stereo speakers, a coffeepot, all of the things I'd use in my freshman dorm room at Wesleyan. As I walked out to the car, I saw Orion rising in the sky above the cherry tree. *A way a lone a last a loved a long the*

My parents came outside. Dad was jangling his car keys. One of his arms was around my mother's waist.

"Okay, old man," he said. "You ready?'

✦

LOTS OF THINGS happened after that. My sister arrived, and we spent a week sitting by my mother's bed. We had been estranged, the two of us, ever since I came out as trans, but without putting the details of our truce into words, we put our differences aside. It was only the second time in eleven years that we had been in the same room together. The first time hadn't gone so well.

Mom switched over to German for long stretches, then she fell silent. One day, she just cried softly, without using words. Then she closed her eyes. A few days later, I was sitting by her side, holding her hand, when all at once she said:

"Oh!"

It was as if, after ninety-four years, something had finally taken her completely by surprise.

I turned to Monica. "Get my sister," I said.

A second later, the two of us were sitting on either side of Mom's bed, each of us holding her hand. My sister ran her fingers through my mother's hair.

"Good-bye, Mom," she said. "Good-bye."

"We're both here," I whispered. "We're together. It's going to be all right."

Mom took another little gasp, once again surprised by something she had not foreseen. Then she didn't breathe anymore.


IN THE DAYS that followed, neighbors and friends came over with station wagons filled with corned beef. My nieces and nephews arrived from England. They were such smart and beautiful young men and women. Oh, how I wished that I had known them for the last decade, and that they had known their cousins. Zach and Sean hung out with them, a little nervous. All six of them went out to the swimming pool.

Zach was a little reluctant to take off his shirt. "I'm the only cousin who isn't buff," he said regretfully.

Later, my sister and I walked arm in arm across a cemetery, holding an urn in our hands. We placed orchids in the tomb.

At the memorial service a few days later, Deedie read a poem my mother had chosen for the occasion. My sister delivered the eulogy. I did not speak, but I did sit down at the piano and play "Träumerei" from Schumann's *Scenes from Childhood*. She had always loved that song. In German, the title means "Dreaming."

Later that night, Sean somehow convinced everyone to go to a Japanese *teppanyaki* house. The adults drank sake. The cousins caught pieces of shrimp tossed adroitly into their mouths. We all sat there in a new and unfamiliar world, watching smoke puff from the cone of an onion-ring volcano.

NINE MONTHS LATER, Zach directed *Our Town*. He cast his own brother as Simon Stimson, the troubled choirmaster who takes his life. There in the graveyard, my younger son looked out at the living and said, "That's what it was to be alive. To move about in a cloud of ignorance; to go up and down trampling on the feelings of those about you. To spend and waste time as though you had a million years. To be always at the mercy of one self-centered passion, or another."

Deedie and I sat next to each other, holding hands, softly sobbing. It was just as I'd promised my son the summer before: All the adults were weeping out their brains. Interestingly, a couple seats over from me was a person whom I could not immediately read as male or female, as mother or father. I'd never seen him or her before.

I looked back at the stage. The Stage Manager said, "Everybody knows in their bones that something is eternal, and that something has to do with human beings. All the greatest people ever lived have been telling us that for five thousand years and yet you'd be surprised how people are always losing hold of it. There's something way down deep that's eternal about every human being."

When the play was over, there was a brief moment, as the house was plunged into darkness and all the adults sat there crying. Then the lights came on, and our children were alive again. They stood there, bowing and grinning, as they basked in the applause of their mothers, and their fathers, and everyone in between.

The cast called out for their director to join them on the stage, and there was Zach, standing before the crowd.

It was just a few hours before his eighteenth birthday. I thought about the night he was born, all those years before. Snow faintly falling. Charles Ryder reaching forward to touch a plover's egg. *Uh-oh.*

The audience cheered. Zach smiled. His eyes searched the house for his parents. It took a moment, but he found us in time.

MY MOTHER HAD DIED on the fifth of July. The night before this, Independence Day, my sister and I sat together on the back porch of the old house, drinking white wine in the dark, together again after all the lost years.

"I always thought this house would last forever," I said, looking up at the ramshackle mansion. "No matter where I lived, or what happened to me, I always knew it was here. Like the mother ship. I could always come home."

"I know, Jenny," she said. "Now, after all this time, this whole world is about to go *psshhhhh.*"

I sighed. She was right. Everything was about to go *psshhhhh.*

"I don't know that I'll be coming back to America anymore," she said softly. "After she's gone. There isn't any reason to, anymore. There's nothing for me here."

In the next room, my mother lay quietly dreaming. Where did she go, that last night of her life? What did she see, as she slowly traveled farther away from shore? Did she see her own father, standing by the sea with his nine fingers? Did she tell him she was sorry that they'd left him on Hart Island?

*That's all right,* he said. *I'm sorry I wasn't around, when you were so small.*

Something went boom. We could not quite see the fireworks, but we could see the sky flickering blue, and green, and white. A neighbor's dog was barking. The sky flickered.

We sat there in the dark, my sister and I. I could smell the fragrance of the newly mown lawn. From the quiet street I heard the laughter of children. Two small figures ran down the side street, sparklers in their hands. It was a great night for them, the stuff of dreams.

*We are but a moment's sunlight, fading on the grass.*

That boy and girl ran down the road and disappeared. Light from the fireworks flickered off my sister's face.

I wouldn't be hearing the voices of those children again. It made me wonder where they'd gone.

TIME OUT III

▼

# CONVERSATIONS with MOTHERS and DAUGHTERS

Christine McGinn

Ann Beattie

Veronica Gerhardf

Susan Minot

# DR. CHRISTINE MCGINN

*You cannot deny the biology of men and women. But where society gets it wrong is the binary. There are plenty of people in between. It's a mystery, and I think it always will be a mystery.*

© Lev Radin/Shutterstock

Dr. Christine McGinn is a surgeon, a mother of two, a backup flight surgeon for the space shuttle program, and a transgender woman. As a man, she saved her sperm before transition; ten years later she used that sperm to have children with her partner Lisa. The two of them are both biological mothers of their son and daughter, and each mother was able to breast-feed the twins. I sat down to talk with Christine at her office in New Hope, Pennsylvania, on a hot summer day in 2011.

▼

CHRISTINE MCGINN: Because I was a physician, I knew that you could freeze sperm and use it later. So that's what I wanted to do. This was in the last few months before I started living as a woman.

At that point of my life, I was really afraid. I didn't realize that the transition could be a success. It was like jumping off a cliff. The whole donation thing was very scary. I had to go down and do something that was very male in order to save the sperm. [*Laughs*]

It was totally opposite of everything I was working on at that time in my life. Producing sperm? I mean, please.

I found out that I had to do it, like, six or ten times. I started off trying to do it at home and race in, and it was so embarrassing. I ended up finding a parking garage, because I would—I could just—I couldn't do it. I couldn't do it at the place, like, the sperm donation room.

JENNIFER FINNEY BOYLAN: I had a friend who donated sperm for an in vitro. He said it was a strange experience to kind of be taken to a very professional environment, and then to close the door and to open the drawer and to find the copies of *Bouncy* and *D-Cup*.

CM: Like that's going to work? You know? I'm a woman. [*Laughs*] You should have, like, some chocolate here. And a candle.

JFB: Maybe some Joni Mitchell. [*Laughs*] All right, so somehow, you managed to save your sperm.

CM: Right. And then, for the next ten years, I just was freaking out. I would read conflicting studies about how long sperm can survive frozen. It was not the typical situation, but I had a biological clock. Because, apparently, the biggest danger to frozen sperm, or embryos, is ionizing radiation from the universe. [*Laughs*] Which you cannot— you, like, cannot shield against.

JFB: Ionizing radiation from the universe?

CM: Yes. These little particles that are zipping through the universe, and right through our bodies; we can handle the direct hits because we have a lot of different cells, but a sperm is, like, one cell. So the longer it sits, the longer it's exposed, they don't know if it's going to work or whatever.

JFB: And you didn't have a relationship at the time?

CM: Well, I was ending one. I was separated and still married, pending divorce.

JFB: How many times have you been married, in all?

CM: I've been legally married twice, and civil union once, with Lisa.

JFB: When you were a husband—and I don't know about you, I always find it weird to talk about when I was a man—did you and your—wives ever talk about having children?

CM: Of course, because it was very important to me. I've always really wanted kids. It's something I never had any doubts about. Ironically, both of my wives never had kids and had no interest in them.

JFB: What kind of husband were you? What kind of father would you have been?

CM: I think answering that question is just going to be kind of, like, making stuff up. [*Laughs*]

JFB: Hey, man, there's a great future for you as a memoirist.

CM: I'm not playing games with you. I think I would've been exactly like I am now, minus the breast-feeding. [*Laughs*]

I mean, I'm a parent, you know. This whole mother/father stuff is kind of random.

JFB: Is it a false binary? As someone who was a father, and who has been a mother, I'm finding that, in most ways, what I've taught my children are the same things I was going to teach them in any case. But as a man, I was a fairly feminine hippie thing. You know, I've never known how to throw a football. But you, Christine. I mean—you were in the navy? I'm going to guess you knew how to throw a football.

CM: Yes. And I look forward to that now. I really do. Like, I cannot wait to take my kids fishing. But there are plenty of women who fish, you know. My sister is a perfect example. She loves to fish. But it's like my brain lives in two worlds, the "Yes, you have to live in this society where these stereotypes exist about what is male and what is female." Then there is me; I just do what comes natural to me, and sometimes it's considered male by everybody, and sometimes it's considered female by everybody, and I don't really care.

Then there's the scientist in me that knows that there is a difference, there is not a binary, but a gender spectrum. There are chemicals that are different in men and women. And when a transgender woman transitions, we are somewhere in the middle. Especially having gone through a simulated pregnancy, in order to breast-feed, I felt the changes of those hormones. I felt my milk let down when not only my baby would cry, but a baby on TV would cry, and even, ridiculously, when a door would close and make a squeak.

You cannot deny the biology of men and women. But where society gets it wrong is the binary. There are plenty of people in between. It's a mystery, and I think it always will be a mystery.

JFB: It sounds like you're saying that males and females really are two different beings, with plenty of territory in between, but motherhood and fatherhood are social constructs, especially if we're not talking about giving birth, going through labor. Post-birth, is your relationship with the child the same whether you're male or female?

CM: I challenge people to define what is male and what is female, and I think you run into the same problem when you try and define what is mother and what is father. Especially now that we have science, and you can have an adoptive mother that breast-feeds.

So the mother produced the egg but didn't deliver the baby. The definitions are changing.

JFB: Is it a good thing, that the definitions have changed?

CM: Yeah, I think so. There is nothing in my life that has compared to the amount of love I have for my children. Anytime there is that much love, it's gotta be a good thing.

Ironically, for as much love as I have for my children, I see a lot of hatred produced by people who are not comfortable with that idea. Like the case of the "pregnant man" on TV a few years ago.

JFB: That case kicked up a lot of dust. I get asked about it a lot. I try to take a middle path and basically say, "You know, whatever— here's a family of people that love each other. How can you be against that?" But it is funny the way even transgender people are sometimes as uncomfortable as anybody with the idea of there being something more than two binary choices.

CM: Right. You know, even though I can throw a baseball, I tend to be more of a binary person. I do get gender spectrum and gender queer. I get it all. But personally, that's not where I fit. So I can become uncomfortable by that as well.

JFB: I saw a T-shirt one time that said, "There are only two kinds of people: those who reject the binary, and those who don't."

CM: That's funny.

JFB: Let's back up. Eventually, you wound up with Lisa. Could you talk about your relationship? When did you tell her you were trans? She didn't know when you first started dating.

CM: It was our third date. We went out to dinner, and it was hard. She was assuming I had been married to a man. She was assuming I was one of these lesbians that wasn't sure of their sexual orientation. She wasn't taking me very seriously, because she thought I wasn't, you know, a true lesbian, a card-carrying member. What we call a gold-star lesbian.

And here I am, nervous, because I'm trying to, like, talk about my former marriages without being too specific. So it was really kind of funny.

JFB: I find that the—sometimes, the simplest, most innocent questions that people ask me can demand that I either lie or else have a conversation that's much more intimate than I want to have, simply in order to tell the truth.

CM: Right, right.

JFB: I'll frequently meet other moms who will say, you know, "What does your husband do?"

CM: And you don't feel like telling them the truth. Like, you don't feel like opening yourself up to their judgment.

JFB: I remember one time I was doing a story for *Condé Nast Traveler*. I was having dinner by myself, as you often do when you're a traveling reporter, in Nevis, which is a Caribbean island. And—

CM: It's also a lesion, in plastic surgery, that could be removed. [*Laughs*]

JFB: [*Laughs*] Well—

CM: How do you spell it?

JFB: N-E-V-I-S.

CM: Is it, like, a little red island or something? [*Laughs*]

JFB: It's next to St. Kitts. Somehow, sitting at the table I made the decision—I'd had a few drinks, and I just decided to be a widow. So I just told them, "Yeah, I used to be married, but you know, he died." And so then I could describe the man I was married to as my former self.

CM: I've had fantasies of doing that, but I've never had the guts.

JFB: Well, can I say, don't do it, because you immediately feel like a creep, because people are sympathizing with you and their eyes are tearing up over something that, in fact, never happened.

CM: It's so George Costanza.

JFB: Exactly. It's the transgender equivalent of George Costanza.

CM: "I'm an architect!"

JFB: So what did Lisa do when you finally spilled the beans?

CM: I said, "I have to tell you something." She's like, "What?" And I said, "Well, you know, when I said I was married?" I don't remember exactly how I said it, but I said something like, "I wasn't the woman in the marriage." [*Laughs*] I was trying not to have to say it.

And this is when I fell in love with her. She just said, "I'm attracted to you. You don't have to go into all that right now. I just want to sit here and have dinner and get to know you. That doesn't matter to me." Which, at that moment, was pretty cool.

JFB: As the relationship deepened, did you have to negotiate your former male identity in any way? Did she have to get her mind around it, or did she essentially say, "Okay, I'm with you, I'll follow you," from that moment onward?

CM: She was, like, an A-student in gender studies. Being a feminist and a lesbian, I—well, that doesn't qualify her, because there are a lot of feminists and lesbians that do not get the transgender thing at all.

JFB: Not to mention gay men. I've seen that. What's the phrase about, "To someone who only has a hammer, everything looks like a nail?"

CM: I agree. But she got it.

JFB: How long after—how long into the relationship did you start talking about kids?

CM: I kind of wanted to get this done by the time I was forty. And yet—this is the kind of thing you don't push somebody into.

JFB: It was a biological clock for you, in a way.

CMG: Yeah, more than one, because I was scared that my sperm wouldn't work the longer they sat.

JFB: Was there a moment when she finally agreed? When she said, "Okay, let's do this"?

CM: It was her idea. She said, "Let's start doing this."

JFB: What was that like?

CM: It took us years to get pregnant. We tried, and then stopped for a while, because it was really emotionally hard to go through that and not get pregnant. The difference with in vitro is that when somebody gets pregnant naturally, you either are or you aren't. When you do in vitro there's, like, ten different steps where you have to sweat it out for each pregnancy. It is tormenting. It is really just gut wrenching. We had a miscarriage.

I felt like I was in Las Vegas. Like, keep rolling the dice.

JFB: Tell me about the birth of your twins.

CM: The day Lisa gave birth, I had been putting furniture together, which, there you go, there's a manly thing. That was my job.

JFB: I did that, too.

CM: I got stuck with that gender role. But then, I wasn't the one that was pregnant.

JFB: I find that there are certain things that still fall to me, that are the man's job, simply because they're not things that Deedie knows how to do. And I keep doing them out of habit, I guess. Like mowing the lawn.

CM: I really think that that's love. Because that really is annoying for you, probably. But you put that aside and realize that it's just easier for you. That's a very loving, selfless thing.

JFB: And also, I guess my transition took away enough from Deedie that—

CM: So there's guilt involved? [*Laughs*]

JFB: I feel like, in addition to everything else that she may have lost, she shouldn't have to mow the lawn, too.

CM: When my kids were born, it all happened so fast. One of the twins became distressed in the womb. They had that baby out in, like, three minutes. And I never felt so helpless in my life. Here I am, a surgeon, and I can't do anything except hold Lisa's hand.

I've never had so much emotion in my life, ever. It was just a flood.

JFB: You had to induce a false pregnancy in order to breast-feed? Tell me how you did that.

CM: As a doctor, I knew that it was possible. I followed the protocol that involves simulating pregnancy with hormones. It's estrogen and progesterone. My simulation pregnancy was over a month before Lisa delivered—with twins, we were expecting them to be born earlier. That entire month I was just pumping nonstop, every two hours. We had a whole freezer full of milk. And you know, the first couple of weeks of it was no good, because it had all of the hormones in it. So we only saved, like, the last week or so. But still, it was a freezer full of milk.

Lisa had no idea about the way breast-feeding takes over your life, because this was her first. It was kind of funny that I went through that on my own, first, weeks before she did. And then it took her a couple of days to actually—for her milk to let down.

The children were so small when they were born. They were only five pounds. At first we had to feed them with a syringe. They were breast-feeding as well, but they weren't latching that great on either of us.

JFB: What was it like when they finally muckled on to you?

CM: Oh, I can't even put it in words. I really cannot put it in words. It was—I was just—oh.

JFB: Were you amazed? Were you afraid?

CM: It was heaven. I was afraid. I don't know, it was uncharted territory. Like, I knew the milk was good. Lisa was a little concerned that it would be like skimmed milk, or something, you know. [*Laughs*] Like—she's like, "Is it the same stuff?"

JFB: Is it the same milk?

CM: And she was a little dubious about, like, is this really all right? I think that's totally natural for a mother, to be concerned.

I will just say that there are things nobody thinks about when two women are both breast-feeding. Like, technical stuff that you don't think about. When you have a mother and a father, the mother decides when the kids get fed. Right? The father doesn't, really. Right?

But you know, when you have two women who are filled with pregnancy hormones and have that, like, mother-bear attitude about how things should be done . . . It was really crazy.

JFB: So did that cause serious conflict between you and Lisa?

CM: Totally not serious conflict, because the most important thing are the babies.

Eden finally latched—I breast-fed her more than Luke. Luke was never really good. Lisa hated breast-feeding. Eventually we decided to stop.

I'm putting on my science hat again—when you decide to stop, there are hormonal issues. The strongest emotion a person can feel in their life comes from oxytocin, which is the love drug.

JFB: Oxytocin?

CM: That's what's responsible for babies' bonding during breast-feeding. So the baby latches on, breast-feeds, your brain just [*makes oozing sound*], just, like, oozes this gooey love substance, oxytocin. Fathers are proven to have higher oxytocin before the delivery, and just stroking your child's head. You know, when the baby—when you smell a newborn's head, it really—that smell, it's like—

JFB: I just saw a friend's newborn on Friday, and I was like, [*makes sniffing sound*]—

CM: My niece said it the best. She came in and smelled them, and she was five years old at the time, and she's like, "They smell like cupcakes." [*Laughs*] And it's universal. When you ask me what that's like, I can't describe it, you know, and I'm a huge fan of food and cupcakes and chocolate, and so that's the closest I can come to it—it's like chocolate. [*Laughs*]

JFB: So when you stopped breast-feeding, was it a kind of a mourning, a loss?

CM: Yes. Lisa wanted to stop before I did. The problem is, once a baby gets a nipple, a plastic nipple, it gives more milk. And so they don't have to work as hard.

It's a unique situation that two breast-feeders in a relationship would experience, but a mother and father would not.

JFB: So did one of you stop breast-feeding before the other?

CM: Yes, Lisa did.

JFB: Lisa stopped. And how much longer did you keep it up?

CM: Not long, because they got the nipple.

They were both so small. We weren't all that successful at it. We were so worried about their birth weight, and making sure they got enough with the syringes. There were definitely times where, you know, we both would breast-feed and, man, I will never forget that. Like, three o'clock in the morning, four o'clock in the morning, in the little cocoon, nursing.

The heat of their body, their naked body on your chest. The

amazing thing is, it really does kind of hurt when they really get going, you know. And you just . . . I don't know how else to describe it. You feel like the life force is just coming out through you. It's so powerful. It relieves that pain that you have in your breast. It releases that oxytocin, and it's just—it's heaven.

JFB: Did you ever do that thing where you would fall asleep with the children in the bed, and wake up with the children in the bed beside you?

CM: Yeah.

JFB: I loved that. It's one of my strongest memories of being a father. Having gotten up in the middle of the night. And they are so small, but such an incredibly powerful feeling, the two of you together surrounding the child. With us, we also had a dog at the bottom of the bed. [*Laughs*]

CM: And we have two, and that was also very important to me, too. We have miniature pinschers.

JFB: So how many months along did you stop breast-feeding?

CM: Three months. It was really emotionally painful, and I cried a lot. I was really sad.

I was pretty sure we were not going to have any more kids. So I'm like, "This is it." It was very sad.

JFB: Is there a moment from the last year and two months where you think, This is what it's like to be a mother, this is it?

CM: Yes, immediately. It was hot as Hades outside. It was, like, a million degrees. We had just had the kids. It was, like, May or June, and my mom was over, and it was, like, we had all this help, initially, because Lisa and I were just not getting any sleep and it was, like, round-the-clock feedings and the kids were small, and Lucas had an apnea monitor that he had to wear all the time, and it was just really hard. And there was a big thunderstorm, and the power went out.

And so, at this point, they weren't really latching very well, so we both had to pump, and then feed them with the syringes. So Lisa and I are totally, like, engorged with milk. And the power's out, and the pumps are electric. Right?

JFB: Right.

CM: So there's no electricity, it's hot as hell, we're worried for the kids. Lisa and I are in pain. We're both leaking. And it was the weirdest, funniest situation. And my mom's there. She runs out to the store to get batteries, and you know, she's just being a mom. She's getting everything, running around like an angel. And Lisa and I are in pain, we're miserable. When she finally came back, the batteries wouldn't work on the pumps—something else was wrong. Lisa and I are dying.

And so, here's the guy part of me. . . . I get the pump that has the backup battery power and the backup car charger. Like, I got all tech on it. [*Laughs*] I'm out in the car trying to get the car charger to work on the pump in the pouring rain. And it's ninety-five degrees out. It's all wet inside, like, the humidity on the windows.

I'm just trying to get some kind of relief.

And this stupid pump didn't work that way, either. We come back in and my mom has candles lit.

And then the electricity comes back on. And we all just laugh and pump and breast-feed. And every one of us is in heaven.

# ANN BEATTIE

*I've got the cherry bomb,
what else am I going to do
with it?*

© Ann Beattie

Ann Beattie is the author of seven novels, including *Chilly Scenes of Winter* and *Picturing Will,* as well as nine collections of short stories, most of which appeared in the *New Yorker.* We sat on her screened porch in York, Maine, on September 3, 2011, to drink iced tea and to talk about mothers and daughters and imagination.

▼

JENNIFER FINNEY BOYLAN: Can you talk about your parents? How did they meet?

ANN BEATTIE: My mother saw a handsome boy skate underneath the porch. It was, like, a second- or third-floor apartment building with a porch, screened porch, in the back. And she said to her aunt, "Who is that?" And her aunt said, "Oh, that's Jimmy Beattie." And my mother said, "You have just seen my husband skate by."

But they didn't marry until—I'm not exactly sure what age my mother was, I think twenty-four, but the Second World War interrupted. And then when he came back on leave from basic training, or something like that, they married. He always insisted they'd given him so many shots, he could hardly stagger up to the justice of the peace. They were only together for a few days, honeymooned at a hotel in DC after they were married, then he went overseas.

JFB: They had one child, you?

AB: They had one child, me.

JFB: So what kind of parents were they? How did being an only child help shape the character of the adult you eventually became?

AB: I was very shy, and I was cowed by them. They were very, very young. I can remember looking at a home movie that they had years later and thinking, Oh my God, those children were in charge of me?

JFB: Were they permissive parents? Were they strict?

AB: They were authority figures. I mean, I think they were a little bit in over their heads. I think they were traumatized by their own childhoods and wanted to do it right, or wanted me not to suffer what they'd suffered. They were very overprotective, as some parents are with only children. But look at their backgrounds. My mother was raised by her grandparents and later by her aunt; her own father died before his thirtieth birthday, and her mother remarried and my mother and her brother lived elsewhere. And my father was raised, for several years, by his grandparents. His biological mother—don't ask me where she was. She returned from the hospital and disappeared.

They were really pretty vigilant about me.

And it wasn't the kind of strictness as in, "You can't do this," but there was no appeal ever to be made to them. If they said no, the answer was no. I learned pretty early that things were not very negotiable there. I could only hope—and sometimes I did, sometimes whatever I wanted I got. Other times just absolutely no. As in a pet: absolutely no. So I never had a pet.

JFB: Not that you're still resentful after all these years. [*Laughs*]

AB: Yeah, that's crazy. I mean, if you've got an only child, why wouldn't you want the kid to have a pet?

JFB: So you were a good girl?

AB: Pretty much. When I was a teenager I was hardly the most horrifying of the most horrifying, but I was in juvenile court when I was a teenager. For one thing, I learned how to blow up toilets with cherry bombs. A friend's brother taught me, and so that wasn't such a great idea to do it, like, toilet number one, two, three, and four, because by toilet number four many of the teachers were simply lined up in the corridor to see who was going to exit the ladies' room. [*Laughs*]

JFB: I'm trying to square the girl who was blowing up toilets with the girl who has her own, I'm going to guess, princess telephone, although it probably wasn't a princess telephone.

AB: It was a princess phone, pink.

JFB: I love those. [*Laughs*]

AB: I was very unhappy when I was a teenager. I could introspect forever, and I would not really have the answer to this. To have been a total D and F student—it wasn't that I wasn't trying, it was that I have the kind of mind that can't be interrupted by bells ringing at twenty- or thirty-minute intervals.

JFB: What was behind all that unhappiness?

AB: I don't know.

I was pretty shy, from being an only child. But as time went on I did worse and worse and worse in school. It certainly did erode my sense of self-esteem.

JFB: So when it was—when the opportunity came to blow up a toilet with a cherry bomb, was it just—?

AB: Why not? I've got the cherry bomb, what else am I going to do with it?

JFB: Were your parents literary in any sense?

AB: They always read me a lot of books. I had a lot of books, Little Golden Books. I had a lot of books when I was young, and I liked them a lot, and they always—both of them read to me when I was a little girl. My father read me the comic strips. I would sit in his lap on Sunday, and they always read me a book before I went to sleep.

My father had a headboard and it contained only a few books, and they were: *Your Life as a*—his astrological sign was Cancer—*Your Life as a Cancer, Help for Your Aching Back, Foot Reflexology,* and *How to Sell Your House Without a Real Estate Agent.* So if that isn't, like, a time capsule, you know, what some guy who didn't read would have around as books, I don't know what is. Perfect.

JFB: In the early seventies, when you first started publishing these amazing stories in the *New Yorker,* what did your parents think?

AB: Well, both of my parents were very pleased, really, and I'm sure somewhat taken aback; you know, where did this all come from? And they must've thought, too: Is this going to last? Even I thought that. I was making—when I say so much money from the *New Yorker,* I mean I was making quadruple what I made teaching freshman comp, but it never occurred to me to let my job go.

My mother called me one time when I was living in Eastford, Connecticut, this little town in the middle of nowhere. And she said, "I've just read your father your first book, *Chilly Scenes of Winter.*" And I knew—I told you what the books were that he'd read. You know, I thought, Read my father *Chilly Scenes of Winter*? Wow.

JFB: Out loud?

AB: Yeah. That must have been a mind-bending experience. What could that have been like? And she said, "I'll put Dad on." So then I hear my father, and he—I mean, this would be like me trying to commend somebody on some physics experiment. So he said, "Well, your mother—yes, your mother has just read me *Chilly Scenes of Winter.*"

And I said, "Daddy, what did you think of that?" And he said, "I'll tell you one thing, it was a hell of a lot better than 'This is the forest primeval.'"

JFB: He was quoting Henry Wadsworth Longfellow? "This is the forest primeval" being the opening line from—is it *Evangeline*?

AB: Yes. I had no idea my father could quote anything, anything from any book ever. That was the first time I had ever heard him quote. The last thing he remembered reading before *Chilly Scenes of Winter* was *Evangeline*. When he was—what? Probably fourteen or something? You know? "It was a hell of a lot better than 'This is the forest primeval.'"

And on another occasion he said something like, "So, some of the things in the stories, the table you describe, that's your aunt's table." And I'd say, "Uh-huh." And he'd say, "But the story wasn't about your aunt." And I'd say, "No, no, the table stuck in my mind, so I—you know, I needed to think about what table would be in the story, and I—yeah, that's her table. That's her table."

And he said, "I'll tell you one thing. You beat the system." So he was proud of me just for not—

JFB: You beat the system?

AB: Yeah, so he was proud of me for not being a nine-to-fiver. My mother was a more sophisticated reader than that, but also some of the stories were painful, not because she thought they were autobiography, because she knew me well enough to understand that they weren't autobiography. I don't see why she would've mistaken them for that, either. But a lot of them were pretty serious, pretty sad stories that I started publishing, pretty cryptic stories, in the *New Yorker,* and certainly in terms of what she was used to reading, and even in terms of what she knew about me, they must've come from a place that surprised her.

JFB: Those stories are not exactly Sherlock Holmes.

AB: That's right.

JFB: Did any of your stories hit particularly close to home? Did they ever admit to that?

AB: One of the things that my mother said—she was very humorous in the way that she expressed herself a lot of the time—and the way she put it was, she'd read a story of mine, she read a story called "Desire" that was in the *New Yorker.*

And she called me, and there was a message on my answering machine when I came home, and she started off with one tone of voice: "Mama has just bought and read your story of, you know, February tenth, 'Desire.'" And then her voice totally changed, and she said, "Mama is so sorry you ever thought that."

JFB: Was your mom one of these moms who was hoping that you'd have children?

AB: I already knew I didn't want to have kids.

JFB: When did you know that?

AB: I'm not saying I've never liked children, you know, individual children and so forth, but I—there was never a time that I really thought, "Oh boy, when I grow up I can get married and have children." Never. I'm not so keen on joining up with the operative system.

I mean, I don't even have many houseplants.

JFB: What do you think the main thing is that you got from her?

AB: A sense of equilibrium and a sense of humor.

JFB: Tell me what you mean by "equilibrium."

AB: A kind of consistency and belief in yourself, not because of anything you can name, necessarily, but because you trust yourself enough to have some kind of consistency that serves you as well as other people.

JFB: So it sounds like your mom was proud, delighted, and a little bit astonished by you? That you became a writer was almost as surprising to her as if you'd been blowing up toilets with a cherry bomb.

AB: I think the blown-up toilets were much stranger to her. Than literature.

# VERONICA GERHARDF

*It was like the shining golden center of my heart was gone. I didn't even have me to replace it with.*

© *Veronica Gerhardf*

Veronica Gerhardf* was my student at Colby College in the early nineties, and later my friend. She was Zach's nanny during his first year. Later, she and her husband moved to Ithaca, New York, and Veronica became pregnant with their first child at age twenty-eight. That's when things got complicated.

▼

VERONICA GERHARDF: I went in for the fifteen-week sonogram. We had the sonogram and saw the baby. Afterwards they put us in an exam room and the doctor came and talked to us and he said, "Well, the sonogram tech thinks that she sees something. She thinks that she sees some swelling or some fluid at the back of the neck. That can be a number of things. It can just be a temporary thing, but it can be an indication of something more serious. So we want to refer you to a neonatologist. We're going to make you an appointment. It's about forty-five minutes away."

JENNIFER FINNEY BOYLAN: So you leave this doctor's office now with this weird shadow hanging over you.

VG: Well, not at that point, because they said it could be the quality

---

* The names of all the individuals in this interview have been changed, at the subject's request.

of the sonogram, it could be the tech. There are so many variables at this point. So we're just going to check it out.

So we thought, Well, huh, okay, well, that's not great, but all right. We still, of course, started to worry, but frankly we didn't know how bad the options could be. We were fairly oblivious, thankfully.

JFB: So how long did you have to wait before you saw the next doctor?

VG: It was within the week. That office was very different. You knew the people in there were there because of high-risk pregnancy.

It wasn't like the happy family practice with babies rolling around on the floor and lots of smiling expectant parents. Everybody that was there did not necessarily want to be there. You could see it on their faces.

So then I went in and they did the sonogram first. This was a much higher-level sonogram. It's like with this unbelievable dildo-shaped sono-wand thing. Nobody had prepared me for that. That was maybe my first indication something was going very wrong very quickly.

The doctor said—couldn't see anything for a few minutes. He was like, "I don't see anything. I don't see what they're talking about." Then he changed the angle of it and he goes, "Oh yeah. There it is. I see it right there."

So the baby had fluid on the back of the neck and then he was able to see that there were some spots on the brain that didn't look right. Really got a very good view that this was not normal.

JFB: So is he saying all this while you're lying there?

VG: Yes. And he's going, he's like, "Yep, there's that. Yeah." He's like, "Yep, I see it. Yeah, I see it. I see it." And we're going, "What?" He's just like, "Yeah, and I see, yeah, okay, yeah."

We're like, "'Yes' what?"

So he said, "I definitely see the swelling on the back of the neck and I'm seeing some things in the brain. We want to do amnio right now."

And then they jabbed a six-inch needle into my stomach.

JFB: So by the time you left there did you know what was wrong with the child?

VG: In these situations there was a high likelihood of Down syndrome. So we thought that was the worst-case scenario. That was hard. That was painful to think about. We left that appointment really quite shaken.

JFB: What were some of the things you were thinking?

VG: I think my mom came up for that because I remember being in the back of the car and she was driving. I was in the back of the car and just trying to stay calm. I'd just been through this horrible appointment where this doctor is just being clinical and we're seeing things we don't want to see and then I have a giant needle stuck in my stomach. It was horrifying.

So I was just mostly in the back trying not to lose my shit. I'm shaken up, hurting, and worried. And thinking, God, what are we going to do? What is happening?

JFB: Do you remember what you did that night?

VG: I laid on the couch mostly.

JFB: How long after that did you get the official word from the doctors?

VG: Oh, it must have been three or four days. During that time I became reconciled to the idea of having a Down's baby. I thought things could be okay. The doctor called Ray at home. I was walking home and I knew that they were calling him. I knew he had been on the phone.

So then when I saw him walking down the street toward me, I was like, Oh, shit, it's bad. Then I just started crying.

JFB: What did he tell you?

VG: They said it was trisomy 18. We had no idea what that was. During this whole time I'd kind of reconciled over the couple of days. I thought, You know what? If it's a Down's baby, it's still my baby. I will love him or her and we'll make it work. We'll figure this out. I had truly reconciled to that. That was really hard and that was painful, but by the time we got the call I felt at peace.

But Down syndrome is trisomy 21. It means the twenty-first chromosome is triplicate. So they said, "Well it's trisomy eighteen. So the eighteenth chromosome is triplicate and that's incompatible with life."

JFB: Is that the phrase they used?

VG: Yes. The fetus's brain is misshapen. Sometimes these babies don't have a brain. It affects significantly the large organs like lungs and liver. It has a lot to do with organ development. There was a ninety percent chance that the baby would die before birth. Then once the baby was born it would have had a fifty percent chance of living through the first week. I don't know if I'm remembering all these percentages right, but it was like it was a death sentence.

Like if this baby is born it will die soon after. If it somehow survives, it will not be able to recognize you. It will not be able to eat. It will probably be born with some or multiple forms of cancer. It lives in a mostly vegetative state. It cannot recognize its own parents.

JFB: So you and your husband, Ray, have been given this terrible news. How did you figure out what to do next?

VG: Immediately we just started crying. We called my mom.

JFB: And she came to be with you?

VG: Yeah. I think she stayed for—she may have stayed for a week. I don't remember.

They said there were three options. One, I could carry the child to term. Second option was to have a surgical abortion. Or they could induce labor and go through the birth process at twenty weeks or so.

We talked to my mom. We talked to our friends. Our friends came to visit, too. We were really on the fence. We were like, well, neither choice is—this is all just a shit show start to finish. There's no good option here. So we didn't really know how to see through it.

JFB: How long did it take you to decide what to do?

VG: I think about a week, week and a half.

JFB: You must have tried to imagine the different scenarios. Tried to imagine the different ways that your life would be different depending on what choice you made.

VG: Right. We didn't really think about how our lives would be different. I thought about, What can I live with and what is the best, what's in the best interest of this baby? I was willing to go through whatever I needed to go through. If it was in the best interest of the baby to carry it to term, then I would do that.

If it was the sort of thing where I could carry the baby and then it could get medical treatment, then I was willing to do that. But the prognosis was beyond that. It wasn't only just death. It was pain. This baby would have no recognition of anyone and would be in a lot of pain and then would die. I couldn't live with that.

JFB: Do you remember the moment you made your final decision?

VG: Yeah, I remember Ray and his friend went out and I was alone in bed. I just had an evening to myself and I was in bed and I just reconciled with saying good-bye and I said good-bye in my head.

I did decide. I didn't want to pretend that this is nothing. I didn't want to do the surgical intervention. I thought, I'll induce labor.

Which they did, two weeks later.

JFB: Veronica, I can't imagine how hard that must have been to go through labor for a child that you know is not going to live.

VG: Yeah.

JFB: The way most women get through labor is you know you're going to have a baby at the end of it. You didn't have that.

VG: No. It was a very small child at that point and they gave me drugs literally because they weren't worried about the health of the baby. I was pretty well medicated. So, the actual labor progressed a lot faster than anyone would have thought.

JFB: Was your mother there?

VG: Yeah, my mother was there and Ray was there.

JFB: How did you get through that?

VG: Oh jeez, it was literally one foot in front of the other. It was, okay, what's the next thing? The next thing is I need a pillow and I'm going to bring it down to the car. Okay, what's the next thing? The next thing is I get in the car. What's next? The next thing is, we get to the hospital. It was moment-by-moment thinking.

JFB: Was the child alive when it was born?

VG: I don't know. I was pretty out of it. If it was, it was only for a minute or two.

JFB: Did you see the baby after it was born?

VG: Yeah, I held her and we all held her and we spent a fair amount of time with her and then my—

[*A lengthy pause.*]

JFB: I'm sorry, Veronica.

VG: It's okay.

[*Another pause.*]

JFB: Do you want to stop?

VG: I'm okay. So.

The visiting minister from our church came and baptized her. So, we were with her for a fair amount of time.

JFB: But she had already passed away by that point.

VG: Yeah. A baby that age can't survive without being intubated and/or receiving very serious medical intervention.

JFB: Can you describe for me that moment you're holding the baby?

VG: I was in a haze. I want to say almost thankfully. It was less emotional than what had led up to it because there was no intellectual turmoil at that point, or emotional turmoil. It just was what it was. Now we were down that road.

There was no more deciding. There were no more surprises. We knew exactly. All the decisions had been made and gotten us to that point. So it was just simply just being there and feeling sad, but knowing that we were moving through it.

JFB: You had the baby baptized. You'd already picked out a name?

VG: Mm-hmm.

JFB: I guess some parents would not have named the child and just not done that. How did you decide to do that?

VG: Well, it was the same rationale behind deciding to induce labor. We couldn't pretend that this wasn't a big deal. We didn't want to say, okay, so let's end this pregnancy and move on. It was about doing it in a very conscious way that mirrored how much it meant to both of us.

I think that honestly I went a little too deep into that.

I was in a very bad spot for a long time because I had intentionally decided to feel it and to experience it very thoroughly and deeply. Then it just got incredibly difficult to pull out of it.

JFB: You mean in the months afterwards.

VG: Yeah. Even within a couple of years. It still affects me.

JFB: How do you think it still affects you?

VG: I have at least three friends who were pregnant at the same time as I was. So, their children now are ten years old and every time I hear about them I think about—it's even on Facebook, what these kids are up to. I always think of how old my daughter would have been.

JFB: You named her Penelope?

VG: Yeah.

JFB: How did you pick that name?

VG: We'd just been hunting through names and then that one sounded nice. So we looked up the meaning and the history of it and it seemed like it was a really suitable name. It's part of the legend of Odysseus. That he had traveled for all these years and he came home to his wife, Penelope, and in the meantime she'd been instructed that she needed to remarry and she said, "Well, as soon as I finish the quilt that I'm making for Odysseus, then yes. I will marry."

So she spent all day making this quilt and then at night she spent her time unraveling it so that she's never done.

For us it meant the task that is not completed, the end that is never met. It meant the promise unfulfilled.

JFB: You said that you felt you went a little too deep into that. Am I remembering that you had a memorial service for her, didn't you? Did you have a funeral and everything?

VG: I did a death announcement that I sent out. I hand-made those.

JFB: I remember getting it.

VG: I made thirty or forty of those and sent those out to our closest friends and family.

JFB: I remember how incredibly sad I was when I got that, Veronica. But I also remember thinking that there was a kind of wisdom in it, of a very dark kind, and it made me admire you so much. I think about the way people keep things inside and live their lives in secret and just carry their grief forever. I thought it was very brave and courageous to share that with people. Do you think it was a mistake though to send those out?

VG: No, although—I know I was taking a risk in being misunderstood. Maybe I would come across as a little hysterical or melodramatic.

JFB: Do you think some people had that reaction?

VG: Not that they shared with me, but yes. I don't know. Mostly we got calls, like, "Oh, I received that and it was so sweet."

JFB: How did that loss affect you over the next couple of years?

VG: Well, it made me incredibly scared of sex. Made me incredibly scared of trying again because it had just been so heartbreaking. So my marriage really suffered.

JFB: How much after Penelope's death was Fletcher born?

VG: Let's see. He was born in 2003 so I think that was—yeah, that'd have been three years later, three and a half years later.

JFB: How did you come to that moment that you could face that again?

VG: Well, therapy and willpower, I guess. It was never a dream that we gave up. It was more like, how do we get our relationship back on track so that we have that kind of intimacy? Yeah, we just had to barrel through, I guess.

JFB: Somewhere in there you also lost your own mother. Caroline died in the midst of this whole terrible period.

VG: Well, she died when Fletcher was about one. So she saw me through my pregnancy. She was there on the day Fletcher was born.

JFB: Did you think about Penelope when Fletcher came into your life or did that shadow disappear?

VG: Well, when I first got pregnant with Fletcher, we had to talk about if we were going to do a larger-scale testing, if we were going to go for more tests earlier. Although the issue with Penelope was not genetic and there was no indication that we would ever have any difficulty again, it's more about they wanted to know what we wanted based on our comfort level.

So I had to make a decision early on. Was I going to worry the whole time? If I started I wasn't going to stop. I could worry about the testing. I could worry about the pregnancy and then the labor and what could go wrong. Then I could worry about will he sleep through the night or do we have to worry about SIDS or dear God, how do I ever put him on a school bus? How do I ever let him go off to college?

So, I remember making a conscious decision: Now I start thinking with faith. I'm going to do all the smart things. I'm going to get the right tests that I need to get, but I'm not going to go overboard. I'm not going to make a habit of worrying.

So from then it was like, okay, this is a new pregnancy. This is all new. Everything's fine. It was like a mantra and a discipline I had to keep. It was hard.

JFB: Veronica, I've heard some couples that I know who have lost children say that it was a thing that just ended up dooming their relationship. The couple just couldn't survive that sorrow. So you had that happen to you, but then you got the great blessing and gift of Fletcher. You and Ray separated six years after that. Do you think that the loss of the baby in any way is connected to that marriage not surviving?

VG: Yes, because Ray was incredibly supportive and caring and he's a very conscientious person. So when he saw that I was hurting he was very respectful and deferred to me. So he was taking his cues from me, which was not exactly in our best interest.

He waited for me to come around. I wound up feeling unwanted because here's the man with the male libido and he doesn't have an inherent desire for me. So it was demoralizing and lonely.

JFB: Did you feel that he didn't have the desire for you because of what had happened with the child?

VG: No, I don't think it was true that he actually didn't desire me. That was just how it came across.

The real problem was when my mother died. Then I realized what a keystone she had been, even in my marriage.

I was in the shower I think the day after she died and I was shampooing my hair. I allowed myself to just cry for fifteen minutes in the shower first off every day. I stood there and I thought, My marriage could really be in trouble now without my mother.

It was like the shining golden center of my heart was gone. I didn't even have me to replace it with.

I had to grow up and figure out who I was and be much more self-determined.

JFB: Do you think you've found that now all these years later?

VG: Yeah, definitely. I'm autonomous to a fault. I really used to look to my mom for a sense of judgment. When I had a decision to make I always considered what she would think.

So what I had to learn very quickly was, hey, there was only me. There is no one else in the world who can live my life for me. There's no one whose judgment I will substitute for my own.

JFB: Do you think of yourself as having two children? Do you think of Penelope as your daughter that died? Or do you feel that you have one child?

VG: Fletcher is an only child. When I think about her at all, she would have been ten years old, I remember, Well, no, she would not have. She was very badly disabled and compromised genetically. She was never going to have a life.

I think it's very different for parents who lose a healthy living child because they can imagine that child growing older and I never could. I never imagined that she was going to live beyond the next moment— maybe a day.

Sometimes I'm sad that I never had a daughter to raise, but I feel a lot of joy with having my boy. He brings me happiness that I didn't know I could have with someone who's so different from me.

JFB: What do you think you know about children now that you didn't know when you were our nanny?

VG: Well, I know that I don't have to love being a mother, which I sometimes don't. It's hard. It's really hard work and it's painful. Sometimes it's aggravating. But I always know when I go to bed that I will love him again when I see him in the morning.

I guess what I've learned is that it's okay to be conflicted about it. It's okay to not love the pain and the fear and the stress and the anger.

I'm still human.

I'm a mother, but I'm still myself.

# SUSAN MINOT

*It was a Monday morning and there had been an ice storm the night before. It was in January. The Boston-to-Maine railroad line goes along the coast there just below our driveway. Usually there was a little ding, ding, ding, ding, ding at the crossing with an arm coming down. . . . That morning [my mother] was on her way to an exercise class. There's a big barn blocking the view of where the train would be coming from. So you couldn't see it.*

© Hugh Foote

Susan Minot is the second of a group of seven siblings and the mother of a ten-year-old daughter, Ava. She is the author of the novel *Monkeys*, as well as the collection *Lust and Other Stories*. Minot lives in a high-ceilinged apartment in the West Village when she is not on North Haven island in Maine. As we spoke, Minot sat on a couch mending a hole in a long black jacket with a needle and thread. She said the fringe was made of monkey fur.

▼

JENNIFER FINNEY BOYLAN: What's the difference in age between your youngest sibling and your oldest?

SUSAN MINOT: Well, the first six of us are within nine years of each other, and that's including the seventh baby, Ellen, who died. Then there was a six-year gap and my youngest sister. So I think it's fifteen years between the oldest and the youngest.

JFB: So what effect does coming from such a large family have on a child? How did it change who you are?

SM: I think it's too many children for two parents to cover. People say, "Oh, it must have been great. So many children in the family, it must have been fun." You'd say, "Well, yes. I'm close to my siblings."

But I think large families may fall short in helping a child's development, if attention from a parent is of primary importance. I mean in our family we can count on our hands the number of times that any of us were ever alone with one parent, much less two. I mean, I can't even picture me ever being alone with both my parents.

JFB: Ever?

SM: Except randomly out on the lawn standing beside both of them.

JFB: Did that make you question their love in any way?

SM: Not at the time. I was one of a group, and that's how our parents were with us. At a certain point, children start parenting each other. We had each other.

I think as a daughter I definitely defined myself in terms of my sisters—we were the three oldest—probably a lot more than I did in terms of my brothers. It's as if the boys—there were three of them too—were another unit down.

My older sister is different than I am. The characteristics that she had of being responsible, looking out into the world to sort of piece things together, made me not, I think, develop so much those characteristics. I felt, "Well, that's being taken care of here." So it allowed me to be a little more dreamy, which I was inclined to be anyway. She would always be the first reconnaissance person to head out into the world and she was very good at reporting back to us what was going on. So I could indulge maybe a little more in my fantasy world.

JFB: Were the rules different for different siblings depending on who they were and how old they were?

SM: Not really, because there were so many of us. There was no talking back. We were always marshaled and told to be quiet. Now I see why. Six young kids must have just been a madhouse.

JFB: I think it is kind of like having your own private army.

SM: Yeah.

JFB: What was your father like?

SM: He was quite idiosyncratic. He didn't appear to need to reveal himself. He had a wry sense of humor and was smart but not particularly intellectual. He was a very good athlete and kind of a—well, not a cynic, but he would say things like, "I never met a man I liked. I only like women."

Then he married this woman full of joie de vivre. I think she loved him and she was happy to be married to him and she loved having lots of children. Since she took care of everything, he could kind of check out a bit. I think there was a little melancholy thing in him, again, that he would never really acknowledge.

He had his shop where he liked to make things out of wood. He'd build boats and he'd build houses.

You were allowed to go down there in the basement with the rocks coming out of the floor and you could build stuff if you wanted. He wasn't overly precious about it. The cans of paint would be crusted over. It was fun playing down there, a place for creating things.

JFB: And then, right in the heart of this, your mother is killed in this terrible way.

SM: Sudden accident, yes.

JFB: She's in a car that was hit by a train?

SM: It was a Monday morning and there had been an ice storm the night before. It was in January. The Boston-to-Maine railroad line goes along the coast there just below our driveway. Usually there was a little ding, ding, ding, ding, ding at the crossing with an arm coming down. We were always told to stop at the railroad tracks when we were on our bikes, even if the signals weren't flashing.

That morning she was on her way to an exercise class. There's a big barn blocking the view of where the train would be coming from. So you couldn't see it. If her windows were up and she had the music on, she wouldn't have heard anything. The train hit her car right smack as she was crossing the tracks like a bull's-eye. The timing wasn't three seconds before or three seconds after. She was killed instantly. My youngest sister was seven.

For my father, it was as if the curtain sort of rose and here were seven children suddenly looking at him, the one parent left. He was a good man, but he had never learned how full-fledgedly to embrace a child.

JFB: So did he learn that on the fly? Or it just kind of—he was never going to learn now? Was it too late?

SM: I think he did learn from my mother, watching her. His own mother had a lot of fortitude.

There was actually a very funny moment right after my mother's funeral. You laugh, you cry, you don't even know where you are. We were all in the kitchen and no one had been sleeping for days and it was maybe the third, fourth day after she died.

There was a pause in the conversation and everyone was kind of looking at Dad. He said, "Well, I suppose we could all go our separate ways."

Everyone laughed really hard. That was his humor. Nothing would ever be surprising now. In a way he was also saying, "This is how out of my depth I am."

JFB: I'm thinking about the differences between fathers and mothers. And here's a father who has left most of the command center to Mom who suddenly is the single parent of seven.

SM: I have two people in my family now, my brother and my stepson, who both have children out of wedlock because they weren't in a committed relationship with the mothers. Both of them are 50/50 down the middle committed as fathers. And this is co-parenting with a mother with whom they had not shared a life. They are totally great and involved fathers.

JFB: It's fathering without husbanding.

I wonder sometimes if I am fathering my children without maleness. Deedie and I have very different relationships with our kids. There was a time when I thought, No, I need to be more womanly with my sons because otherwise I'm shortchanging my identity as a female. But now I believe that parenthood is a mutable experience. There's a lot of room for me to be whoever I want to be with my children without having to lose any of my own identity.

SM: It's interesting to think about how much sexuality does or doesn't come into parenthood. When I look at my brother and stepson, they maintain a whole parenting attitude, not letting the mother take certain areas, if you follow. I see a lot of maternal behavior coming out in those fathers, or what would have been traditionally considered maternal.

JFB: And by "maternal behavior" you mean . . . ?

SM: Good question. I guess, a more gentle handling of disciplinary things. And being aware of the trivial things that have to do with the particulars of a child's life, really tracking with them.

JFB: You think of that as maternal?

SM: In my generation the father would kind of swoop in, have his say or be the final word on something, whereas the mother was more constant and there.

JFB: Yeah, the father was like the Supreme Court and the mother was more like the—

SM: The mother was all the lower courts.

JFB: Did your father become more maternal? After you lost your mother? Did his manner of parenting you change now that he was the only one responsible?

SM: He was forced to be more clued in to his children, but his manner didn't change, not really. He was an isolate, in a family of many children! My sisters and I turned into Mum.

JFB: So how many years between when your mom died and when he got remarried?

SM: A year.

JFB: Was there the traditional resentment, "Oh, no one gets to marry our father"?

SM: Just the opposite. It was more along the lines of, "Please marry him, someone. Because we can't keep looking after him."

JFB: Were you worried about him? I remember that the father in *Monkeys* turns to drinking.

SM: Yes, there was worry. He had had this huge shock and his whole life had changed. So drinking was definitely an issue for him, especially that year after.

JFB: What would he do when he was drunk? Was he angry? Was he a singer?

SM: My father was a nice man with bits of anger buried in him. He'd turn into sort of a bobbing head with a smile that made you cringe because you knew it wasn't real. He became sentimental and gentle but you knew he was just out of it and therefore, as a father, lost to us.

JFB: Later, after you'd left home and moved out in the world, did you think, I'm never having kids, or, I want a big family just like the one I grew up in?

SM: I did think, I'm never having kids.

JFB: Never?

SM: I thought so—for about ten years.

JFB: Because . . . ? Enough was enough already?

SM: It more had to do with the domestic life as I saw it. I was not interested in having a domestic life.

JFB: So it wasn't even children so much. It was the idea of kind of signing on to the grid? Ann Beattie said something like that to me. She said, "I'm not so keen on joining up with the operative system." But you did have children in the end.

SM: I knew I wanted an artistic life. Earliest on, I wanted to be an actress. When I was very young we watched a lot of movies and put on plays. Then I loved painting and art and did that. Then, I think because it was easiest to be compulsive with it, I concentrated on writing.

JFB: Some people call you a minimalist. Is there a connection between that style and the family that you grew up in?

SM: I prefer the term *brevetist*.

JFB: A brevetist. Is there any kind of line you can draw between your artistic style as a brevetist or as a subtractionist—as Mary Robison calls it—and that house that you grew up in with all those brothers and sisters and wanting to get out on your own, and finding a more simple life?

SM: Interesting thought. I would say the style has more to do with my taste in fiction, with the kind of fiction that I aspire to write. Because being minimal does not come naturally to me. In fact, it is the opposite. It's like my house. I think, I want to live in a simple, unfettered house. And look, I can't stop gathering things that have meaning to me, they just keep piling up.

JFB: So how did you get to the point where you decided to have a child?

SM: I've been married twice, both quite surprising to myself since

I didn't think, again, I would ever get married. I didn't think I needed to. I believe in partnerships and union and love between two people but not marriage necessarily. But I have been married twice.

The first time I got married I was in my early thirties. The urge for a child initially was, "Let's make a creature together." But we didn't. Our marriage didn't last. It lasted three years. After that I started to travel. I went about. I liked being free. I definitely liked not being in a house in a domestic situation. I wanted to see the world.

Then, in my late thirties, early forties, not in any major relationship, I thought, If I don't have a child I'm going to be sorry. A strong maternal urge came over me. It didn't have to do with making a creature with someone else. I just wanted to use the part of myself not being used which wanted to be devoted to the nurturing and raising of a child.

I don't know if that's because my mother had been such a strong figure in my life or if it had just finally appeared in me.

JFB: What amazes me is the way our feelings towards babies and children change. When I was a single man—I love being able to say that—I remember getting on an airplane and somebody, some mom with a screaming baby, would sit down in the seat next to me and I would freak out. Ask to change seats. Whereas now if a woman, or a man, for that matter—it's usually a woman—sits down with a baby, I'm all over that baby and I'm all over helping that mom. "Here, I'll hold the baby while you go to the bathroom. It'll be okay." I'm just fascinated by kids and I'm drawn in. Is that because I'm female now or is it because I have children of my own and I know how cool it is?

SM: Well, I think it's partly because you're female. If you were a man the mother would be less likely to hand you her baby. She's thinking, Oh, you're a sister so you get it. With a man you're not sure if he gets it. Nothing against men, just how it is.

JFB: How old were you when Ava was born?

SM: I was almost forty-four. I adopted her at birth. She's brought her own biology with her.

I was single. But by the time she arrived I was with her dad and he was there at her birth. He's been her dad since the moment she came out.

JFB: Do you feel that you understand your parents better now that you have been a mom? Is there a way in which suddenly you go, "Oh, now I get it"? Or was it not that much of a mystery in the first place?

SM: It's very hard to see your parents as people, I mean really. I've spent a lot of time thinking about them and have hashed it out in therapy. I've tried to think of my mother as a person I could meet, to imagine what she was like at age forty. But I can't do the flips in my mind it requires to think of her as only a person and not my mother. I know what her personality was and how she was socially but to me she was that kind of godlet in my life and there's no way I can switch that impression.

JFB: What do you think you know now that you didn't at the time your mother died?

SM: Well, I'm not sure this is about being a mother, but it has to do with being older. The older you get the more you realize how much you don't know. I feel that as a mother.

JFB: The wisdom of realizing how stupid we are?

SM: I thought then that my mother knew more than I feel I know now.

JFB: I don't know, Susan. Looking back, it's amazing to me that your family origin could not be more different from the family that you—

SM: That I made. Yeah, short of being married to a woman, which would have added one extra level—

JFB: Or changing genders completely. Which is more than we can say about some people.

SM: Then I would have really gone and done everything as much the opposite as possible.

JFB: Well. The day is young.

# POSTLUDE

# ANTI-VENOM

We were driving up a dirt road together, Zach and I, fighting about this essay he'd written for school, "Where I'm Going to Be Ten Years from Now." His prediction? Australia. Developing anti-venom, for the Australian Death Adder.

I offered my opinion. "No," I said.

"You should be proud!" he said. He was eighteen now. "Me, getting a PhD. In toxicology. Helping to save lives."

"You're not handling poisonous snakes. For a living. Okay? You're just not."

"It's my life!"

"I know it's your life, but if you're dead, it's my life. Plunged into darkness!"

"I'm not going to die."

"Of course you're going to die! Australia has the deadliest snakes in the world!"

We were driving toward the cabin of his former fiddle teacher. She was having a party. My son cast a glance at me. "You should believe in me," he said.

"Of course I believe in you. I just don't want you to get hurt."

"I'm not going to get hurt."

"You're going to handle deadly snakes, how can you possibly not get hurt?"

"You pick them up with a long stick."

"A long stick. Wow! That really puts my mind at ease!"

He shook his head. He was irritated now. "You don't believe I can milk the venom from snakes."

"Zach, you failed your driver's license three times. You've lost every pair of glasses you've ever owned. Of course you're going to get bitten by a poisonous snake! And die! And then my life will be plunged into darkness! Darkness!"

"They have anti-venom for the death adder," he explained. "If there's any trouble, I'll just take the anti-venom. Okay?"

"If they already have the anti-venom, why do you have to handle the snakes in the first place?" I was pretty sore at him. "I thought developing the anti-venom was the whole point! Why would you handle the snakes if you already have the anti-venom?"

"You're shouting," Zach noted.

"Of course I'm shouting!" I shouted. "This is why I changed all those diapers? This is what I gave my whole life to? You, dead in Australia! Poisoned! Alone!"

He just shook his head. In lieu of conversation, he turned on his iPod, which was wired to the car stereo. The car filled with blarney, the pipes and fiddles and all the rest. *To Dublin town I made me way, then to Cobh, and Amerikay. Now I'm in the land of liberty, a fig for all me foes!*

I guess his theory was, a little music from the Olde Countrie would soften me up. He was wrong about this, though.

Something ran across the road before us, and Zach jammed on the brakes. It all happened quickly. One minute we were listening to Irish music, the next we were spinning through space, waiting to see if we would live.

We skidded into the ditch. From the woods, a coyote paused and looked back at us. I saw the wildness in its eyes.

"Good driving," I said. "Excellent reactions."

Zach started the car again and got us out of the ditch. We started up the hill again. "I told you that you could trust me," he said.

A few months before this, he'd been admitted to Vassar College, early decision. I loved telling people my son was going to be "a Vassar Man."

In April he'd been cast in the school's musical, *The Wizard of Oz,* as the Cowardly Lion. The director had his actors talk about their characters. "What's the most important thing in the world for the Cowardly Lion?" he'd asked Zach. My son did not hesitate with his answer. "His tail," he said.

Deedie and I had sat in the dark theater, watching our child sing and dance. *Put 'em up, put 'em up.* At the end of the third act, he bid farewell to Dorothy. *I would never have found my courage,* he said, *if it wasn't for you.*

One Saturday he went to the barber and cut off all his long hair; he gave it to an organization, called Locks for Love, that makes wigs for cancer patients.

Then he fell in love with the girl who played the talking apple tree in Oz. Her name was Hana, and she came from the Czech Republic, a land where the word for *beloved* is *amado.* They went to the prom together.

*Hey,* she had asked, *how would you like it if someone came along and picked something off of you?*

Seannie was in South Africa. He'd been accepted as an exchange student for the last third of his sophomore year at a school in Cape Town called Bishops Diocesan College. A month earlier we'd taken him to Logan airport and loaded the fifteen-year-old on the plane.

"Please, please, please be careful, Seannie," Deedie had said.

Sean gave her that sly grin. "I got it," he said, and then walked off toward Africa without his mothers. What did he do in South Africa, by way of being careful? He went bungee jumping, and skydiving, and rock climbing, and shark-cage diving.

Now the sun was sinking toward the ridge to my right. The long shining mirror of Long Pond was visible in the valley. Silence hung in the air between us, and not for the first time. My sons were leaving me, going out into the broad world.

"Zach," I said at last, "if you really, really want to milk the poison from deadly snakes in Australia—if that's your dream—I'll support you."

"Thank you," he said, and rubbed my shoulder. "This means a lot to me."

"I'll always support you, and your dreams," I said. "Even if your dreams . . . are stupid."

My throat closed up. The tears rolled down.

Of course, if it was the stupidity of dreams we were considering, I was one to talk. I mean, please. I thought of the hours I'd spent at Zach's age, lying in bed, staring at the ceiling, imagining a world a lot farther away than Australia.

We pulled up at the violin teacher's house, right at the top of Buttermilk Hill. The pastures of her farm were all around us, and beyond that the mountains and the lakes. Her husband's single-engine plane sat at the edge of a long field. A wind sock dangled from a pole just beyond a field of tomatoes and cabbages.

From the cabin came the sound of skirling mandolins and fiddles.

My son looked at me, incredulous. "You're crying now?" he said. "About me getting bitten by an imaginary snake? In Australia? In the future? You're actually crying?"

"A little."

I wiped the tears away and we got out of the car. The sun was almost gone now, sinking behind the mountains.

We walked toward the cabin. The music grew louder. His teacher was playing a reel. "Farewell to Erin."

In the twilight it was hard for me to see the stairs. I paused at the bottom step, unsteady on my old legs, uncertain.

My son turned to me. He took me by the arm. "Come on, Mom," Zach said. "I got you."

# AFTERWORD

© Joyce Ravid

# SAME MONKEYS, DIFFERENT BARREL—

[A Conversation with Jennifer and Deirdre Boylan]

BY ANNA QUINDLEN

Jennifer Finney Boylan's account of her transition from male to female, *She's Not There: A Life in Two Genders,* has become a touchstone not only for people who are transgender but for all those interested in exploring what it means to be male and female. As James, Boylan published several critically acclaimed novels; as Jenny, she has also written *I'm Looking Through You: Growing Up Haunted* and the Falcon Quinn series for young readers.

Constant throughout it all has been Boylan's work as a professor at Colby College in Maine and Deirdre Finney Boylan, known as Deedie, the woman Jim married in 1988 and the mother of their two sons, Zach and Sean. In 2003 Anna Quindlen wrote in a *Newsweek* column about the acuity and humor of *She's Not There,* beginning a relationship with the Boylans that resulted, one summer afternoon, in this conversation about motherhood, marriage, and masculinity. In the spirit of Jenny Boylan's writing, there was extraordinary honesty on the part of both partners, and lots of laughs. Below, an edited version.

▼

ANNA QUINDLEN: Deedie, I actually want to open the conversation with you. It's been more than a decade since the pivotal events of *She's Not There.* I think most readers would have two questions: How have your boys' reactions changed as they've matured, and what has your journey been like?

DEEDIE FINNEY BOYLAN: I think in some ways it's easier to talk about the boys, obviously. Over time, I think the boys continue to see Jenny as the parent that they've always loved. Because they were so young during transition, the youngest one doesn't really have clear memories of Jenny as a male, of Maddy as Daddy. We have pictures, and we talk about things. I think they still continue, in the way that most teenagers do, to have very, very little interest in talking about their parents to their peers, in terms of "Why do you have two women parents?" Zachary wears his heart on his sleeve and Sean is an enigma to us most of the time. But, you know, if you say to them, "Do you ever wish our family was just like other families?" I think they don't necessarily understand the question. And then they'll say, "Well, it'd be nice if we didn't have to explain things to people," but it doesn't worry them. I don't think they worry about bringing a new friend over to the house. I don't think they worry about what the neighbors will say, or what will peers say.

JENNIFER FINNEY BOYLAN: I hope that having me as a parent, having us as parents, has made them more accepting of people who are different. More openhearted. It's hard to imagine what our lives would be like otherwise.

AQ: You pose the question "Do you ever wish our family was more like other families?" But in most ways that matter, isn't your family just like other families?

JFB: Yeah, I think mostly that is totally true. I don't know, sometimes I think what makes us different is the fact that we . . . um . . .

AQ: Are still married? [*Laughs*]

JFB: Of the dozen or so people that we knew in the mideighties when people were coupling up and getting married, I think we might be the only couple that's still together. [*Laughs*] My friends from high school, my friends from college. I do sarcastically say sometimes that if more husbands became women, more couples would stay together.

DFB: But I think that goes back to what my greatest fear was at the time of transition, that I didn't think I wanted to be married to a woman. I was afraid that this was the end of our marriage, and our family.

JFB: Can you say confidently that you do want to be married to a woman?

AQ: Well, the point in the book is she wants to be married to you.

DFB: Yes. Although my first visceral reaction, was, "Thank God we have two houses."

AQ: But the other visceral reaction that comes through loud and clear in *She's Not There* is a sense of a loss of control. That you basically have no say in this. Did you lose that feeling of helplessness after a while?

DFB: Yes, I did lose that feeling after a while. But, especially at the heart of transition, when things were changing very, very fast, I felt like I was on a train, and if I stayed on the train I might be ripped off, and if I jumped off, I'd be killed. I was hanging on for dear life and just had to wait and see what happened. I didn't have any control. And it had nothing to do with me. What I did get to decide is that I still do want to be married to Jenny. We do still love each other and we have a life together which is rich and rewarding. Our family is very close and very happy and very successful, and everybody appears to be doing what they want to do. As you know, with teenagers sometimes it's hard to tell [*laughs*], but the boys are thriving, our lives are rich and rewarding. We live where we want to live and we do what we want to do, and we're doing it together as a family. And that's not something that I feel trapped in, it's something at this point that I totally embrace and am happy with. At first I didn't know if I could be sustained in whatever new incarnation of our life was going to evolve. And I think the thing that is most surprising is perhaps how little has really changed, in the foundation of our relationship, in the foundation of our family and the way we operate. It seemed like that was being dynamited at a certain point, but in fact, those sorts of connections and values and beliefs and shared things are still the same.

JFB: Also, within the context of a good family, as a father, I think I was playful and loving. I was around a lot. As I went through transition, I don't think they ever felt the fundamental building blocks of the family were being torn apart. The transition may have seemed like a superficial difference to them.

AQ: And the two of you already had what sounds like a pretty egalitarian marriage.

DFB: I think it was fairly egalitarian. We joke that our division of labor is that when I cook Jenny cleans, and when Jenny cooks *Jenny* cleans. That's remained true. Jenny does the dishes.

JFB: Deedie does the laundry, I'm sorry to say. To me it's not the laundry, it's the folding. Dear God, the folding! And also, I know I never do the folding right. You turn to me and say, "Oh, that's not how you fold that!"

DFB: That's true. [*Laughs*] Again, we do the same things we always did. I do most of the grocery shopping. I do most of the cooking. But Jenny has things she loves to cook and cooks every week. Jenny makes pizza on Fridays.

JFB: Right, and I'm the straightener in the house.

DFB: I'm a terrible housekeeper, which has always been funny because Jenny is so energetic and her energy can be really wild—

JFB: I'm the crazy one.

DFB: Right, the crazy manic energy, so she must be really messy, right? And I'm a little bit more steady, less flamboyant, but I'm actually the slob. I'm a total slob. Jenny picks up behind me all the time. And Jenny's still the breadwinner. In her Colby career, her teaching career, her work in academics, her publishing has always brought in at least twice as much as my work as a social worker.

JFB: Which isn't to say you don't work as many, if not more, hours a week than me.

We were talking about the kids before; I just wanted to mention that in my experience of, by now, the thousands of other transgender parents, the ones that are most able to keep a good relationship with their kids are the ones who go through transition and go public when their kids are small, and the ones who have the hardest time are the ones who come out when the kids are in the heart and the onset of puberty and adolescence. It's funny, we often think about adolescence as opening up to the world—

DFB: —but it's not. The cultural experience, the social experience of adolescence is actually that things get much more narrow.

JFB: What being a man or being a woman means, exactly, it narrows, in so many ways.

AQ: Well, I really want to talk about that, because I have two sons and a daughter. I was horrified when my boys were born and I realized that, in some ways, the straitjacket that we defined as masculinity was even worse than the old straitjacket we know as femininity. People had such stereotypes about what they were going to be. "Oh, little boys! Oh, they'll run you ragged! Oh, they'll want trucks! Oh, they'll hit and bite." And none of it happened to be true of the particular little boys . . .

DFB: . . . that you raised. Or that you got.

JFB: That's the question, isn't it? Got or raised? We had some friends over to my mom's house yesterday, and they had two sons who were—I believe the term is *roughhousing,* in the pool. They were splashing each other, kind of pushing each other around, stealing things from each other and not letting the other have it back. And our boys, I wouldn't say they've never done stuff like that—

DFB: Oh, they do some of that, but it's not as . . .

JFB: Their interactions are less . . . oh, help me out with this, Deedie. They seem . . .

DFB: They're less overtly physically competitive with each other.

JFB: They're not feminine boys, whatever that means.

AQ: There we go with "whatever that means." I mean, at some level, gender was clearly very, very important to you [ *JFB laughs* ], and at another level, given the fact that the person who was Jim seems very much like the person who is Jenny, it raises all sorts of questions about how permeable that gender membrane is for our kids. And how the pernicious thing is to force them into a series of little boxes that the world out there has defined as narrowly as possible, yes?

DFB: I agree with you.

JFB: Every parent who has more than one child has the experience of raising the second child, and the third, and the fourth, if there are that many, using more or less the same basic techniques. And yet, children from the same family, as we all know, can be wildly different characters. And so we've wondered, what is it that caused that? And our boys, the ways in which they're stereotypically masculine are that they are competitive, they are . . . well, Sean, in particular, is an athlete. Sean has always loved sports. But Zach takes fencing very seriously. Does fencing count? Zach is the co-captain of the fencing team. But they are not stereotypically masculine in that they each have a certain gentleness of spirit. But even as I say this, I'm like, so wait, gentleness? Women are like that?

AQ: When you're talking about competitiveness and athleticism, you're describing my daughter.

DFB: I was a competitive athlete.

AQ: Certainly your experience, Jenny, raises interesting questions about nature versus nurture, because the book indicates that from the earliest possible age you kept thinking right wine, wrong bottle.

JFB: I was going to call the book, originally, *Same Monkeys, Different Barrel.*

[*AQ laughs.*]

JFB: What I wanted to change was a physical body. It just didn't feel like home. But the great surprise through all this has really been how much like my male self I am. And I think that's a thing to celebrate. I think one of the things that Deedie and I were struggling with back when I was going through this was the question of whether I was about to become a stranger. I often meet transgender people, male-to-female people, who say, "When I was young, I wanted to play with dolls, and I love to bake cookies." And I want to say, "For heaven's sake, make cookies! You don't need a vagina for that!"

AQ: But it also sounds like what you're saying is that for certain people, perhaps people who are unhappy with their lives, there's the sense that "I will change genders and be a whole different person!" And what you're saying is, "You're the same person, but with a different gender."

JFB: I think that's true. One of the things that is different, I think, there's less free-floating anxiety and moodiness. Yes?

DFB: You mean for you? [*Both laugh.*] I think that's mostly true.

JFB: I used to get these stomachaches. Every other month. Serious, just, what do you call it . . . when someone is having a physical reaction . . .

DFB: Somatic?

AQ: Hysterical?

[*All laugh.*]

JFB: Such a girl word!

I would have these terrible stomachaches because of everything I was keeping a secret, and everything I couldn't put into words. They're gone. I haven't had one of them in twelve years.

AQ: That was some secret!

JFB: You know, the fact that I kept it secret from Deedie for ten or twelve years is still something I carry around. I guess you never really get over the guilt of that.

We got married with my thinking, I will be able to keep this locked up. It was a private calculation, and it was a miscalculation. It's kind of a mild word to use for something so large.

AQ: Have you had these kinds of conversations with your sons? Or is it too soon? Is it too much?

JFB: Conversations about what?

AQ: Conversations about the spiritual and psychological underpinnings of what you went through.

JFB: No, not really.

DFB: They're not there yet.

AQ: Let me ask this in a different way, then. Have they read the book?

JFB: They have read the book. Zach read it I think three years ago, and Seannie read it last summer. When I asked them what they thought, Zach's biggest reaction was, "I didn't know how hard it was for Mommy." Meaning Deedie.

AQ: But obviously you were able to insulate them from that when they were very young, because it was clearly a period of some tension during the transition.

DFB: There was a lot of other turmoil going on at the same time. My sister was dying of ovarian cancer at exactly the same time. And the kids were so young that there was a way in which I couldn't even imagine splitting up our family, even if it meant I was going to be married to this crazy woman.

AQ: And now you are married to this crazy woman.

JFB: How'd that work out?

[*All laugh.*]

DFB: I know! And I still am! But part of it was they were really little and part of it was that my sister was dying, and I had to spend a lot of time and psychic energy with that and with her. I really needed Jenny to look after the kids while that was going on, and to keep the home fires burning, and to let me go when I had to go, and to let me come back when I had to come back. Because of all the different things that were going on, it actually bought her a lot of time. We needed each other tremendously at that moment. I needed her support, and she was able to support me. And she and my sister were very close, so that was . . .

JFB: It's funny, because your sister was one of the few people to think that my becoming a woman was, like, one of the best things ever. She was the one who said, "I'm so glad it's only that you're a woman. I thought it was something serious."

AQ: I love that line.

JFB: Are we going to talk about menopause? I only mention that because what I'm facing now, at age fifty-three, is the question of, at what point do I stop taking hormones? Because for one thing, they're not feminizing—I hate that word—they're not feminizing me anymore.

AQ: So if you stop taking the hormones . . .

JFB: I'll go through hot flashes. I'll go through a pretty uncomfortable few months. I'll be grumpy. Maybe I'll get over it. So one of the things we've talked about is whether or not, when Deedie's all done, whether I should be all done too.

AQ: Boy, you two have some interesting issues. So how do you introduce one another to strangers? "This is my . . ."

DFB: I usually say "spouse." Jenny usually says "partner." And there are times where I'll say we're married, imagine that! Figure that out!

JFB: As people came into my mother's memorial service, Deedie and I were at the door, shaking hands. Well, there were a lot of my mother's old friends there. I know most of these people, and Deedie knows about maybe half of them. So I'm shaking hands. "Thank you for coming, and this is Deedie."

AQ: And what would you say, Deedie?

DFB: "I'm Hildegarde's daughter-in-law."

AQ: That's good.

JFB: That's dodging a bullet.

DFB: Or I'd say, "I'm Deedie, I'm married to Jenny." I said that several times.

JFB: The introduction is often about what the space is. When I went through transition in 2000, I was uncomfortable with saying *wife,* because I thought if Deedie's my wife, I'm her husband. Ooh, awkward.

[*DFB laughs.*]

JFB: And now, there are so many examples of two women together. It's funny though, if I say *wife,* people think we're lesbians, which we're not.

DFB: But who cares?

AQ: But we've moved so far that we've passed into an entirely new country. Now there are transgender kids who want to be seen as transgender. In other words, they don't want to claim a nation-state of male or female, they want to be something completely different.

JFB: I understand that as a philosophical and emotional sensibility. I think I've told you before that I've been protested four or five times over the years. And about half of those times when I've been protested, it's been by transgender people who are—

DFB: —disappointed in your polarity?

JFB: Disappointed that I'm not more radical.

DFB: That you wanted to be a soccer mom and drive the minivan. Except you aren't.

JFB: Yeah, that's right, because you're the soccer mom.

DFB: You never went to those soccer games! I coached the team!

JFB: I went to a couple! But when they say they want to be free from gender, a lot of young people mean they want to be either completely androgynous or that they want to be completely fluid so they can be masculine one day and feminine the next. And that's fine. But for me, freedom from gender means waking up in the morning and not having to think about it. I just kind of put my blue jeans on and go downstairs and feed the dogs. I don't really want to fight the gender fight every day. I don't have anything more to prove. And also, that there are as many ways of being trans as there are of being gay, or lesbian, or straight, or Irish, or anything else.

AQ: Deedie, when you look at Jenny, do you ever see Jim?

DFB: [*Pause*] That's a good question. We've just spent the last month going through the loss of Jenny's mother. There are all the pictures, and all the albums, and the lifetime Jenny had before I came into her life. I don't look at Jenny and see Jim. But we do have photos across both decades of our marriage. We were talking about this yesterday with friends of ours from Wesleyan who were looking at . . .

JFB: The wonderful photograph of one of our first dates that your sister took. And I was looking at that young Deedie, and I realized, you know, everybody goes through transition. The transition from young Deedie to . . . uh . . . less-young Deedie—

DFB: Fifty-one-year-old Deedie. From twenty-seven to fifty-one.

JFB: —is every bit as profound. You're the same person, but, of course, you're also not the same person. Can't remember if I wrote about this, about the ship of Theseus, in *She's Not There*. Theseus has a ship and he replaces the sails, he replaces all the planking on the decks, and after ten years, someone's been saving all the pieces that were replaced and has built them into another ship. So now there's two ships: one of which has all the original pieces, and one that Theseus now sails. So this is a Philosophy 101 question: Which is the true ship of Theseus? And it's usually defined as the ship that Theseus sails. So if you had the twenty-five-year-old Anna Quindlen here, right now, I mean, I'd love to talk to her, but . . .

AQ: There's so much she needs to know.

JFB: But I'd much rather talk to you. Because you're the Anna Quindlen that I know. So I was looking at that photograph of two young lovers in their twenties, and we're both looking off into the distance. I didn't look at that photograph to think, Wow, I used to be a guy! Phew! How weird was that! I was looking at it thinking, Wow, she's beautiful. And I'm still married to her. And the version of her that I'm married to I love even more than this beautiful young twenty-eight-year-old. There are a lot of long roads that we travel.

AQ: That all of us travel.

DFB: Right, that everyone travels.

AQ: I wanted to ask you a question about your sons. Over the years, I've had friends split up, and I watch them over and over again thinking, It's because we got divorced. He won't talk to us because we got divorced. He's acting out because we got divorced. He doesn't have a steady girlfriend because we got divorced. And I wonder if you had to stop yourself from thinking that everything was about Jenny's transition.

DFB: I think it was harder for Jenny than it was for me.

JFB: Oh my God, yeah.

DFB: Sean went through a period in fourth grade when he didn't want to get out of bed, and he didn't want to go to school. . . .

JFB: And the relief we felt when we discovered it was because he really just didn't like his math teacher, rather than something terrible I had done.

DFB: Or that he was afraid of what people were saying in school. Jenny worried a lot.

JFB: I still worry. I think I'll always worry.

AQ: And what about the peer group? I mean, my kids have great friends, but from time to time, during their adolescence, I would think of them as the incubus in the house. Were there people who sowed discord?

DFB: You know, so far, that has not been true.

JFB: No, they think I'm cool. And not just me. In some ways, you're cooler than I am, because you're deranged enough to stay with me. They'd say, "Zach, you have the coolest parents." And I think, *Yeah, he does.*

DFB: Who says that?

JFB: Bridget says that.

DFB: Oh, well, Bridget.

[*AQ laughs.*]

JFB: And Robbie says that. And Kit.

DFB: I'm not sure if that's true. But I think that they have had good friends. There was one parent ever, one parent ever, who ran into Jenny at a birthday party and said, "You really look like Jim. Are you his sister?" And Jenny had to take her aside and say, "I'm not Jim anymore, I'm Jenny." And the woman said, "My child will never come to your house, you're not allowed to invite him over, and I will be civil to you in public but I completely disagree with this and will not have my child exposed to it." One kid. Out of everyone we went to school with. It wasn't someone we wanted to be friends with anyway, they just happened to be in the same class. Other kids and parents and families have been only curious and supportive and welcoming.

JFB: I think we're protected—by "we" I mean not just the two of us but the whole family—because I'm so public and I'm so out. It's not like the Boo Radley house, where people are afraid to knock on the door.

AQ: I love the idea that Zach might start his college essay with—

DFB: "Oprah asked me what my family was like."

AQ: Exactly.

DFB: When Jenny told them that she was writing another memoir, Zach just said, "You know, Maddy, this time, could you use our real names?"

AQ: They still call you Maddy?

JFB: They do. Once in a while I'm introduced as the other mom. Rarely. I'm still Maddy, if only to differentiate me from Deedie. You know, I didn't want to use *Mom* or *Mommy* early on, because I thought I was taking something away from Deedie. I'm not the one who was pregnant for nine months. I'm not the one who went through labor and had a cesarean.

DFB: Two.

JFB: And got mastitis. And had the epidural fall out. So, I felt like saying, "Oh yes, I'm a mother too, now!" was kind of cheeky. *Maddy* feels like that's me.

AQ: Are there any of your friends who just couldn't make it through the transition?

DFB: A couple.

JFB: There are some friends we have who I know liked it better when we were husband and wife and are still not thrilled about the whole transgender thing. It's very common for me, if I'm at a Colby event with friends that I've had for more than a dozen years, for people to use the wrong pronoun. Which, I admit, still drives me crazy. I'd like to say I know they don't mean any harm by this, but after a dozen years . . . Deedie is much more forgiving than I am about this.

DFB: Well, it's not me.

AQ: Deedie, I want to ask you what I think is a pretty hard question. *She's Not There* is filled with a sense of what you've lost. At some point, you say, "This isn't what I signed up for." So it's all these years later—what have you gotten out of this? Instead of loss, what did you gain?

DFB: You know, I go back to what we were saying when we first started talking. I get to be married to the person that I love. I get to have a family and a life that I find rewarding and exciting and fun. It is now ten, eleven, twelve years later, and I'm still here. I don't have to be here. I want to do it. What we have built together, as our life and our marriage and our family, is really rewarding.

JFB: But I will say—this is going to sound defensive; ready?—frequently people will say, in response to *She's Not There,* "The person I really want to hear from is your wife. That's the real story." Or, "I get the sense in *She's Not There* that we haven't really heard the real story from Deedie." Or, "Poor Deedie. She's the real hero of the story." And while I do think Deedie is a hero, there's a way in which—this is the self-defensive part—I feel for Deedie to be defined as a hero implies that I must be—

DFB: The villain? [*Laughs*]

JFB: Well, yeah, and that anyone who would stay with me has to be seen as a martyr or an object of pity.

AQ: I actually think that it suggests that she had to settle for less, at some level. And what I think she's just said pretty eloquently is, "I got what I wanted."

JFB: She got what she didn't know she wanted. Which is what happens to all of us.

AQ: Right.

JFB: But I guess I'll put it differently. I will say, in spite of all the losses, in spite of being transgender, instead of all the other things I have to apologize for, on a good day, I'm a lot of fun.

[*AQ cracks up.*]

JFB: I'm a pleasant person to be around. I make great pizza. I play the piano and I can sing. I think I'm a loving person, and that I bring that to people. And that our family is better for having me around, and Deedie's life is better for having me in it. And with this narrative of, "Oh, the poor thing. I don't envy her!"? I mean, jeez. What I want is for people to envy her. I want people to sob tears of misery that they're not Deedie, that they can't be married to me, because—

[*Deedie gives Jenny a look of exasperation and love.*]

JFB: Oh, look at that face! Oh my God! All right.

Maybe not sob, but do you know what I'm saying?

[*Deedie gives Jenny another hard look.*]

JFB: Should I shut up now?

[*Deedie nods. The three women laugh.*]

JFB: Okay. I'm all done.

# RESOURCES

A DONATION HAS been made in the name of the interview subjects of this book to the PEN American Center, the global literary community protecting free expression and celebrating literature. www.pen.org

▼

OTHER ORGANIZATIONS AND NONPROFITS DEAR TO THE PARTICI-
PANTS IN THIS PROJECT INCLUDE:

• Little People of America. LPA is a national nonprofit organization that provides support and information to people of short stature and their families. www.lpaonline.org

• Evan B. Donaldson Adoption Institute. The institute provides leadership that improves adoption laws, policies, and practices through sound research, education, and advocacy. www.adoptioninstitute.org.

• ASAN (Autistic Self Advocacy Network). The Autistic Self Advocacy Network is a 501(c)(3) nonprofit organization run by and for autistic people. ASAN's supporters include autistic adults and youth, cross-disability advocates, and nonautistic family members, professionals, educators, and friends. ASAN was created to provide support and services to individuals on the autism spectrum while working to educate communities and improve public perceptions of autism. autisticadvocacy.org

• National Center for Transgender Equality. Dedicated to advancing the equality of transgender people through advocacy, collaboration, and empowerment. www.transequality.org

• GLAAD (the Gay and Lesbian Alliance Against Defamation). For twenty-five years, GLAAD has worked with news, entertainment, and social media to bring culture-changing stories of LGBT people into millions of homes and workplaces every day. www.glaad.org

• The Edward Albee Foundation. The Albee Foundation exists to serve writers, visual artists, and composers from all walks of life, by providing time and space in which to work without disturbance. www.albeefoundation.org

• The Papillon Center, run by Dr. Christine McGinn, provides transgender care in Bucks County, Pennsylvania. drchristinemcginn.com

▼

FOR INDIVIDUALS SEEKING RESOURCES FOR TRANSGENDER PEOPLE AND THEIR FAMILIES:

• In addition to the NCTE, readers might investigate www .transparentday.org, a group advocating for the celebration of the lives of parents and children without the stereotypes of gender.

• The Sylvia Rivera Law Project works to guarantee that all people are free to self-determine gender identity and expression, regardless of income or race, and without facing harassment, discrimination, or violence. srlp.org

• *En|gender* is the blog run by writer Helen Boyd, author of two smart memoirs about transgender marriage, *My Husband Betty* and *She's Not the Man I Married;* her site also contains a thoughtful community message board. www.myhusbandbetty.com

▼

BOOKS ABOUT TRANSGENDER EXPERIENCE:

*Whipping Girl: A Transgender Woman on Sexism and the Scapegoating of Femininity* by Julia Serano. Seal Press. ISBN: 978–1580051545.

*Transgender History* by Susan Stryker. Seal Press. ISBN: 978–1580052245.

*True Selves: Understanding Transsexualism—For Families, Friends, Co-*

*workers, and Helping Professionals* by Mildred Brown and Chloe Ann Rounsley. Jossey-Bass. ISBN: 978–0787902711.

*Stone Butch Blues* by Leslie Feinberg. Firebrand Books. ISBN: 978–1563410291.

*Becoming a Visible Man* by Jamison Green. Vanderbilt University Press. ISBN: 978–0826514578.

Organizations advocating for nontraditional families:

• PFLAG (Parents, Families and Friends of Lesbians and Gays) promotes the health and well-being of lesbian, gay, bisexual, and transgender persons, their families, and their friends through: support, to cope with an adverse society; education, to enlighten an ill-informed public; and advocacy, to end discrimination and to secure equal civil rights. community.pflag.org

• The Family Equality Council works at all levels of government to advance full social and legal equality on behalf of the approximately one million lesbian, gay, bisexual, and transgender families raising two million children. www.familyequality.org

Websites of authors participating in this project:

- Richard Russo: www.randomhouse.com/knopf/authors/russo/
- Ralph James Savarese: www.ralphsavarese.com
- Trey Ellis: www.treyellis.com
- Augusten Burroughs: www.augusten.com
- Edward Albee: www.albeefoundation.org
- Timothy Kreider: www.thepaincomics.com
- Dr. Christine McGinn: drchristinemcginn.com
- Ann Beattie: authors.simonandschuster.com/Ann-Beattie/1926455
- Susan Minot: www.openroadmedia.com/authors/susan-minot.aspx
- Anna Quindlen: www.annaquindlen.net

▼

JENNY BOYLAN'S WEBSITE is www.jenniferboylan.net and contains a wealth of material, some of it specifically related to this title. Jenny can be contacted at jb@jenniferboylan.net; she attempts to answer all mail, except when things get a little backed up. She can be followed at JennyBoylan on Twitter and as Jennifer Finney Boylan on Facebook.

▼

THE BOYLAN FAMILY maintains two endowments, which are sustained by proceeds from this book and other JFB projects. The Boylan prize in nonfiction at Wesleyan is a small fund supporting undergraduate writers at Wesleyan University in Middletown, Connecticut. More information is available at www.wesleyan.edu/writing/community/prizedetails/boylan.html.

The J. Richard Boylan Scholarship in the Humanities at Johns Hopkins University provides major support for undergraduates at JHU in Baltimore, Maryland. www.jhu.edu/~admis/catalog/misc/scholarships_awards_prizes.pdf.

Sympathetic readers and other supporters of undergraduate education wishing to contribute to these endowments can contact the schools directly at the links listed above, or write to the author at jb@jenniferboylan.net.

# ACKNOWLEDGMENTS

I WISH TO EXPRESS my sincere gratitude to everyone who helped with this project—the parents and former children who suffered through my endless questions; to Anna Quindlen, for agreeing to perform (and edit) the interview that provides the afterword to this work; to editors Deb Futter, Gerry Howard, Christine Pride, and Lindsay Sagnette at Random House; and to my agent Kris Dahl at ICM, for standing by me these last twenty years. I want to particularly thank my assistant, Grant Patch, for all the research he did on my behalf, as well as for transcribing many of the interviews. Other interviews were transcribed by Verbal Ink Transcription Services (www.verbalink.com).

I'm especially thankful to Augusten Burroughs, who first suggested that I write this book over a dinner of burning-hot food at Spice Market, in Manhattan; it's probably worth mentioning that in reply I told Augusten that I was "all done with memoir" and "all done with gender." Augusten is also responsible for the photograph of Edward Albee as well as the author photo.

I'm grateful to my colleagues and students at Colby College in Maine, as well as at Ursinus College in Collegeville, Pennsylvania. It was Ursinus's president, the late John Strassburger, who, along with English professor Jon Volkmer, brought me to that campus for the fall of 2010 and invented the position of Grace Hoyer/John Updike Distinguished Visiting Creative Writer for me. I miss him.

Above all, I'm grateful to my family—my parents and my sister; my brave, glorious sons, Zachary and Sean; and to the incomparable Deedie Finney Boylan, whose love has made my life possible.

# STUCK IN THE
# MIDDLE WITH YOU

# A Reader's Guide

1. On page 7, author Jennifer Finney Boylan compares her own marriage to Deirdre with that of Grenadine Phelps, whom she meets at a fencing match. "By almost anyone's measure," she writes, "Deedie and I are the dangerous outliers, and Grenadine and her husband Mr. and Mrs. Normal. Even though Deedie and I love each other beyond all understanding, and Grenadine's fondest hope was that her husband would be murdered by insurgents." Do you think of Jennifer and Deirdre as "outliers"? What makes a family "normal"?

2. Boylan writes, "I would like to think that [having a transgender parent] has been a gift to [my sons] and not a curse. It is my hope that having a father who became a woman has made my two remarkable boys, in turn, into better men." Do you believe this is true? How do you think having a parent who is "atypical" affects children? Does it strengthen a family, or place it at risk?

3. Throughout *Stuck in the Middle with You*, we ob-

serve Boylan worrying that her sons will suffer by not having a father, that it will be harder for them to learn what they need in order to become men. And yet, her sons appear to flourish and thrive, and she notes that she has taught them some "masculine" things, like splitting wood, regardless of her gender. How important is having both a mother and a father for raising well-rounded children? Is it possible that the sex of the parents is less important than the values they teach or model?

4.  Deirdre Boylan says that "marrying Jenny was the luckiest thing that ever happened to me." Do you think this is true? If you were married to a spouse who emerged as transgender, would you be able to stay married to him or her? How important is gender to a relationship? Do you believe that we fall in love with a person, with a body, or both?

5.  Boylan writes that "a woman cannot be defined solely as a person who has borne children, or who has a menstrual cycle, or who has nursed a child. As the years have gone on, I've come to accept that *womanhood*—like *manhood*—is a strangely flexible term." She even notes that there are "genetic" women who have a Y chromosome. Is there a single thing that you believe defines someone as a man or a woman? Is, as Boylan suggests, our gender identity more "strangely flexible" than we first suspect?

6.  "One of the things about manhood I learned from my father," Boylan writes, "is that it's a solitary

experience, a land of silences and understatements, a place where a lot of important things have to be learned alone. Whereas womanhood, a lot of the time, is a thing you get to share." Later, she suggests that fathers are more playful than mothers, and that mothers worry more about their sons and daughters. How do you think mothers and fathers are different in the way they interact with their children?

7. Richard Russo, in describing his largely absent father, says, "[I] can either take what he's offering . . . enjoy it and let the rest go, or . . . be bitter and resentful. For me [it was] just an easy choice. . . . Just to have fun with him." Are you surprised about Russo's remarkably forgiving approach to his father's many shortcomings? Have you ever been able, in your own life, to choose to "take what someone's offering" and "just have fun," instead of giving in to the very human instinct to feel resentment or anger?

8. Boylan's children, at a remarkably young age, seem to adjust to the change in their parent, and go so far as to come up with a new name for her—"Maddy," their combination of Mommy and Daddy. Are you surprised by the way the boys so lovingly accept something that many adults might have struggled with? Do you think the boys might have struggled more if Boylan's transition occurred when they were older?

9. Edward Albee asks, in his interview with Boylan, whether parenthood "mean[s] making or is it the being?" He says, Boylan "never birthed

[her two sons]. Isn't that a different quality of parenthood?" What do you think? Are parents who are not biologically related to their children different from parents who are? Does the experience of actually going through labor and giving birth change the relationship between parent and child?

10. Dr. Christine McGinn notes in her interview that the definition of motherhood and fatherhood are changing. She tells the story of being transgender (from male to female), saving sperm, and later using that sperm so that she and her female partner could have children. Both mothers breast-feed, and both mothers are the biological parents of their children. Do you view this, as Boylan seems to, as primarily a story about love, and adaptability? What does it mean to be a mother or a father in the twenty-first century, when the definitions are changing so rapidly? Will all this change have a positive effect on children, making them, possibly, more accepting of the diversity of human experience?

11. Cartoonist Tim Kreider discusses his affection for the biological mother and half sisters he first meets in his forties. What do you think accounts for the connection that biological siblings can feel? Later, he suggests that while he's glad to have found his biological mother, he is unlikely to undergo a similar search for his biological father. Does this surprise you? Why would an adopted child be more curious about his or her biological mother than his or her father?

12. Boylan's mother, Hildegarde, seems to accept Jennifer as her daughter, even after raising her as her son and in spite of the fact that she is a conservative person, both spiritually and politically. What do you think explains Boylan's mothers' ability to put aside her confusion and simply believe that "love will prevail"? If your child came out to you as transgender, would you be able to accept him or her with the same love that we see from Hildegarde? Is there anything that could happen that would make you turn your back on your child? Or should the love between parents and their children be a love without conditions?

# Recommended Reading:
## *Stories of Triumph in the Face of Change*

I have always been drawn to stories of metamorphoses. Here's a short list of books about men, women, and children who find their families, and themselves, challenged as their identities evolve.

*Far from the Tree,* by Andrew Solomon. Stories of parents who find that their children's lives—and identities—are very different from their own.

*Raising My Rainbow,* by Lori Duron. A mother tries to figure out the best way to nurture and love her "gender creative" child.

*The Yellow Wallpaper,* by Charlotte Perkins Gilman. This short story, first published in January of 1892, shows us a young mother recovering from a nervous breakdown. The "cure" inflicted upon her—to live a life without any intellectual or creative outlets—threatens to make her crazier.

*My Husband Betty,* by Helen Boyd. A feminist comes to terms with the changes in her marriage, and herself, as her husband evolves into her wife.

*Orlando,* by Virginia Woolf. The classic novel whose title character undergoes a fundamental and mysterious change at the books halfway mark. Whether he—now she—is a different person, or the same, is one of the novels' most delightful inquiries.

*Running with Scissors,* by Augusten Burroughs. The literary memoir of a young man whose mother gives him away to her eccentric psychiatrist.

*The Riddle of Gender,* by Deborah Rudacille. A science writer explores the many different forms of gender variance, combining a look at neurology and psychology with a series of heartfelt interviews.

*Stone Butch Blues,* by Leslie Feinberg. The groundbreaking novel, one of the first works to capture transgender experience in fiction, tells the story of Jess Goldberg, a trans-man who comes to accept the many contradictions of a gendered existence.

*Fun Home,* by Alison Bechdel. Bechdel's lyrical, thoughtful graphic memoir tells the story of coming of age in a family that runs a funeral home.

*The Awakening,* by Kate Chopin. First published in 1899, this novel brings us the story of Edna Pontellier, a woman who has to weigh the life of her family against her own quest to live a life of authenticity.

# Meet the Author

Jennifer Finney Boylan is a widely praised author and professor. She is an activist for LGBT people in general and trans men and women in particular, through her writing as well as through her involvement as national cochair of GLAAD. She supports the expansion of our scientific understanding of gender through her service on the board of trustees of the Kinsey Institute. And she advocates for storytellers of all stripes, in part through her support of the PEN American Center, and, above all, through her work with her students at Colby College in Maine, where she has been part of the English Department for twenty-five years.

Edward Albee summed up her oeuvre in 1988: "Boylan observes carefully, and with love. [Her] levitating wit is wisely tethered to a humane concern. . . . I often broke into laughter, and was now and again, struck with wonder."

Jenny is the author of thirteen books: three novels, a collection of short stories, three memoirs, and six young adult books, four of them written under a pseudonym. Her next published work will be a novella, *I'll Give You Something to Cry About,* available as an Amazon e-single as well as through Shebooks, Inc., the online portal for long reads by and for women.

Jenny's memoir *She's Not There,* published in 2003, was one of the first bestselling works by a transgendered American. The book won an award from the Lambda Literary Foundation in 2004 and has since been published in many foreign editions. Anna Quindlen called it "a very funny memoir of growing up confused, and a very smart consideration of what it means to be a woman." In 2009, Boylan received the Stonewall Legacy Award from the University of Massachusetts, for the "contribution she has made to the lives of LGBT individuals."

Her 2008 memoir *I'm Looking Through You* is about growing up in a haunted house. While trans issues form part of the exposition of the book, the primary focus of *I'm Looking Through You* is on what it means to be "haunted," and how we all seek to find peace with our various ghosts, both the supernatural and the all-too-human.

Jenny has been a frequent guest on a number of national television and radio programs, including three visits to *The Oprah Winfrey Show.* She has also appeared on *Larry King Live,* the *Today* show, and *The Barbara Walters Special,* and has been the subject of a documentary on CBS News's *48 Hours.* In 2007, she played herself on two episodes of ABC's *All My Children.* She has spoken widely around the country on gender and imagination, at venues including the National Press Club in Washington, DC, and the New Jersey State Theatre. She has given plenary and keynote speeches at conferences on diversity and scholarship around the country, and at colleges and universities including Amherst, Yale, Wesleyan, Harvard, Dartmouth, Columbia, Vanderbilt, Duke, Bucknell, and Johns Hopkins.

Her nonfiction has appeared on the op-ed pages of the *New York Times* and in *GQ, Allure,* and *Glamour.* She is also an ongoing contributor to *Condé Nast Traveler* magazine. Her story on the graveyards of New England appeared in the October 2009 issue of *Martha Stewart Living.*

Since 1988, Jenny has been a professor of creative writing and American literature at Colby College, in Waterville, Maine. She was chosen by students as the Charles Walker Bassett "Professor of the Year" in 2000.

Jenny lives in rural Maine with her family. She has been married to Deirdre "Grace" Finney since 1988; their sons Zach and Sean turned eighteen and sixteen in 2012. (The boys were instrumental in the creation of the Falcon Quinn series.) The Boylans' lives revolve around soccer, fiddle, the French horn, big meals, two black labs named Indigo and Ranger, and, of course, each other.

For additional Extra Libris content from your other favorite authors and to enter great book giveaways, visit **ReadItForward.com/Extra-Libris.**

**ESSAYS, READER'S GUIDES, AND MORE**

Also by Jennifer Finney Boylan

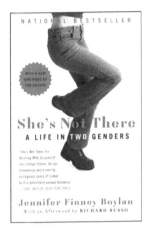

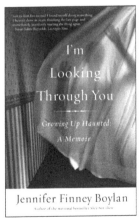

B\D\W\Y
Broadway Books

Printed in the United States
by Baker & Taylor Publisher Services